This I Believe

This I Believe

AN A TO Z OF A LIFE

Carlos Fuentes

TRANSLATED BY KRISTINA CORDERO

RANDOM HOUSE

NEW YORK

Grateful acknowledgment is made to the following for
permission to reprint previously published material:
New Directions Publishing Corp.: Excerpt from a poem from
Early Poems 1935–1955 by Octavio Paz, translated
by Muriel Rukeyser, copyright © 1973 by Octavio Paz and
Muriel Rukeyser. Reprinted by permission of the
New Directions Publishing Corp.

Zephyr Press: Excerpts from *The Complete Poems of Anna Akhmatova,*
translated by Judith Hemschemeyer, edited and introduced
by Roberta Reeder. Copyright © 1989, 1992, 1997
by Judith Hemschemeyer. Reprinted by permission of Zephyr Press.

Library of Congress Cataloging-in-Publication Data

Fuentes, Carlos.
[En esto creo. English]
This I believe : an A to Z of a life / Carlos Fuentes ; translated by
Kristina Cordero.
p. cm.
ISBN 1-4000-6246-2 (hardcover)
I. Title.

PQ7297.F793E5413 2005
863'.64—dc22   2004054732

Printed in the United States of America on acid-free paper

Random House website address: www.atrandom.com

2 4 6 8 9 7 5 3 1

FIRST U.S. EDITION

To the memory of my beloved son

CARLOS FUENTES LEMUS

(1973-1999)

Contents

Contents

This I Believe

A

Amor

In Yucatán, you never see the water. It flows underground, beneath a fragile sheath of earth and limestone. Occasionally, that delicate Yucatec skin blossoms in eyes of water, in liquid ponds—the *cenotes*—that attest to the existence of a mysterious subterranean current. For me, love is like those hidden rivers and unexpected streams of Yucatán. On occasion our lives come to resemble those infinite chasms that would be fathomless if we did not find, at the very bottom of the void, a flowing river, at times placid and navigable, wide or narrow, at times steep, but always a liquid embrace that helps keep us from disappearing forever into the deep gulf of nothingness. While love may be that river that flows and sustains life, love and its most treasured qualities—goodness, beauty, affection, solidarity, memory, companionship, desire, passion, intimacy, generosity, and the very will to love and be loved—are still not necessarily free of the one thing that seems to negate love: evil.

In political life, it is possible to convince oneself that one is acting out of love for a community while driving that community into destruction and inspiring hatred from both within and without. I do not doubt, for example, that Hitler loved Germany. But in *Mein Kampf,* he made it clear that the notion of loving his country was inseparable from the hatred of all those things that he perceived to be at odds with Germany. The kind of love that is cultivated out of hatred for others was made explicit in a regime of evil that has no parallel in all of history. From the beginning, Hitler declared that he would practice an evil brand of politics in order to achieve good. He made no attempt to hide this, unlike Stalin, who wrapped himself in a flag of humanistic Western ideology—Marxism—to perpetrate an evil comparable to that of Hitler, but that did not dare utter its name. Hitler's love of evil led him to a Wagnerian apocalypse against the backdrop of a Berlin in flames. Stalin's love of evil was translated into the slow collapse of a Kremlin built of sand, washed away by the waves, slow but constant, of the same history that the Dictatorship of the Proletariat hoped to embody. The Nazi regime collapsed like a horrid, wounded dragon. Soviet Communism dragged itself to the grave like a sickly worm. Fafner and Oblomov.

The Marquis de Sade also proposes a love of evil that seeks carnal pleasure as a way of grounding the body's pain and its subsequent disappearance from earth. Sadistic love, the Marquis tells us, may be a bad thing for the victim, but represents a supreme good for the executioner. De Sade, however, did not intend actually to put his monstrous evil-as-good vision into practice. He was not a politician; he was a writer who was almost continuously locked up in prison and thus incapable of acting except in the kingdom of fantasy. There, he was the monarch of creation. And he warns us: "I am a libertine, but I am neither a delinquent nor an assassin."

There is another covert form of evil that presents itself as love. This consists of imposing our will upon another person "for his own good"—that is, for the love of someone whom we rob of his liberty in the name of love, effectively leading him away from the path of his own destiny. This is one of the eternal themes of literature, and for me, the person who captures it with the utmost clarity is one of the great authors who blazed through my youth, François Mauriac.

Thérèse Desqueyroux, Le Désert de l'amour, Le Nœud de vipères, Le Baiser au lépreux, and *Le Mal* itself are all novels about a perverted evil that, intending to do good, either destroys or debases the ability to love through the manipulation of religion, money, and, above all, social convention and hypocrisy. Thérèse Desqueyroux, at the height of this drama about good intentions paving the way to hell, kills in the name of an old offense, and at the price of her own health, in order to save family face. Society, family, and honor thus determine, in the name of love owed to those institutions, the heroine's erotic slavery and crime of passion.

The praise of love as the supreme reality or aspiration of human beings cannot and should not overlook the fraternity of evil even though, in essence, love overcomes evil in the majority of cases. It can crush it, but it will never vanquish it fully. Love needs a cloud of doubt to hover above, against the evil that preys upon it. Inevitably, though, the cloud and the rage of the heavens will dissolve into pleasure, tenderness, sometimes even blind passion or the fleeting happiness of love as men and women experience it. The most ardent romantic passion can languish and fall into habit or irritation with the passage of time. A couple begin to know each other because, first and foremost, they know so little of each other. Everything is surprise. When there are no surprises left, love can die. Sometimes love yearns to recover the wonder of its earliest moments but inevitably comes to realize that the second time around the wonder is nothing more than nostalgia. Some people perceive the notion of habit as a terrible burden—a conclusive, repetitive, tedious desert whose only oasis is death, television, or separate bedrooms. But then again, aren't there also many couples who have discovered, through habit, the truest and most lasting form of love, the love that is best able to welcome and protect the companionship and support that also signify love? And doesn't another kind of desert exist as well, one that is fiery by day but frozen by night? I mean the desert of endless passion, so excruciating that the great protagonists of romantic love have preferred premature, passionate death at the very height of the love experience to the slow loss of passion through the monotony of day-to-day life. Can Romeo and Juliet grow old together? Maybe. But young Werther cannot end his days watching *Big Brother* on television as his only form of vicarious participation in passions less lethargic than his own.

Love wishes to be, for as long as possible, the pinnacle of pleasure: desire blossoming from inside and extending out to the hands, the fingers, the thighs, the waist, the open flesh; caresses and an anxious pulse; the universe of love-blessed skin, the lovers reduced to the discovery of the world; voices that speak in silence; the interior baptism of all things. It is when we think of nothing at all so that this moment will never end. Or when we think of everything possible, precisely so as not to think of this and give the pleasures of the flesh their freedom and their longest brevity; when we concede that St. Augustine was right, and yes, love is *more bestiarum* (in the manner of animals) but with one difference: human beings are the only animals that make love face to face (complications notwithstanding, of course). For the animal, there are no exceptions. For us, the animal exception is the human rule.

When is the felicity of love greatest? In the act of love or in the leap forward in the imagination of what the subsequent lovers' union will be like? The exhausted joy of memory and then, once again, abundant desire, enhanced by love, a new act of love: is this felicity? The pleasure of love leaves us stunned. How is it possible that the entire being, without any kind of waste or abandon, can lose itself in the flesh and the gaze of the beloved, and at the same time lose all notion of the exterior world? How is this possible? How can one pay for this love, this pleasure, this illusion?

The prices that the world exacts for love are many. But, just as in the theater or the sports arena, there are various entrance prices and even preferred seating. The gaze is the essential ticket of love. As the saying goes in Spanish, love enters through the eyes. And it is true: when we fall in love, we have eyes for no one but our beloved. One night when I was in Buenos Aires I discovered—not without a mixture of modesty, poignancy, and shame—yet another dimension of the amorous gaze: its absence. Our friend Luisa Valenzuela had taken my wife and me to a tango bar on the endless Avenida Rivadavia. It was a genuine dance hall—no tourists, no light shows, no paralyzing strobe lights. A popular neighborhood haunt, with its orchestra of piano, violin, and accordion. Everyone sitting on chairs lined up around the perimeter of the wall, like at a family party. Couples of all ages and sizes. And a queen of the dance floor. A blind girl, in dark glasses and a flowered dress. The reincarnation of Delia Garcés, the fragile Argentine actress. She was the most sought after dancer in the place. Resting her white cane on her chair, she would get up to dance without seeing but being seen. She was a marvelous dancer. She evoked the tango exactly as Santos Discépolo defined it: "a sad thought that is danced." It was a lovely and strange kind of love that was danceable in both light and darkness. Half-darkness, yes.

In time, the *crepúsculo interior* or "interior twilight" of the Donato and Lenzi tango also teaches us that it is possible to love the imperfection of one's beloved. Not despite the imperfection but because of it. Because some specific shortcoming, an identifiable defect, makes the person we love that much more adorable; not because it makes us feel superior—the Greeks, in fact, punished hubris as a tragic offense, not just against the gods, but against human limitations—but rather because of the very opposite, because it allows us to admit the things that we ourselves lack and, as such, compensate for with someone else. This is different from the form of love that can be defined as the will to love: an ambiguous condition that can wave along with the flags of solidarity, but can also show off the rags of self-interest, cunning, or that brand of friendship-out-of-convenience that Aristotle so aptly described. We would do well to distinguish very clearly between these two forms of love, because the first is an exercise in generosity while the second revolves around egotism.

"A perfect egotism between two people" is Sacha Guitry's very French definition of love, placing a rather ironic twist on intimacy. On the one hand, shared egotism implies accepting, tolerating, or remaining discreet in the face of the many miseries that, in the words of Hamlet, "flesh is heir to." But, on the other hand, bald egotism—radical, miserly solitude—implies both separation from the other as well as separation from oneself. There is always someone who will say that the greatest moment of love is separation, loneliness, the melancholy of remembrance, the solitary moment . . . And this situation is certainly preferable to the melancholy of a love that never existed—out of shyness, indifference, or haste. There wasn't the time, we say to ourselves. There wasn't the time for the last word. There wasn't time to say so many things about love.

Love, whether it is will or habit, generosity or imperfection, beauty and plenitude, intimacy and separation, is a human act that pays, as do all human acts, the price of finality. If we make love the worthiest goal and most worthwhile pleasure of our lives, it is because in order for it to exist at all (or perhaps because it does in fact exist) we must envision it as limitless precisely because it is so fatally limited. Love can only conceive of itself without limit. At the same time, lovers know that their love has limits—even if they are blinded by passion and deny this—if not in life then surely in the death that is, according to Bataille, the empire of true eroticism: "The perpetuation of a love more intense in the mortal absence of the beloved." Cathy and Heathcliff in *Wuthering Heights,* Pedro Páramo and Susana San Juan in Juan Rulfo's novel *Pedro Páramo.* But in life itself, can even the most absolute, abundant love ever fully satisfy us? Don't we always want more? If we were infinite, we would be God, the poet tells us. But we want, at the very least, to love infinitely, for this is our only possible brush with divinity. It is our gaze of farewell and our gaze upon God. *Dios y adiós.*

I hope the reader of this book will discover the various kinds of love that are contained in each chapter of my personal alphabet. There is one kind, however, that I would like to highlight so as always to keep it present in my mind. I refer to the quality of attention. Love as attention. Paying attention to the other person. Opening oneself to attention. Because extreme attention is the creative faculty, and its condition is love.

Agnes Heller, the philosopher of Hungarian extraction, writes of how ethics are concerned with the personal responsibility we assume on behalf of another person; our response to the call of the other. All ethics culminate in a morality of responsibility: we are morally responsible for ourselves and others. However, how can one single person assume responsibility for everyone? This is the central theme of all Dostoevsky's novels.

How can we begin to absorb the full experience of a suffering, humiliated, yearning human race? This is the question that Dostoevsky posed, with youthful desperation, to the greatest Russian critic of his day, Vissarion Gregorievich Bielinsky. The critic's reply was overwhelmingly succinct: start with one human being, the person closest to you. With love, place your hand in the hand of the last man, the last woman you have seen, and in their eyes you will see the reflection of all the needs, all the hopes, and all the love known to all of humanity.

B

Balzac

I believe in Balzac. Next to Cervantes and Faulkner, he is the novelist who has influenced me the most. And like all great writers, he has many dimensions. But there may very well be no other writer quite as deft as Balzac when it comes to articulating social reality—*"Moi, j'aurai porté toute une société dans ma tête"* (I will have carried a whole society in my head)—and, at the same time, creating a specter that serves as a harbinger of things to come: the story of the fantastic. Realistic and fantastic. His reality includes the reality of the imagination. His characters are ambitious social climbers but they are also the defeated, the humiliated. His obsession is money as well as terror and illusion. His passions are personal as well as collective. The *études de mœurs* (*Le Père Goriot, Les Illusions perdues, Eugénie Grandet*) live on alongside his philosophical studies (*Louis Lambert, Séraphita, La Recherche de l'absolu*).

"The novelist of energy and will," as Baudelaire called him, is also the novelist of man's constant battle with terror. The energy so prodigiously expended by Balzac's *arrivistes* has its rewards—social status, money, fame. But it also leads to inevitable consequences—debilitation, old age, loss, surrender. . . . For Balzac, *La Peau de chagrin*—*The Wild Ass's Skin,* the skin of pain—comes to symbolize the world of objects. It is the supreme object, the thing-in-and-of-itself, the possession that is able to accumulate more possessions through simple desire.

There is a price to pay for this: each time we desire something and discover that our desire has been granted, the skin dispossesses us of our own life and offers us, in exchange, final and everlasting possession: death.

The possession of things is a central theme for the social Balzac. But the loss of things is the central theme of the mythic Balzac—the myth being that of Tantalus, eternally condemned never to touch the fruits that are just beyond his reach. "Slender shadow, bloodless and cold, see, your own thirst torments you," wrote Quevedo, tantalized by death. Balzac, however, moves both closer to and further away from the myth. Closer, we find social activity. Raphael de Valentin, the protagonist who acquires the wild ass's skin as a kind of poisoned gift, is a gambler. His wager is that life and death are the only numbers worth playing in the casino of life. The roulette wheel of life and death gives and takes away the things we possess. And in Balzac's social world, what you are is what you possess.

Like a grand opera, *The Wild Ass's Skin* opens with a first act that unfolds in a gambling house, a place where monetary things are lost and won from one moment to the next. In the second act, which takes place in a money-lending house, a talisman saves Raphael from financial ruin. The third act is a prolonged orgy of property and death in which Raphael wins and then loses everything he has, all because of the magical object that he possesses and that possesses him.

Balzac's genius resides in the tension between time and space in his novels. In *The Wild Ass's Skin,* the skin itself is the symbolic narrative space. Raphael desires things, and the object-space grows smaller and smaller with each successive wish. But right along with the space, his time runs out as well. The hero's will is annihilated by the fulfillment of his desires. There are few moments in fiction quite so terrifying—and absurd—as the moment when the banker asks him, "Do you want some asparagus?" to which the terrified Raphael cries out, "I want nothing!" Or later on, when he lashes out at the solicitous manservant, Jonathas, "Monster! Have you sworn to bring about my death?"

In this desperate novel, time and space, possession and dispossession, life and death become fused together amidst erotic passion. Sex is practically invisible in Balzac: Raphael desires the body of the courtesan Foedora but prefers the wild ass's skin to the skin of Eros. Sexual desire could destroy the skin and thus destroy Raphael's life. In Freudian terms, the wild ass's skin would be the proof of a "triumph over castration." It also possesses the fetishistic quality of being unknown and, as such, permissible. Nobody prohibits Raphael from keeping the skin because the object's price is unknown. Nobody, in other words, can prohibit Raphael from being the owner of his own death.

The erotic surprise of this particular Balzac novel comes when we discover that sexual plenitude has been reserved exclusively for Pauline, the purest of heroines. This virginal woman of populist melodrama conceals and demands the most complete sexual surrender, and Raphael exhausts his destiny in his desire for her. The wild ass's skin disappears and he dies—in a horrific final scene—gnawing at Pauline's breast. It is not the cruel Foedora, but the sweet Pauline who kills Raphael because she cannot allow him to live without desiring her—or, in other words, she cannot allow him to die without desiring her. Separating Raphael's dead body from Pauline's breast proves to be an arduous task, for our hero continues to cling to her like a ferocious beast.

Two other works by the visionary Balzac have always struck me as particularly disturbing. In *Séraphita,* the he/she protagonist, who is sometimes a man, sometimes a woman, or rather half-man and half-woman, makes sexual ambiguity an unattainable and thus infinitely and hopelessly coveted object of desire. Wilfrid's longing for Séraphita is as unattainable as Minna's longing for Seraphitus. Wilfrid, in his desire for the woman Séraphita, runs the risk of finding himself in the arms of the man Seraphitus, and in the same way Minna may find herself embracing the body of the woman Séraphita. Once again, the Tantalus myth illuminates Balzac's fantastic iconography, and Mme Potocka, one of the writer's refined lovers and correspondents, is absolutely right when she tells him that with regard to Séraphita one must think in terms of a "creation" and not a "creature." How can Wilfrid or Minna possess such a person if they do not understand that this is someone who is neither man nor woman but rather a creation in the fullest sense, a creation which demands that they—and every lover—surrender unabashedly to the movement of a soul in which we—characters and readers alike—risk our lives? This, we might say, is the difference between *Séraphita* and *Orlando*, the very lovely and innocent novel by Virginia Woolf, which plays such marvelous games with the constant metamorphoses of time and sex. But Woolf does not ask us to choose, nor does she choose anything herself. Orlando travels seamlessly through time, alone. Séraphita demands that we be something that we don't want to be, while at the same time we fervently desire to be either Him or Her. Séraphita demands that we give up life so that we may possess it beyond the realm of sex. Séraphita demands eroticism.

Louis Lambert, Balzac's most autobiographical novel, offers another illuminating prophecy. The young and brilliant Lambert is, in the words of Balzac, "a soul crushed under the weight of thought." Flaubert was wrong when he read it as a nightmare and judged it to be the story of a madman. As mad as Nietzsche, because this Louis Lambert, even when locked away in a darkened room without uttering a word, is not mad. He has been defeated by the velocity of his thoughts, which move so fast that he is unable to express them verbally. Thought annihilates the thinker. Louis Lambert, then, is the most astounding harbinger of Friedrich Nietzsche.

Can literature defeat death? This is Balzac's insidious question, and it accompanies many of his characters: Lucien de Rubempré and Eugène de Rastignac in their ambitious ascent of the social ladder; Père Goriot, the modern-day Lear who is victimized by the cruel vanity of his ungrateful daughters; Cousin Bette, who hatches her sinister plot so that vengeance may finally liberate her from the humiliation she has endured; and the great puppeteer of *The Human Comedy*, Vautrin—Abate Herrera/Collin/Trompe-la-Mort—who manipulates everyone else's fate so that he himself may avoid confronting his own unbearable burden: his own destiny. These characters live in the company of ghosts, though none quite so intensely as Colonel Chabert, when he introduces himself in the home of his wife, who has remarried, having believed him to be dead. "Colonel Chabert," he says. "He who was killed at Eylau."

In response to a letter from the Duchesse d'Abrantes in which the noblewoman chastized Balzac for not coming to visit her often enough at her country home, the novelist simply replied, "Please don't blame me. I work night and day. You may be shocked, rather, by the fact that I am not yet dead."

The skin shrinks, but the novel grows. Balzac has given death a name. He has seen that possession gives life, but in the end takes it away. Yet he has only been able to do so insofar as he has been able to identify his novel as a text, a verbal structure that gives permanence and content to all the things that resist having permanence and content—that is, the brevity of life and material possessions.

Beauty

Socrates knew that he was ugly and prayed for "inner beauty." I cannot think of a more accurate disposition for judging "the beautiful": to ask the body to guide us toward the soul and to ask the soul to help us understand the possibility of harmony between body and spirit. The question of how body and soul relate to each other is implicit in our lives. Are they inseparable? Divisible only by madness and death? Does the soul outlast the body or do the two die together, locked in a mutual embrace?

Ugliness is body without form. The artist tries to assimilate and assemble all that is disparate. The theme—pain, death, birth, revolution, power, pride, vanity, dream, memory, or will—is irrelevant. What inspires the body is irrelevant as long as it gives the body form, because then the body can no longer be ugly, and we discover that Socrates was right. Beauty belongs exclusively to the person that perceives it, not to the person who possesses it. Beauty is nothing more than the truth within each and every one of us. The truth and beauty of bodies as well as the truth and beauty of games, dreams, solidarity, the attention we devote to people and things, food and drink, poem and song, memory and imagination, the beauty of nature, death, and the mystery of day and night.

In my novel *Los años con Laura Díaz* (*The Years with Laura Díaz*), these words are spoken by Frida Kahlo, wounded and bleeding in a hospital bed:

> You can look at me without modesty, Laura Díaz . . . you can say that I look horrible, that you wouldn't dare show me a mirror, in your eyes today I am not beautiful, on this day and in this place I am not pretty, and I won't answer you with words, I will ask you instead for some colors and a sheet of paper and I can turn the horror of my wounded body and my spilled blood into my truth and my beauty, because you know, my best pal, my true confidante to the end, knowing ourselves makes us beautiful because it shows us what we desire. When a woman desires, she is always beautiful . . .

And when she is desired? The eroticism of plastic representation consists of the illusion that flesh possesses permanence. Like everything in our time, plastic eroticism has been accelerated. For many centuries, a trinket or a painting had to serve as substitute for the beloved. Photography accelerated the illusion of presence. But only the cinematic image is capable of simultaneously delivering both the evocation and its immediacy. This is her as she was then, but this is also her as she is now and forever.

It is her image, yes, but it is also her voice, her movement, her beauty and youth, all everlasting. Death, the great godmother of Eros, is conquered and justified at the same time by our reunion with the beloved who is no longer at our side, breaking the great covenant of passion: always together until death, you and I, inseparable.

But there is also such a thing as the beauty of the horrible, and it is something that has always existed.

The beautiful and terrible warning we hear in the poetry of the Spanish Baroque is that the soul "will abandon the body," as Francisco de Quevedo writes, "not its love; they will be ashes, but it will still have its feeling; they will be dust, but dust in love." (Quevedo, "Amor constante más allá de la muerte.") To foresee the death of the body accentuates rather than deprives it of its presence, yet it still does not free us from introducing the body to the soul and the soul to the body, in life, asking the question: "Are we one? Are we in harmony with one another?"

Does the harmony between body and soul depend on the ideal of beauty that so many different cultures and historical moments have envisioned in their own ways? Rubens liked his women voluptuous, while Modigliani liked them skinny, and Botticelli's limpid ideal has nothing at all in common with Schiele's sickly anti-ideal. Nevertheless, our judgment about what is beautiful depends on our individual concept of beauty. Why is one body beautiful and another not? We are attracted to what comes closest to resembling our own ideal. A spectacular fashion model of our time would have been perceived as tubercular to nineteenth-century eyes: Cindy Crawford would be a consumptive in Delacroix's harem.

Not long ago, the Chilean novelist Marcela Serrano described the modern woman as having the capacity to change skin like a snake, freeing herself from the inevitability and servitude of more obsolete times. Through this vision, the symbol of renewed skin brings me back to the question of the dissociation or harmony between body and soul. Why is one body beautiful and another not? Why do we speak of beautiful souls and ugly bodies, or comely bodies and abhorrent souls? Disharmony exists, there is no doubt about it. But what also exists is the form that both harmony and disharmony can and should assume. What did the decapitated, dehumanized Mother Goddess Coatlicue represent to the Aztecs? Perhaps the notion that a divinity demands inhumanity. But aren't the lovely actresses of the big screen—"the women who saunter down Fifth Avenue, so close to my eyes, so far from my life," as the Mexican poet Tablada wrote—as distant from us as Coatlicue?

The artist knows that there is no such thing as beauty without form, but the artist also knows that the form or shape assumed by beauty will depend upon the particular ideal of beauty prevalent in the social context from which the art emerges. The artist transcends the dilemma—partially, momentarily—by adding a factor: that beauty cannot exist without the gaze. It is natural for the artist to favor the gaze. A great artist, however, invites us not only to gaze but to engage the imagination. The feminine form as a form of beauty is also an object of olfactory sensitivity (Don Giovanni's *odor di femmina*), of aural sensuality (Goya, Buñuel, and Beethoven, as deaf men, have to imagine the voices of the body), and, finally, imaginative sensuality. (The jealous Proust and Catullus, Romeo and Quixote separated from Juliet and Dulcinea, Samsa transformed into an insect, *imagine* another body, either lost or desired.)

The art of visual beauty would be far poorer if it were to exclude the extension of the gaze to all that is tactile, aural, olfactory, *gostoso* as the Portuguese would say. Because we, as humans, seek an infinite pleasure that can satisfy all our senses. Nor are we content with that alone. We always want something more, something that we may not even be able to articulate, something our imagination and senses seek, demand, imagine, even if they cannot conceive of it in a concrete manner. "Oh, intelligence, solitude in flames, that conceives all without creating." This very deep intuition of José Gorostiza, in what is the greatest Mexican poem of the twentieth century ("Muerte sin fin," or "Endless Death," 1938) puts the great dilemma of our residence on earth into words: to desire a satisfaction that is infinite, but temporal at the same time, a here and a now.

Beauty does not surrender her body to tell us to be content with what the world gives us, to limit our desires and ask for a kind of perfunctory conformity. No: rather, beauty surrenders her body to give us the gift of a body in the present, a body here

and now that nevertheless does not sacrifice any of its possibilities, none of its *maybes* and none of its *nevers.* For the person who
knows how to see, the body's ideal and its negation are brought
together in art: the harmony of the body with the soul as well as
their possible disharmony; the presence of the body as well as its
inevitable absence; its pleasure but also its pain.

Buñuel

In 1950, while studying at the University of Geneva, I attended a film club in the city. It was there that I first saw *Un Chien andalou* by Luis Buñuel, presented by a gentleman who spoke to us of a reprobate filmmaker who had died in the Spanish Civil War. That was when I raised my hand to correct him, for Buñuel was alive and living in Mexico—in fact he had just finished *Los olvidados,* which was to be premiered that spring at Cannes.

Los olvidados arrived at the Cannes Film Festival despite the objections raised by the puritanical, chauvinistic bureaucrats in the Mexican government who considered the film to be "denigrating to Mexico." Octavio Paz, who at the time was the secretary of the Mexican embassy in Paris, defied the official denunciation of the picture and personally distributed a lucid essay on Buñuel and his great film at the entrance to the Cannes Festival Palace. Buñuel never forgot this act of courage and generosity.

I met Buñuel while he was filming *Nazarín* in Cuautla. The cast included Rita Macedo, my first wife, as well as Marga López and the extraordinary Francisco Rabal, whose air of mystical remove and tender mercy magnificently sustained the fury and ultimate pain of the character of Galdós. The essence of Buñuel's secret religiosity is patent in *Nazarín.* His famous quote, "I'm an atheist, thank God," may be an amusing *boutade,* but it was also a necessary disguise for a creator who personified, as no one else could, the unsettling declaration of Pascal's Christ: "Thou wouldst not seek me if thou hadst not found me." In this light, Buñuel was part of one of the most compelling, if uncategorizable, intellectual tendencies of the twentieth century: that of religious temperament without religious faith. Camus, Mauriac, and Graham Greene, to varying degrees of intensity, bear witness to this inclination, as do filmmakers like Ingmar Bergman, a Protestant to his own chagrin, and Luis Buñuel, an atheist but for the grace of God.

Has anyone ever struggled so valiantly with the drama of Christian conscience as Buñuel did in *Nazarín* and *Viridiana?* And has anyone arrived at such bitter realizations regarding the deformations of institutionalized faith and the abuses of power invoked in the name of Christ as did Buñuel in *L'Age d'or, Simón del desierto* (*Simon of the Desert*) and *La Voie lactée* (*The Milky Way*)? Heresy is the theme of this last film, which reminds us that the word *heretic,* in etymological terms, means "he who chooses." A brief but brilliant scene from *Tristana* reveals the protagonist in a moment of indecision as she faces two identical chickpeas in a casserole dish. At times, Buñuel makes his decisions categorically: "The horror I feel toward science and technology brings me back to the detestable belief in God," says a character in *Le Fantôme de la liberté* (*The Phantom of Liberty*), as Buñuel whispers in my ear, "That is who I am."

Patriotism, chauvinism, and political ideologies were among the things Buñuel found intolerable. He did, however, tend to qualify some of his anarchist commandments. For Buñuel, anarchism was a marvelous but ultimately impractical idea. Its only altar was that of pure thought. As an idea, blowing up the Louvre was splendid, but in practice it was nothing less than atrocious.

Buñuel, ever wise, was able to distinguish the freedom of imagination from the limitations of reality.

As a Surrealist, however, he did share the belief that the world could be liberated simultaneously by art and revolution. And as revolution succumbed to political terror, Buñuel used tradition to lend startling weight to Surrealist creation. Oddly enough, French Surrealism never went beyond the realm of ideas, magnificently articulated by André Breton, who wrote in a language as classic as that of the Duc de Saint-Simon. The Spaniard Buñuel and the German Max Ernst, however, discovered the anchor of the unconscious along with Surrealist illusion and liberation in their own cultural roots. For Ernst, it was through German fairy tales and legends, while for Buñuel, it happened through the picaresque—Fernando de Rojas, Cervantes, Goya, Valle-Inclán.

Fuelled by the culture of Spain, Buñuel liberated the gaze with a remarkable technique. He fills his films with medium and long shots, occasionally gray and monotonous, that suddenly reveal a convulsive detail through a deft, swift close-up: a skull inscribed on an insect's head, blood burbling from a woman's thighs, a crucifix that doubles as a switchblade, a chambermaid's erotic ankle boots, an eye slit through the middle as a cloud moves past the face of the moon. . . . This dialectic between the world and its infinitesimal secrets is what allows Buñuel to create these climactic shots, true cinematic epiphanies in which passion sometimes rears its grotesque animal face (the hidden Catholic inside Buñuel saw St. Augustine's *more bestiarum* act in the sexual relationship, although he did admit that the act "of love without sex is like an egg without salt"). Yet at other times, he recognizes natural instinct as the necessary condition of poetry. The grotesquely savage passion of the violently intertwined lovers in *L'Age d'or.* The incomparably dreamlike tenderness of the moment when the social castaways of *El ángel exterminador* (*The Exterminating Angel*) abandon their anguish, pretensions, vocabulary, and treachery, united by the night, to succumb to the overwhelming beauty of the dreamworld. . . .

Just as Buñuel attacked the hypocrisy hidden beneath the trappings of false religious devotion, he also attacked what he perceived to be the alienation and insincerity of modern life—and not just the life of the bourgeoisie but that of the dispossessed as well. Clearly, it is far more delightful and tantalizing to observe the discreet charms of a group of bourgeois people who can never sit down to dinner than to contemplate the hideous cruelty of abandoned children in the slums of Mexico. Buñuel, as such, refused to ascribe any intrinsic virtue to the poor simply for the fact of their being poor, nor did he ascribe fatal vices to the rich simply for the fact of their being rich. As far as Buñuel was concerned, the human capacity to injure one's brother transcended all social barriers. The diabolical blind man or the fearsome Jaibo of *Los olvidados* are as cruel as the perverse Fernando Rey victimizing Viridiana or Tristana, but there are also those who are equally victimized by the double feminine Medusa, the two faces of Conchita, in *Cet obscur objet du désir* (*That Obscure Object of Desire*), Buñuel's final, masterful work of art.

In the end, Buñuel's hero-heroine is an individual: Robinson Crusoe, Nazarín, Viridiana, Belle de Jour, and the chambermaid played by Jeanne Moreau. They each wage their battles through their solitude and incomprehension, but in the end, the only way they can save themselves is through solidarity. Alone on his island, Robinson shouts so that the echo of the mountains may provide him with company. Man Friday finally gives him the companionship he seeks, rescuing him from his solitude as well as a far more appalling fate: that of becoming master to a slave. Nazarín discovers that his lonely imitation of Christ permits him to perform acts of charity and also to receive it from others, though in the incongruous form of a pineapple. Viridiana must abandon her frustrating attempts at charity and finally join the Spanish trio of grifter, procuress, and saint, and from there, she is able to reawaken her Christian humanity. It is the prolific relationship between Buñuel's personal vision and his camera's eye, however, that most explicitly expresses the image of his art and his world. Catherine

Deneuve, in *Belle de Jour,* finds the culmination of all her erotic fantasies in a brothel. But the four walls of this house of ill repute dissolve over and over again as the actress's gaze, never frontal, always oblique, searches beyond the frame of the screen. It is a liberating gaze that constantly looks toward a world beyond, penetrating the walls of the brothel as well as those of the movie theater, transporting us to the exterior, social space that belongs to the *others.* And these *others* should not be taken lightly: one need look no further than Jeanne Moreau's ironic, sovereign gaze in *Le Journal d'une femme de chambre* (*Diary of a Chambermaid*). In this, the great actress's greatest role, Moreau looks upon everything with ironic distance—an old man's shoe fetish, the conventions of a wealthy home, the brutality of a servant—until at last she wraps them all up into one social and political whole. What Jeanne Moreau observes is nothing less than the rise of fascism in Europe.

A congenial man, incomparable friend, possessor of a singular sense of humor. I recall with intense affection the hours I spent with Buñuel in Mexico, Paris, and Venice, and regard them as among the great privileges of my life. Together we discovered that the essence of friendship lay in knowing how to be together without ever saying a word, in contemplating and assimilating the things we said before speaking again, always with a glass of *buñueloni* in hand. Recipe: half English gin and equal parts of Carpano and sweet vermouth.

C

Children

I have witnessed the births of all three of my children. My first daughter, Cecilia, was born in Mexico City in 1962. Her mother, my first wife, was Rita Macedo, a beautiful actress of *mestizo* appearance—dark-skinned, with large, almond-shaped eyes and prominent cheekbones. She had just begun filming *El ángel exterminador* with Luis Buñuel when she became pregnant and her doctors told her that bed rest was in order: the birth would be a difficult one. In fact, Rita appears in the last scene of the film, when the people who have escaped from their confinement convene in the church to offer their thanks, only to discover, once again, that they cannot leave. . . . As often happens in the movies, that last scene was the first to be filmed. That is why Rita only appears at the end.

As things turned out, Cecilia's birth was not difficult. It was, as this natural, universal event always is, in every part of the world, unique and miraculous. Every father confers upon the birth of his child a series of marvelous, singular qualities that are difficult for anyone else to understand; every father also knows that he too will add his own unique quality to the birth of his child. Cecilia's birth was a musical event. I might have heard or remembered words, images of flowers or fruits, animals or birds, rivers, oceans. But all I heard was music. I cannot explain it. Nor can I imagine it. I can only bear witness to it. The moment Cecilia emerged and cried out for the first time, I knew that I was hearing a proclamation of nature, the newest, but also the most ancient. To hear the voice of a human being coming into the world is to hear the echo of the origin of all things. To hear an impassioned song. When a little girl is born she doesn't cry out simply because it is the most natural thing to do. Her true nature is asserting itself at that moment, through her voice, the conduit that carries her toward society, culture, love. The miracle of birth is nothing more than that.

When Cecilia arrived she was quick to reveal the voice of tenderness, and as I held her in my arms for the first time I felt my body and hers fully, freely expressing themselves. Father and daughter, different—yet both of them, in the beauty of that single moment, possessed a free sexuality, the kind in which desire and the joy of the amorous-filial relationship become fused and confused.

"La Fuentecita," "La Gordita," "La Ex Gordita" (Little Miss Fuentes, Little Miss Chubby, Little Miss Ex-Chubby) were the nicknames Luis Buñuel bestowed upon Cecilia as she grew up, and he abandoned his cruel fantasy of yanking off my little girl's round head so that he might play soccer with it. She grew up with tension, with feelings of abandonment, and a keenly critical, realistic view of things. Even today, as she approaches the age of forty, she increasingly demonstrates a tender strength and a manner of being that is never complacent—with either herself or others. I, however, am exempt from this severity and am welcomed into her affections.

Nevertheless, as I watch my daughter's life unfold, I still find myself caught in the moment she appeared for the first time, when I heard that music of necessity and desire. A voice of supplication, happiness, sadness, that would all eventually dissipate because the sounds of words and song are simply not the same. The practical aspects of life do not allow this. The privilege of birth is to arrive in song. And that is why, then and there, I named her Cecilia, patron saint of music, condemned to death by suffocation in her own bath, decapitated only after a Roman soldier tried and failed three times, leaving her to die over three agonizing, slow days. We give names to exorcise.

In 1972 I married Silvia Lemus, my second wife. Natasha, my second daughter, was born in Washington in 1974. She was a bouncy, happy baby, bubbling over with imagination and glee. A father's greatest wish is that his daughter will always be a source of tenderness, that she will always come skipping her way into the living room. But the photographs fade, the organdy snags, the silks grow yellow with age. The First Communion is not an eternal event.

"Melanie," Natasha called out to her playmate as the two little girls, just having celebrated their fourth birthdays, bounded their way through my library, "this is my father. He's a hundred years old." We all age at our own pace. In between separations and reunions, conflicts emerge. When the separation wins out, there shouldn't be innocent or guilty parties, just the eternal effort to settle old issues and find balance within ourselves, with our parents, with our children.

Natasha and I have been as close to and as distant from each other as we have been from our respective inner selves. She speaks of the "sad winter" of her childhood, and of her repeated attempts to become a woman, to invent and reinvent herself over and over again. She wanted to please. She wanted to shock. At times she was the hungry exile in her own home. On a desert island she found a box filled with books and came back to surprise her teachers—and to correct them, now that she was far ahead of them, to the point of exasperating them: "You have been doing too much reading, little girl."

She knew too much, and she shielded herself with a culture as brilliant as it was damned. She didn't know how to invent herself on a stage, on a piece of paper. She needed to leave behind the prison of foggy, intangible places and come out into a space where she might communicate with others—writing, acting, giving her talents a chance. She needed to discover the place where being everything you want to be is a virtue.

I named Natasha after the lovely Natasha Rostova of *War and Peace,* although her name is also an ode to Dostoevsky's Filippovna.

My son was a young artist, embarking on a destiny that nobody could wrest from him because his was the destiny of art, works of art that would long outlast the artist. Touching the feverish temples of her son, the mother wondered, nevertheless, if this young artist that was also her son had not created too close a bond between starting point and ultimate destiny. The tortured, erotic figures of his paintings were not a promise but a conclusion. They were not a beginning. They were, irremediably, an ending. Understanding this was anguish for his mother, because in her son she wanted to see the full realization of a person whose joy depended on his creativity. It was unfair that his body was betraying him, that the body was calamitously independent of his will.

She would watch her son at work, absorbed and fascinated: my son will soon reveal his gifts, but he will not have the time for conquests, he will work, he will envision things, but he will not have the time to produce. His painting is inevitable—that is the reward, she said, my son will not replace or be replaced in the thing that only he can do, it doesn't matter for how long, there is no frustration in his work, even though his life will be cut short. . . .*

---

*Fuentes, Carlos, *Los años con Laura Díaz* (*The Years with Laura Díaz*), 2000.

Children

When I wrote these lines some years ago, I envisioned them as a kind of exorcism, not a prophecy. I thought about my son, Carlos Fuentes Lemus, who was born in Paris on August 22, 1973, and died in Puerto Vallarta, Jalisco, on May 5, 1999. Just as he started to take his first steps—his mother Silvia and I were living on a farm in Virginia—bruises began to appear all over his body and his joints swelled up. We soon found out why. Carlos, as a result of a genetic mutation, was suffering from hemophilia, the illness that prevents blood from coagulating. From a very early age, he had to receive injections of the coagulating agent he lacked, factor VIII. Although it was tedious, we believed that this procedure would bring him relief from his affliction for the rest of his life. The contamination of blood banks as the result of the AIDS outbreak left hemophiliacs dangerously unprotected—sometimes because of erroneous medical decisions, sometimes because of acts of criminal irresponsibility on the part of European and American authorities. Because of this, the hemophiliac was completely vulnerable and exposed to dire infections and the weakening of the immune system.

Carlos's childhood was filled with aches and pains, but very early on, in a way that was more than intuitive—it was as if his precociousness was an augury of his own death and a catalyst for his creative life—he dedicated his hours to the art of words, music, and forms. When he was five years old, he won the Shankar Prize for Children's Drawing in New Delhi, India: without our knowledge, the teachers at the elementary school in Princeton that Carlos attended had submitted his very first works to be considered for the prize. From that point on, Carlos never abandoned the pencil that came first, the paintbrush that followed soon after, and the early artistic influences to which he was devoted and which would stay with him always: Vincent van Gogh and Egon Schiele. I remember one summer trip through Andalucía: he made us stop the car every other second to photograph, admire the landscape, and occasionally pluck sunflowers from the ground as if picking up a painting by the great Dutch artist and taking it away with him. He planted sunflower seeds in the garden of our house at Cambridge University, which we assumed would perish in the English chill, but we returned in the spring to find them blooming, just like in a painting. . . . Then, taking a remarkable leap into the past, Carlos discovered the precise, luminous work of the Renaissance artist Giovanni Bellini and the expressive formalism of Utamaru, the Japanese painter. This was his pictorial legacy.

Images became the center of Carlos's life. First it was the pictorial image, soon afterward the literary image, eventually the immobile photographic image, and finally the fluid image of the cinema. He seemed to understand that the image resists reductive definition and encompasses, in a manner that is almost an act of love, all the senses . . . sight, sound, smell, taste. That was why the meningitis that almost destroyed him in January 1994 was so particularly painful, because it practically robbed him of his sight and his hearing—the most intimate and sensual company his ailing body knew. His passions were Elvis Presley, Bob Dylan, the Rolling Stones, but most of all Elvis: every year, every August 16, Carlos would travel to Memphis to commemorate the anniversary of Elvis's death. The collection of photographs he took constitute a singular archive and testament to the immortality of the King.

Like many parents who remained stuck on José Alfredo Jiménez and Ella Fitzgerald, I had quite a time following my son in his musical meanderings. I did, however, feel a very affectionate identification with his literary tastes. The poetry of Keats, Baudelaire, and Rimbaud, the plays of Oscar Wilde, the novels of Jack Kerouac, the philosophy of Nietzsche . . . I realized that when Carlos read, he transcended the image eagerly to seek out—though perhaps not necessarily to find—the metaphor, the incarnation of worldly things in their most mysterious form, more distant but more accurate: the most forgotten relationship but also the most natural—simply, the relationship between *this* and *that*.

Carlos, from the many hospital beds he had to lie in as he miraculously recovered his sight and hearing but lost other vital functions—at times because of irresponsible and unforgivable surgical errors—never abandoned his pen and paper, drawing and poetry, in his feverish search for the profound meaning of all the things that both illuminated his life and stole it away from him. I say "miraculously," and the miracle has a name: the attentions of a preeminent Mexican epidemiologist, Dr. Juan Sierra, who time and again gave Carlos back his creative life.

Carlos forged his artistic path with urgency, with joy, with pain, without a single complaint. His deep eyes, occasionally brilliant, occasionally absent, told us of how the body's individual pain can be neither transferred nor imagined by others. And if that pain could not be transmitted through a poem or a painting, then the pain would be forever silenced, alone, inside the suffering body. There is a tremendous difference between saying "My body hurts" and "The body hurts." How to ascribe a voice to some pain or other is the enigma that Elaine Scarry considers in her excellent book *The Body in Pain.* My son Carlos conceived this experience in terms of visual and verbal urgency. "Will I live tomorrow?" he asks himself in one of his poems.

> Will I live tomorrow, just can't say.
> But I ain't goin' away without a fight.
> This room is my nucleus.
> To think huddled under a blanket is my escape,
> I close my eyes
> and hear my fear hidden within silence.
> My fear: when broken it becomes
> the evil unknown.
> Welcome, my mystery.

But my reaction, unknown as well,
frightens my soul.
Except when it's really unexpected.
My fear, then, has no time
to think its own terror
and the fullness of beauty takes over
my soul.

I hide my things away,
not out of fright,
but because I refuse to deal
with half-thinking brains.
"Ignorances liberate."

I want to see you
in the same position, rocking yourself
in tears,
deprived for just one week
of your weak supporters.
"Each man kills the thing he loves."
Each woman will let herself
be loved to death.
Which is the love that lasts
to death?
Is it only a pilgrim
of all resemblance?

My son identified strongly with artists who died young: John
Keats, Egon Schiele, James Dean, Henri Gaudier-Brzeska. . . .
They didn't have the time, Carlos would say to me, to be any-
thing but themselves. At one point I told him the story of his
long-dead uncle, my father's brother, Carlos Fuentes Boettiger,
who died of typhus as he was beginning his studies in Mexico
City at the age of twenty-one. Just like my son Carlos, our uncle
Carlos began to write from a very early age and in fact published

a literary magazine in Jalapa, Veracruz, with the support of the poet Salvador Díaz Mirón. There is a strange resemblance between the poem of my son, dead at twenty-five, and the poem of my uncle, dead at twenty-one. In the magazine *Musa Bohemia,* I found a poem that my uncle Carlos Fuentes wrote when he was fourteen.

> I am frightened of repose, I despise rest . . .
> The night intimidates me.
> Because that is when my life rises up in reproach,
> looks at me, leaden, and then shows me
> the tremendous ghost, the horror of old age . . .

Neither Carlos my son nor Carlos my uncle reached "the horror of old age," but that fear of the unpredictable is something that has brought my wife and I, parents of Carlos Fuentes Lemus, closer to the pain we understand so much better now, the pain that so many of our friends have suffered through, the death of a child.

Confederacy of shadows, intertwined destinies and death, along with people and all they leave behind, inert, in a drawer, in a closet, on an empty canvas or a blank page. And despite everything, we fight to hold on to the heat of the object, the force of the brushstroke, the footprint of the man who walks. . . . What joy it was to learn that Carlos, gifted with an intuition that was both wonderful and terrible, spent the last evening of his existence, in Puerto Vallarta, phoning all his friends, all over the world, telling them about his plans to finish his movie, publish his book of poems, exhibit his artwork, telling them he was happy, strong, full of creativity, in love with his girlfriend Yvette. The following morning he collapsed under the weight of a pulmonary infarction.

We were left alone, Silvia and I. Our warm and wonderful friend Carmen Balcells understood, better than anyone, the relationship between mother and son.

I think of Silvia most especially, because she has always been so extraordinarily devoted to your boy and has lived in a perpetual state of terror about his health. I remember so clearly one time when I visited Carlos in New York, and how startled I was by his fragility and Silvia's fatigue—more than a mother, she seemed like a girlfriend or a confidante offering her unyielding support to a boy full of that childish desire and eagerness to enter a kind of normality that would never be possible for him. . . .

Exorcisms of death sometimes become prophecies for life. Carmen Balcells was right. In *The Years with Laura Díaz,* I evoke the death of my uncle Carlos Fuentes in Veracruz at the turn of the twentieth century, but as I wrote I wanted to prevent the death of my son Carlos, embodied by the second Santiago of the Laura Díaz genealogy:

Silence. Tranquillity. Solitude. That's what unites us, thought Laura, holding Santiago's burning hand in her own. There is no greater respect or tenderness than that of being together and silent, living together but living the one for the other without ever saying so. With no need to say so. Being explicit might betray that deep tenderness which was only revealed in a tapestry of complicity, intuition, and acts of grace . . . Laura and Santiago experienced all this while he was dying, both of them knowing that he was dying, but both conspiratorial, knowing, and thankful to one another because the only thing they wordlessly decided to banish was compassion. The shining eyes of the boy, sinking deeper and deeper by the day, asked the world and the mother, the two forever identified in the son's spirit, "Who has the right to pity me? Don't betray me with pity. I'll be a man to the end."

The person who works by night inevitably ends up feeling like the creator of the world. If he doesn't work through the night, the sun will not come out the following day. As I would be getting ready for bed, Carlos would come in to say good night, wrapped in an old beach robe. Only once, thinking that I was asleep, did he retreat from me murmuring, "I am damned." Then the night would come and give him all the education he needed. The night was his metaphor. The night came and no one could stop it. It is the hour for the creation that battles with darkness and death.

Carlos's death left his mother and me with the reality of all that is indestructible. He already lived inside us, even though we were unaware of this. I don't know if this solace is enough to answer the nagging question left behind by the loss of such promise. "Dying young is a bitch," our friend Terenci Moix commented. We feel the spontaneous, happy obligation of doing for the dead person the things that he can no longer do for himself. But this vicarious experience is not enough. One must come to learn that children, dead or alive, happy or miserable, active or passive, have what the parent does not. They are more than their parents and more than themselves. They are our time out. And they oblige us to assume the paternal courtesy of being invisible so as not ever to diminish the honor of the creature, the responsibility of the child who needs to grow up in his own freedom and see himself as the shaper of his own destiny. Our children are ghosts of our descendants. And the child, as Wordsworth so marvelously put it, is "the father of the Man."

Carlos's sisters remained with him beyond his death. Natasha wrote of him, "Carlos was romantic at heart and I think that for his world and his mind—healthier than most—his death was more beautiful than two months in the hospital. Prince Creole, there is no one who does not love you." And Cecilia, who was at our side every step of the way, put together a video of all the moments of her brother's life that had ever been recorded. Watching the tribute my daughters had made for my only son, I realized that a child deserves the gratitude of a father, even if only for one single day of existence on earth.

Christ

I have searched in vain for a historic figure more complete than Jesus, the Christ. There are perhaps figures that have walked across time's stage with a more forceful gait, yet they lack, specifically because of their intense external activity, the interior spiritual realm of Jesus. The mystics themselves, given their intense interior life, cannot claim their place in the town square as Jesus can, for he was an active historical being. The greatest scientists, in the interest of and in obedience to the indispensable objectivity of credible results, abstain from attributing spiritual or even moral dimensions to their work. One cannot blame Albert Einstein for the deaths at Hiroshima, though one can blame Himmler for the deaths at Auschwitz. The personal shortcomings of the great mystical creators are as anecdotal—fascinating, but anecdotal—as their virtues. But in the end, the obscenity of Mozart, the slovenliness of Beethoven, the insolence of Gogol, the gluttony of Balzac, and the vices of Coleridge and Baudelaire do not affect our appreciation of their works. Nobody would want a character as neurotic as Dostoevsky for their next-door neighbor. And Bach would have been, without a doubt, a placid, invisible fellow resident in an apartment building. The ideological sphere, how-ever, is where the public personality and the private life of an artist produce a more problematic combination. Aragon, Eluard, Neruda, and Alberti as protagonists of Communism, and Benn, Pound, D'Annunzio, Céline, and Brasillach as bulwarks of fascism have earned themselves severe recriminations that nevertheless do not damage the intrinsic quality of their work. Victims of intoler-ance, on the other hand, of dictatorship and dogma, often tran-scend the extraordinary quality of their artistic work to become recognized and remembered, above all, as martyrs—from Vives to Lorca and Miguel Hernández, from Giordano Bruno to Osip Mandelstam and Isaac Babel, from Sor Juana Inés de la Cruz to Anna Akhmatova. And the long list of those expelled from their homes by Nazi Germany, Soviet Russia, Franco-era Spain, the Latin American dictatorships, McCarthyism in the United States.

The singularity of Jesus is that the permanence, fame, or value of his work arises from obscurity and anonymity. Had he not been rescued by the apostles and propagandized by St. Paul, it is highly likely that the preacher from Galilee would have be-come lost among the hundreds of holy men who traveled the paths of the ancient world. But nothing—not the Gospels, not St. Paul, not even the Christian Church itself—can divest Jesus of his condition as a humble man, stripped of all power, unadorned by luxury, a man whose humility and poverty transform him into the most powerful symbol of human salvation.

Can we then attribute that power to the notion that Jesus is God the Son, yet also a partner in the power and the virtue pos-sessed by God the Father and the Holy Spirit, the other, winged member of the Trinity? The Church has condemned as heresy the seductive and very literary theories regarding the relationship between God the Father (Yahweh) and God the Son (Jesus). The Syrian gnostic Saturnilus maintained that there existed only one Father, completely unfathomable, who, upon coming to the world as Savior, is an uncreated savior—without body, without form. Only his appearance (as Jesus of Nazareth) is human. Why?

So that the human world might recognize him. Basilides and the Egyptian gnostics proposed that God had never been born at all and never had a name. Christ was only a particle in the mind of the Father. Patripassian Monarchianism earns its fascinating name from the belief that God is one and indivisible. The Father introduced himself into the body of Mary, was born of her, and suffered and died on the cross. In this sense, men actually crucified God the Father. The Sabellians swore that Father, Son, and Holy Spirit were one and the same Being: one singular God with three different worldly manifestations. The Apollonian dualists defended the existence of two Sons, one sired by God the Father and the other by Mary the Woman. The Nestorians carried this double-personality theory to an even greater extreme, stating that Jesus is really two people—one, the Man, and the other, the Verb. And it is up to us to distinguish between the actions of Jesus the Man and the words of Christ the Lord. Finally, the most influential of all the heretics, the Arrians, believed the Son to be a mere influx, projection, or co-non-creation of the Father, derived from the substance of the Father.

Of all the heresies revolving around the figure of Christ, the one that attracts me most is the one that, respecting all the fictions regarding his nature, focuses on the man who lived among men and who offered, here on Earth, the most conclusive and lasting evidence of what it means to be a human among humans. Jesus as the living nucleus of all human possibilities and contradictions is, for me, the most appealing and lasting of all the Christs. The man who preaches innocence and goodness and at the same time displays active fury against the Pharisees and the merchants in the temple. The Jesus who asks us to "turn the other cheek," along with the Jesus who says he brings war and not peace. The Jesus who asks us to "let the children come to me," but also the Jesus who exhorts us to abandon father and mother so that we may participate in the world.

This is the incomparable power of Jesus. From poverty, humility, and anonymity, he preaches much more than the salvation of the world. He preaches and practices salvation in the world. He offers us the world as an opportunity for salvation, not as a land irredeemably condemned to evil. Eternal life, in this light, becomes a spiritual dimension of human desire. The loss of Jesus to the world beyond human existence vanishes when we witness the power of his earthly example. This is a man who considers the loftiest possible aspirations for the human race to be those of learning to live with one another, caring for one another, and not falling prey to hypocrisy, the Phariseeism and Simonism that, in the end, tarnished the Church created in his name.

Jesus's greatness lies in his temporality. His obscure, mysterious life is what makes him eternal. His personal relationships are with the most unworthy and unbelieving of souls. He does not preach to the converted. He espouses no dogma. His own contradictions would not permit it. After all, we know nothing of Christ's adolescence and youth. With whom did he spend his time? Was he heterosexual, homosexual, or did he abstain from sex altogether? Was he, like the saints Francis and Augustine, a sated and reformed sinner? Precisely because he works within the constraints of time, Jesus encourages us to believe in time. His words reveal an extraordinary temporal faith, for even when eternity seems to appear at the horizon of his words, the goal of Christ's faith is the future of the human race. Jesus's faith exhorts us to work in the world. The heaven of Jesus Christ is found in solidarity with one's brothers, not in some kind of celestial empiricism. And his hell is found in earthly injustice, not in some bottomless pit consumed by flames. Jesus does, however, extend the values of life on earth to the realm of the eternal: "For I was hungry and you gave me food; I was thirsty and you gave me drink; a stranger and you welcomed me; naked and you clothed me; ill and you cared for me; in prison and you visited me." "When did we give you all this?" his listeners ask him. And Jesus replies, "Amen I say to you, whatever you did for one of these least brothers of mine, you did for me."

The very metaphor of the Resurrection is a way of telling us that we are obligated to complete life, not just continue it, and that the continuity of life, in spite of death, is the reality of eternal life. Salvation is found in the world. Hell exists in the world. And the world has chosen to believe Jesus. Jesus did not revive the dead. He resurrected the living.

The relationship between God the Father and God the Son, which caused heretics and doctors of the Church so many sleepless nights, cannot escape the fact that nobody knows the Father, whereas the Son allowed himself to be seen. We can devise fictional stories. Perhaps the Father does not tolerate the Son no matter how much Jesus tells him, "Look, I'm doing everything possible to reveal your existence." The Father might resent the fact that the Son is seen not as his delegate but as the True God, given that he is the God that assumed an earthly form. And to cap it all, Jesus does not only redeem Man. He redeems God the Father himself, and rescues the God of Israel from his cruel and vengeful image. Jesus gives God the Father "a human face," as they would have called it during the crisis of Communism. Does the Father resent it? Is the end of Calvary Yahweh's punishment of the insurrectionary humanity of Jesus? "Father, why have you forsaken me?" So painful, these words; so tragic, the ending; and so problematic, the issue of Jesus's death and Resurrection. Abandoned by God, what choice is there for his legacy other than Resurrection, which ends up being his compensation for the Father's abandonment, the promise that he will return to the Father's side, united with him, in a perfect and trinitarian symbiosis, or forever punished by the Father, reduced to silence, to a mean existence, to silence itself?

The battle between Father and Son—if it existed at all—would ultimately be useless. The Son already achieved eternal triumph on Earth, no matter what God the Father—if He exists at all—may say or think. For that reason all heaven is in a rage, to borrow William Blake's profoundly intuitive phrase. Jesus is the Disobedient Son. God the Father is fed up.

As I said earlier, had it not been for the apostles (and, most especially, Paul of Tarsus), Jesus might have been forgotten for all posterity. Beyond the testimonies found in the Gospels, it was St. Paul who ensured that Christ would reign over the institution that is the Church. What ensures Jesus's place throughout history, however, is the same thing that prevents him from being truly present in history: the Christian Church, subject to the ebb and flow of political life, to obligations and exceptions, to betrayals of Christ, to the seduction of the very things Christ harshly denounced—Simonism, Phariseeism, the faith of petty lies, the hunger for earthly power—things that transformed the Church into the industry of Christ, an industry that takes us further and further away from Christ himself. The Church is God the Father's vengeance against an intolerable Christ. St. Augustine, brilliant Sophist that he was, predicted what was to come. The priest, like the Church, may be weak or mad. But the priesthood dignifies him. The Church places its ministers above their own condition as humans. What the saint of Hippo does not say is that the Church is an institution that forgives itself, and as such places itself, in the name of Christ, far above and beyond its earthly condition. Origen was condemned for believing that God's mercy, being infinite, would eventually forgive the Devil. He should have said that it would eventually forgive the Church as well. And I am not referring to Luther and the Protestant revolution. I need look no further than my own era and my own lifetime to reject the Church of Pius XII, Pacelli, and their collusion with Franco and the Nazis. And then, following the Allied victory, their collusion with the CIA, various mafias, and the corrupt Christian Democrats in Italy. The Church's honor has been rescued, of course, by popes like John XXIII and bishops like Oscar Romero in El Salvador, but once again shame has fallen upon the Argentine Church, for example, which gave its blessing to dictatorships led by criminals, assassins, and torturers. . . .

The extraordinary thing about all this, however, is that two thousand years of betrayals have still not managed to kill Jesus.

The empires of evil were relatively short-lived—the Reich, which, according to Hitler, was destined to reign for a thousand years, or the Communist future promised by the Soviet bureaucracy: "How many divisions has the Pope?" Stalin asked mockingly. Far more than the Kremlin, as it turned out. Yet those armies of Christian faith exist in spite of—not because of—the Vatican institution. The Church may administer and take advantage of the Christ figure, but it has not managed to appropriate Jesus, who has always been so far beyond the Church that was created in his name. Jesus is the eternal reproach to the Church. But the Church has to tolerate Jesus if it wants to keep going. Jesus slips from the hands of the Church by becoming a problem for those who remain outside it. In the hunt for heretics and nonbelievers, the Church has been unable to remain exclusively of and for Jesus because Jesus extends the values of eternal life to the values of earthly life and that is where he becomes something much more than a fragile God who became man. He becomes the God whose power resides in his humanity. And Christ's humanity is what keeps him alive as a problem for a modern world that may have religious temperament if not religious faith. Luis Buñuel, the lapsed Catholic; Ingmar Bergman, the Protestant who lived outside the tenets of the Church; Albert Camus, socially and civically religious. But there are also men of faith who are able to put faith to the test in the real world: François Mauriac, Georges Bernanos, Graham Greene. And most of all the woman of faith, Simone Weil, who asks herself, "Can you love God without knowing Him?" and answers yes. That is the terrible answer to Dostoevsky's terrible question: "Can you know God without loving him?" Stavrogin and Ivan Karamazov answer yes. This is the dilemma and only Jesus can resolve it. A person is not God, but God can be a person. And that is why millions of men and women believe in Jesus and represent his strength, far beyond churches and clergy. Jesus does not resurrect the dead. He revives the living. Jesus is the copy editor of human life.

Cinema

Of all the art forms of the twentieth century, none is quite so startlingly reflective of its age as cinema. Painting, architecture, sculpture, and music all descended from the past, paid it tribute, and reinvented it. Film is the only art form that was born and raised along with the twentieth century, the only art form that belongs exclusively to the twentieth century. Its aesthetic and literary debts are massive. But the very presence of the cinematic image, the creation it inspires and the mythology it weaves have had perhaps the deepest influence of any art form on the identity of our time.

I have always thought that some great writers could have been born in another age without losing their eternal qualities. Marcel Proust comes to mind as one example. The novelist from Paris would have been no less significant a writer had he been born into the seventeenth or eighteenth century. And Laclos, the master of the eighteenth century, would have been a grand twentieth-century writer. On the other hand, there are writers without whom we could never understand "our time," writers who are indispensable to the age in which they lived.

They are universal and will always have readers, but they bear the mark of their era like an indelible seal. Dickens and Balzac can only belong to the nineteenth century. And Kafka is the essential writer of the twentieth century. Without *The Metamorphosis, The Trial, The Castle, Amerika,* we could never understand our era.

Film, because of its inherent novelty, has had to undergo a constant process of transformation. Because of this, yesterday's innovation grows old in an astonishingly short period of time. Luis Buñuel often complained of film's dependence on the technical. The sheer speed of progress renders the majority of older films obsolete. To conquer the instantaneous nature of time with lasting images is the filmmaker's great challenge, and as I write about Buñuel, I begin to evoke images from *Un Chien andalou* and *L'Age d'or,* which live on even though their techniques have long since been improved.

I mention two silent films because there is such a profound abyss between silent and spoken films. The development of cinematography without words achieved heights of beauty and eloquence that the spoken film has never been able to match. It makes one tend to agree with Montaigne: *"Tandis que tu as gardé silence, tu as paru quelque grande chose."* A great deal of comic cinema—Chaplin, Keaton, Harold Lloyd, Laurel and Hardy—relies on the purely visual to execute its gags properly. Sound ruined, cheapened, or transformed them. It ruined Keaton and Lloyd. It cheapened the "fat one" and the "thin one." But it transformed Chaplin, who gave the world of talkies two masterworks with *The Great Dictator* and *Monsieur Verdoux.*

The plastic narrative of films like Dreyer's *Passion of Joan of Arc,* Eisenstein's *Battleship Potemkin,* Pabst's *Pandora's Box,* Sjöström's *The Wind,* Griffith's *Broken Blossoms,* Vidor's *The Crowd* and, finally, Murnau's *Sunrise* (perhaps the most beautiful film of the silent era) was crudely interrupted by the rather insipid novelty of Al Jolson singing "Mammy" and the succession of static theatrical melodramas with no virtue other than the novelty of the spoken word. Hollywood made valuable contributions to genre film—cowboy, gangster, and social protest films, not to mention the screwball comedy and the sublime eroticism of the ritualized dancing films starring Ginger Rogers and Fred Astaire—but these achievements cannot in any way match the technical, narrative, and visual revolution sparked by Orson Welles's *Citizen Kane,* the first film in which the ceilings were visible, the close-ups and middle shots were equally focused, sound and image came together, time and space came alive, and biography and cinematography coalesced.

Rouben Mamoulian's experiments with sound gave the camera back its mobility. And then there was Busby Berkeley's resplendent musical extravagance; Flaherty's magnificent use of film as documentary; George Cukor's calibrated direction of film, not stage, actors. Or the deliberate theatricality of Carné's *Les Enfants du paradis,* alongside the urban misery embodied by figures such as Jean Gabin, Arletty, and Michel Simon, broadening the scope and legitimizing a multitude of genres within the cinematic sphere. And while spoken comedy may never be as eloquent as silent comedy (Cantinflas is no Chaplin, Abbott and Costello are no Laurel and Hardy), film dialogue does manage to distinguish itself from theatrical dialogue, most notably in the crackling marriage of word and action in the comedies of Lubitsch and Hawks, and in the purely cinematic spoken performances of such actors as Cary Grant and James Cagney, Bette Davis and Barbara Stanwyck—the best of the best.

The creation of a personal style beyond obedience to generic norms and despite the potency of certain stars and the commercial demands of studios is what confers greatness on the few true creators of cinematic works of art.

In one miraculous moment Orson Welles managed to unite, through his own highly personal style, the possibilities of spoken cinema, one man's biography, and a societal dynamic in which having it all is equivalent to losing it all. *Citizen Kane* is possibly the greatest film of the twentieth century. But for me it is also inextricably linked to other films of that period that both build and destroy the illusion of what is called the American Dream. Stanley Donen and Gene Kelly's *Singin' in the Rain* is perhaps the purest and most delicious work of American optimism. Gene Kelly and the marvelous, adorable, breathtaking Cyd Charisse are the embodiment of the neo-Cartesian nature of the United States: "I dance, therefore I exist." Martin Scorsese's *Taxi Driver,* on the other hand, is the American nightmare: pure, gratuitous, desperate violence because everything is there and everything is nothing. Orson Welles had ambition. Gene Kelly had dancing. Robert De Niro had self-destruction.

Other personal versions of cinematic beauty emerge from societies less confident and less self-celebratory than the United States. Jean Renoir is perhaps the epitome of the French spirit, in which irony illuminates and rescues us from the illusion of reason and the disillusion of misfortune—a humane, insightful, expansive, clear intelligence that pushes us beyond easy Manichaeism. Pierre Fresnay and Erich von Stroheim understand each other because they are so alike, whereas Jean Gabin and Marcel Dalio understand each other despite their differences.

The Grand Illusion is the twentieth-century European film that competes for the laurels bestowed upon *Citizen Kane* (although many would argue in favor of another of Renoir's great works, *The Rules of the Game*). But not so far behind them we find the filmmakers who, beyond the great political imagination of Welles and Renoir, were able to create a visual context for spiritual concerns, conceived perhaps as religious temperament without religious faith: Luis Buñuel, a Catholic to his own chagrin, Ingmar Bergman, a Protestant to his own chagrin, not to mention Robert Bresson, Jansenist to the core. And do we misrepresent Alfred Hitchcock when we question whether fear—the English director's great theme—is in fact the greatest modern dramatization of the Fall and of the distance that separates man from God? This is the true nature of Hitchcock's suspense: where is God? And why has He left us so alone in a world of unforeseeable traps? Fear indeed!

Film also has an exceptional ability to be poetry, as in Vigo's *L'Atalante* and Laughton's *The Night of the Hunter.* With remarkable consistency, film continually manages to combine social commentary with dramatic narration. This, in fact, is the great Italian contribution of Rossellini, De Sica, and Visconti. Film is masterful in its ability to create atmosphere, from the sinister American film noir to the luminous. Is there any film with more interior and exterior light than *The Wizard of Oz*? And if the notion of "genre" has burdened even great directors like Ford and Kurosawa, two Asian directors should be cited for having given the cinema back its supreme creative freedom to fight the tyranny of the genre: Japan's Kenji Mizoguchi, in one of my favorite films, *Ugetsu monogatari,* and India's Satyajit Ray, in his Apu trilogy. Mizoguchi's miracle is that of showing us the emotion that lies within all that is ghostly, while Ray's is that of teaching us how merciful the gaze can be.

In the end, there is something else that cannot be separated from the love of film, and that is the love and fascination one feels for the cinematic face. Once, while watching Dreyer's *Passion of Joan of Arc* with Buñuel, the great filmmaker from Aragón confessed his fascination with the *facies,* the cinematic face. In the end, there can only be one Falconetti, and perhaps that is why Dreyer's Pucelle made only one film in her lifetime.

But repeated yet unique, enchanted dust that we are, what would our lives as twentieth-century humans be without the beauty, illusion, and passion granted us by the faces of Greta Garbo and Marlene Dietrich, Louise Brooks and Audrey Hepburn, Gene Tierney and Ava Gardner? For this reason, I adore finding references to the gaze within the gaze in the movies.

Bogart to Bergman in *Casablanca:* "Here's looking at you, kid."

Gabin to Morgan in *Port of Shadows:* "You got pretty eyes, you know that?"

This is the great miracle of the cinema: it conquers death. Garbo's face in the last scene of *Queen Christina,* Louise Brooks's face and profile with that crow's-wing hairstyle in *Pandora's Box,* Marlene's face amid the gauze and baroque filters of *Shanghai Express* and *The Scarlet Empress,* María Félix daydreaming as she is serenaded in *Enamorada,* or Dolores Del Rio seeing her own death in that of Pedro Armendáriz in *Flor Silvestre,* or Marilyn's face as she descends the diamond-studded staircase or as she fights the New York summer steam that rises up beneath her white skirt revealing her white thighs in *The Seven Year Itch.* These faces, ultimately, are the final and absolute reality of film: none of them can grow old or die. Film made them eternal. They are the cinema's victory over old age and death.

No theory or artistic triumph can eclipse or eliminate that simple truth. It is our reality, our most intimate yet most shared love affair, and we owe it all to the cinema.

Civil Society

A modern state, in any part of the world, must now confront a global economy that surpasses all national laws and borders.

How can the inequalities brought about by globalization be corrected?

How are individuals to be prepared for the age of new and ever-increasing competition in all walks of life?

How can social welfare programs be restructured so that the most vulnerable citizens will not become victims of global Darwinism?

The Latin American state, in particular, must not proceed from protecting its inefficiency to protecting its injustice.

In a globalized world, local government plays a critical role in maintaining the social equilibrium within each nation, and this cannot be achieved unless public spending is kept at a level of at least 30 percent of the gross domestic product. This, in turn, requires promotion of internal savings and liberation from the vicious cycle that leads us to attract external capital with high interest rates, instead of encouraging productive capital with high savings rates. To achieve all this, there must be a complementary relationship, not a hostile confrontation, between the public and private sectors.

This is precisely where civil society—the third sector, the social sector—can play a critical role by building bridges between the public and private sectors, by putting an end to pointless antagonisms, by advocating the compatibility of collective interests, and by acting on its own in areas that the other two sectors cannot occupy, describe, or even, occasionally, imagine.

Sometimes, when bureaucracy is blind, civil society is better equipped to identify, with greater speed and accuracy, the needs for development: for example, the problems of the forgotten village, the invisible neighborhood, the working mother.

And at other times, when private enterprise sees only a lack of profit, the social sector can discover or invent the best way to employ local resources and set up initiatives that will allow the less fortunate to help themselves: day-care centers, cooperatives, credit systems, shared medical and pharmaceutical plans, personal and public health programs, educational support, and door-to-door illiteracy programs if that is what is needed.

Or reading groups, or incentives for encouraging local theater. Savings banks, neighborhood associations, family medicine programs. Small, flexible, original, and renewable, third-sector organizations can be pioneers for governmental or private sector initiatives.

And they fulfill a political function that may be less visible but certainly not less critical. They help establish the public agenda. They empower people.

This is particularly true in Latin America, where we continue to be two nations, the term used by Disraeli to describe mid-nineteenth-century England caught between industrial development and social backwardness. We are indeed two nations: Brazil rather wryly calls itself "Belindia"—part Belgium, part India. In Latin America, the Mercedes and the mule, the skyscraper and the slum, the supermarket and the garbage dump, the baroque and the barock 'n' roll all coexist, and the television aerial is the new cross of the neighborhood parish.

I believe that the third sector's principal challenge in Latin America is that of creating bridges between these two nations, advocating human development as the starting point for sustained economic development, with the understanding that global problems can only be resolved by tackling local problems: the village, the isolated community, internal migration, small farms, trades, neighborhood roads, rural schools, vocational training, and traditional craftsmanship.

Global health cannot exist without local health.

The success of the new democracies in Latin America will be determined by their ability to relate the notion of political liberty to that of social welfare.

The function of civil society is to "socialize" both the public and private sectors. And I will even venture a step further: civil society should colonize them, though always recognizing that civil society itself is constantly being colonized by the State and the corporate world.

This, then, is not about stagnant, hermetic compartments. To a certain degree, civil society is not unlike political parties that have one foot in society and the other in the institutional world.

For this reason, the oft-invoked notion of civil society as an entity uncontrolled by the public and private sectors is insufficient. Civil society criticizes public and private institutions but it can also enrich them, contaminate them, and offer alternative solutions for real prosperity.

The aim is to broaden the horizons of this mutating world, so that new structures can emerge, strengthened by new institutions that will be able to adapt to change with justice.

With respect to Latin America, I insist upon the need for raising our level of savings so that our production levels may grow; with this change, Latin America would be less dependent on speculative capital. And that, in turn, would attract productive capital.

This is an extremely broad topic, but its nuances are so minute that they often go unnoticed. Nevertheless, they are important enough to constitute a basis and a framework for what we understand to be the "third sector" or "civil society."

To open up the channels between savings and productive investment, social welfare funds are necessary, as are savings banks, credit unions, and, in a general sense, access to credit in the interest of expanding the financial system and its scope. At the same time, systems of micro-credits must be encouraged and expanded. I will give one example that I think is sufficient to illustrate this point.

In various rural regions in Asia, a democracy of credit is being created. Since its inception twenty years ago, the Grameen (rural) Bank of Bangladesh has designated 2.5 billion dollars to 2 million clients at current interest rates. In one year alone the bank dispensed some 500 million dollars' worth of credits to the poor, with an average individual loan of around 200 dollars, and a 98 percent rate of return. The poor—unlike certain banks in Mexico, Russia, the United States, or Indonesia—pay back their loans punctually. They do not require taxpayer-subsidized economic bailout plans. The majority of micro-credit recipients are women, and 90 percent of the money they receive is used for their children's health and education; in other words, for the development of citizens.

In Mexico, Manuel Arango proposes private administration for public ends and Jorge Castañeda proposes cooperative programs with defined parameters and specific goals that would be able transversally to cut through class differences and unify efforts in the interest of resolving concrete, if small-scale, problems.

Public interest does not have just one champion. Increasingly, solidarity and the desire to participate enable the creation, across the board, of nongovernmental organizations whose work could very well be as important as the efforts of government and private enterprises.

I can offer two examples: they are far-flung on the map but complementary. In the Brazilian city of Curitiba, the mayor, the architect Jaime Lerner, spearheaded a joint effort between public administration, private enterprise, and civil society to fight pollution, create more green space, recycle garbage, rehabilitate the urban center, and decentralize urban growth. The result was an improved quality of life for this Latin American city, and it was achieved thanks to the cooperation of all three sectors.

The other, more dramatic example is that of the extraordinary achievements of Hungarian civil society, operating within—and in spite of—a totalitarian system in its most radical incarnation: as a social underground in a dictatorial regime. The great Hungarian novelist Gyorgy Konrad describes how, with all they had to endure, including the Stalinist bureaucracy and the Soviet tanks, a chain of infinitesimal acts of love, sensuality, creativity, and friendship allowed the country's civil society to survive on a day-to-day basis, despite all the unhappiness they lived with.

An experimental school, a research project, a new orchestra, the chance to publish in the underground, a tiny restaurant, a mathematics association, an attractive boutique, independent publications, semiclandestine newspapers . . . all of these in the Hungary beholden to the Warsaw Pact were minimal but transcendental manifestations of civil society. When? How? Where? Humbly, the great Hungarian novelist reminds us: "in retreat, in trenches," and ever conscious of the dangers and the obstacles, willing to wait one or two generations to achieve the socialization of the system. . . .

If they could achieve this, filled with courage and hope, as active members of civil society in a totalitarian state, do we, living in democratic, free-market systems, face a far less onerous task or is it the other way around—has liberty dulled us, illusion duped us, and complacency weakened us?

The paradox of Latin America is that we have a strong culture and weak institutions. The Latin American challenge, then, is to channel its cultural constancy and strength toward its political and economic institutions, and this cannot be achieved without the sustained impetus of civil society. Social explosion is the alternative—the return to military regimes, the resurgence of that time-honored Latin American tradition of authoritarian, centralist governments, along with the old lust for corruption and the more recent proliferation of narcotics empires.

If we can overcome these ills, we will strengthen both society and culture. They are inseparable. Without them, we will suffer from a fragile economy and a constantly threatened political sphere. Democracy with development and justice. This is the clarion call of Latin America. We have had, on occasion, political democracy with neither development nor justice (the Colombia of the liberal-conservative rotation); development with neither democracy nor justice (the Mexican revolution until 1960); and justice with neither democracy nor development (the early stages of the Cuban revolution). There are many other examples, many other variables. Currently, we rely too heavily on external and not enough on internal factors to achieve the balance we need. And so it falls to the third sector—civil society—to activate the citizens' initiatives that can create useful jobs for the workforce that has been expelled by the state and private sectors as the result of an exclusionary modernization process.

Give the people back their power. Create the conditions to achieve real prosperity, from below—it will be far more solid than the flimsy prosperity that provides indispensable fiscal discipline but does not eradicate poverty or unemployment, and gives priority to financial capital while undermining faith in human capital. In her seminal book *¿Qué Hacemos con los pobres?* (*What Do We Do with the Poor?*), Julieta Campos very succinctly assesses the situation: Latin America must move away from exclusionary modernization toward an inclusive one. The logic of the market, in and of itself, "accentuates the asymmetries." Can't we create a new model of modernity based on local initiatives and the participation of communities—that is, civil society? "Without renouncing global economic efficiency . . . without weakening the control on spending and the stability of both the exchange rate and prices," we must "address the priorities of human development."

The mobilization of civil society can provide answers to these questions. But civil society does not live on air. It needs the protective shelter of democracy and the nourishing life force of cultural legacy.

D

Death

When one must walk with Death, what time is valid for life? Freud advises us that all things without life existed previously to all things with life. The end of all life is Death, an all-powerful queen who preceded us and will remain long after we are gone. Did Death mark us before we existed? Will she remember us after we are gone? In other words, did the nothingness that preceded us, the same nothingness that will survive us, only become a conscious entity in nature, and not in its own nothingness but rather as the result of our journey through life? Death awaits the bravest, the wealthiest, the loveliest. But the same is true for the meanest, the poorest, the ugliest—not through the simple fact of dying, not even through human awareness of Death, but rather because we all ignore Death. We know that one day it will come, though we can never know what it is. We await it with varying degrees of acceptance, rage, sadness, bewilderment, remorse, with what the Mexican poet Xavier Villaurrutia characterizes as "nostalgia for death." We can assess and judge our lives, but we know that in the end the real prosecutor is Death, and we know the verdict before it is handed down. The final, inevitable companion. Friend or enemy? Enemy. And when it robs us of a loved one, rival. How unfair, how wretched, how utterly hateful is the death that kills not us but the one we love. Yet Death as enemy is the one death we can conquer. Occasionally, as I take my daily stroll through Brompton Cemetery in London, I walk past a vast space filled with white crosses. They contrast sharply with the elaborate designs of the majority of the tombs in that burial ground. They are the simple white crosses of the young men who died in World War I. I read their birth and death dates and am always shocked, because I cannot find a single man who reached the age of thirty. The death of a young person is the very definition of injustice. Revolted by such utter cruelty, there are at least three things we can learn from it. The first is that when a young person dies, nothing can separate us from Death any longer. The second is the understanding that some young people die to be loved more. And the third lesson is that the young person whom we love and lose to Death is alive because the love that united us continues to live on in our lives.

Are these mere consolations? Do they constitute a triumph over Death? Or do they do the exact opposite—aggrandize its power? Death tells us: you are fooling yourself, what *was* no longer *is*. And we answer: we are fooling you, what *was* continues to *be* even more than it ever was. Death laughs at us, daring us to think not of the other person's death, but of our own disappearance from earth. Death challenges us to believe that the memory of those who survive us will be our only life after death. Whether or not that is true, we will never know. What we do know is that the guardians of our memory will also eventually disappear as well, with the false hope that there will always be some living witness to remember them. Death mocks us: after all, do we remember more than four or five generations back of our own dead? Do we have enough family lore, ancestral portraits, unforgettable events to save the immense legion of our ancestors from mortal oblivion? Are there not thirty ghosts behind every individual soul?

While very few of us can pick out a hero or a genius from our own personal genealogies, we all certainly have access to the great verbal heritage of one of the two greatest poets of the Spanish Golden Age, Francisco de Quevedo (the other being Luis de Góngora). Evidence of death: *"¡Cómo de entre mis manos te resbalas! ¡Oh, cómo te deslizas, edad mía . . . ¡Oh, condición mortal, oh dura suerte! / ¡Que no puedo querer vivir mañana/sin la pensión de procurar mi muerte!"* (How you slip from between my hands! How you slide away, years of my life . . . Oh, human condition, oh hard fate! / That I may not hope to live tomorrow / without the payment toward my own death!) But there is evidence, also, of a love that is constant beyond the grave. *"Alma a quien todo un dios prisión ha sido . . . /su cuerpo dejará, no su cuidado; /serán ceniza, mas tendrá sentido; / polvo serán, mas polvo enamorado."* (Soul which has been a prison to a whole God . . . / will abandon the body, but not its love; / they will be ash, but it will still have feeling; / they will be dust, but dust in love.)

John Donne puts another spin on premature death. In his "A Funeral Elegy," the young woman was fourteen years old, and fate did not allow her through the door to the future; she took the liberty of her own death. But each survivor became a delegate that would fulfill the destiny that might have been hers. And so, a victory over death: "For since death will proceed to triumph still, / He can find nothing, after her, to kill."

This is the death that belongs to all of us. The death that is shared with the word that conquers Death.

The fact remains, however, that whether we are preceded or succeeded, forgotten or remembered, we nonetheless die alone and, in a very radical sense, we die for ourselves alone. Perhaps we do not die entirely for the past, but we certainly die for the future. Perhaps we will be remembered, but we will no longer remember. Perhaps we will die knowing all the things that there are to know in the world, but from then on, we will only be a thing. We came and were seen by the world. Now, the world will continue to be seen, but we will have become invisible. Whether we are punctual or not, we live according to life's schedule. But Death is time without schedules, without hours. Is there any greater glory than that of imagining my death to be singular, exclusively for me, with preferred seating in the great theater of eternity?

There are those who hope that Death will liberate them from their own memory. So many suicides. There are people who for their entire lives (or what is left of them) will regret not having paid attention, offered a helping hand, or listened to some person or other who is now gone forever. There is the silence of that very masculine love that must wait until death to emerge, and only then tells the dead person all the things that he never could have said, out of modesty, while he or she was alive: a tapestry of burdens and lamentations that are like a second shroud laid upon the dead person. And will the dead person have exercised his right to carry a secret to his grave? Is that not one of the great rights of life, to know that we know something that we will never reveal to anyone?

For all the denials and inevitabilities that pile upon our heads, for all the testimonies and certainties of the impossible that the prosecutor of Death presents to us, we resist giving up the notion that Death is nothing—it is something, it is important, we tell ourselves, even when Death herself tells us otherwise. We reassure ourselves that death today will grant presence to the life of yesterday. With Pascal, we repeat, "Never say 'I lost it.' Better to say: 'I have returned it.'" And we must believe this to be true. That there are some people who die to be loved more. That our beloved ones who are dead live on because the love that united us still lives on in our lives. That only the things that do not wish to survive at any price truly have the chance to live. And to want to live at any price is the curse of the vampire that lives within us.

It is also an erotic opportunity. In *Wuthering Heights,* Cathy and Heathcliff are united by a passion that knows it is fatally doomed. Heathcliff's somber greatness lies in his awareness that all his social actions—vengeance, the acquisition of money, the humiliation of those who humiliated him, the childhood days shared with Cathy—will never return. Cathy knows this too and for this reason, because "I am Heathcliff," she leaps prematurely into the only thing that resembles the lost land of original love: the Land of Death. Cathy dies so that she can say to Heathcliff, "Death is our true home, meet me here." Death is the true kingdom of Eros, the place where erotic imagination replaces physical absence and, most especially, the radical separation created by Death.

Death, Georges Bataille tells us in his magnificent essay on *Wuthering Heights,* is origin disguised. Given that it is impossible to return to the original time of love, the lovers' passion can only be consummated in the eternal and immutable time of death. Death is an endless moment. Why? Because Death, in the most extreme sense, has renounced the calculation of interest. Nobody who is dead can say "This works for me" or "This doesn't work for me," "I win" or "I lose," "I rise" or "I fall." In Juan Rulfo's *Pedro Páramo,* this is the novelist's final victory over his own cruel, calculating character who, unlike Heathcliff, remains anchored in the immortality of his unrequited love for Susana San Juan. In exchange for this defeat, Rulfo introduces us, along with the entire town of Comala, to our own death. Because of this novelist, we have been present at our own death. We are better able to understand that the life/death duality does not exist, that the life-or-death option does not exist, that Death is in fact part of life, that everything is life. We can imagine, then, that every child born every minute is the reincarnation of every person that dies every minute. There is no way to know whom we reincarnate because there are never witnesses on hand to recognize the reincarnated person. But if there was one single witness able to recognize me as the person I was before, then what? He stops me on the street . . . as I get into a car or walk into a restaurant . . . he takes me by the arm . . . and forces me to participate in a past life that once was mine. That person is a survivor, the only person who can possibly know that I am a reincarnation. The only person who can possibly tell me, "One life is not enough. Many existences are required to create the character of a single person."

But if one life is not enough to fulfill all the promises of our individual characters, truncated by death, do we run the risk of going to the opposite extreme, of thinking that spirit is everything and matter nothing? That one is eternal, the other temporal? Or does nothing really die fully, neither spirit nor matter? Do they evolve in the same way? We know that thoughts are transmitted beyond death. Can bodies be transmitted as well?

Ideas are never fully realized. At times they retract, hibernating like some beasts do, waiting for the most opportune moment to reappear. Thought does not die. It only bides its time. The idea that seems dead in one time reappears in another. The spirit does not die. It moves. It duplicates. Sometimes it supplants, and even supplicates. Disappeared, it is believed to be dead. It reappears. In reality, the spirit announces its presence in every word we utter. There is not a single word that is not infused with memory and forgotten thoughts, imbued with dreams and failures. And nevertheless, there is not a single world that cannot conquer Death because there is not a single word that is not the carrier of imminent renewal. The word fights Death because it is inseparable from it—stealing it, announcing it, inheriting it. . . . There is not a single word that is not the bearer of imminent resurrection. Every word we utter simultaneously announces another word that we do not yet know because we have forgotten it and another word we do not know because we desire it. The same thing happens with bodies, which are matter. All matter contains the aura of what it was before as well as the aura of what it will be after it vanishes. For that reason we live in an age that is ours, but we are also the ghosts of an older age, as well as the foreshadowing of an age that is yet to come. Let us not lose sight of these promises that Death holds.

E

Education

Education has come to be the basis for productivity. As we enter the twenty-first century one thing is clear: economic growth depends on quality of information and this, in turn, depends on quality of education. The most privileged positions in our modern economy are occupied by those who create and produce information rather than tangible products. Film, television, music, and the telecommunications industries, as well as manufacturers of equipment and technology for information processing, are at the center of global economic activity today. Years ago, the wealthy amassed their fortunes in things like steel (Carnegie, Krupp, Manchester). Today, however, the wealthy make software equipment (Bill Gates, Sony, Silicon Valley). This is a basic truth that can and should be contrasted with certain facts. The depths of poverty found in the countries of the so-called Third World have resulted in decreasing education levels. There are 900 million illiterate adults in the world, 130 million children who do not attend school, and 100 million children who stop attending school during the primary years. The countries of the Southern Hemisphere contain 60 percent of the world's student population but control only 12 percent of the world's budget for education. In Mexico, the average level of schooling is six and a half years. In Argentina it is nine, and in Canada, twelve. At high school and college preparatory levels, only twenty-eight of every 100 teenagers between the ages of sixteen and eighteen receive any kind of schooling in Mexico, and at the universities only 14 percent of those between nineteen and twenty-four actually earn their degrees. At the graduate level, only 2 percent of enrolled students earn master's degrees, and only 0.1 percent reach Ph.D. level. Only 6 percent of the world's scientists come from the Third World. Of this figure, only 1 percent are Latin American. Ninety-five percent of all scientists come from the First World.

The right to education, as Nadine Gordimer says, is as basic as the human right to air and water. Every year the world spends 800 billion dollars on armaments but cannot seem to put together the 6 billion dollars annually necessary to place all the children of the world in school by the year 2010. "A reduction of as little as 1 percent in military spending, throughout the world, would be sufficient to get all the children in the world in front of a blackboard" (information provided by UNESCO and the World Bank). The cost of one warplane for the air force of a Latin American country would be enough to pay for 80 million schoolbooks.

Exclusion from the educational system is the cause of inequality in Latin America. Political stability, democratic achievements, and economic well-being will not be sustainable if the population does not gain increased access to education. Can progress be possible if only 50 percent of all Latin Americans who enter school are able to graduate? Can progress be possible when a Latin American schoolteacher earns only $4,000 a year while his or her counterpart in Germany or Japan earns $50,000?

Solutions. Strengthen educational yield, the chain of steps that can bridge the dramatic gap that currently exists between the most basic level of education and education for technology and the information industries. Strengthen the teaching profession. The Latin American schoolteacher cannot be expected to expend more energy and assume more responsibility when salary scales continue to wane and professional tools are increasingly harder to obtain. The future of Latin America becomes brighter every time teachers receive better training, when their status improves and their social presence is strengthened. Moreover, in the accelerated but still difficult process of democratization in our countries, teachers have the right—as do all citizens—to participate in politics, but they are also bound by a higher obligation: that of using the classroom as a forum for broadening the concept of politicization. This is something that goes beyond partisan militancy, and it is achieved not through abdication or lies, but through the understanding that school is where the concept of politicization can begin. School is where this concept can move from the notion of "power over the people" to "power with the people." In today's world, the broadening of democracy in school means understanding what power is in the first place— how it gets distributed among individuals, groups, and communities and how resources are allotted in wealthy countries inhabited by millions of people living in poverty. School is where people may learn that civic militancy is not limited to political parties but can be carried out effectively and profoundly from a person's identification through social class, sex, neighborhood, ethnicity, or association.

Capitalism triumphed over feudalism because it multiplied opportunities for the citizenry, starting with education. Latin American capitalists should contribute to the creation of national banks for education in every Latin American country, with funds and combined administrations as well as representatives from private enterprise, the state, and civil society, all of whom may work to take best advantage of their combined resources, in a spirit of justice and efficiency, so that they may invest in the educational foundations of the country by offering loans, donations, and scholarships to the most needy as well as the most necessary educational institutions, from vocational schools to centers for high technology. And, of course, to universities.

I believe in the concept of the university. The university does not divide, it unites. It acknowledges and recognizes, it neither overlooks nor forgets. Universities are a meeting place for things that have survived, things that are present, and things that are yet to come in terms of culture. But in order to live and thrive, culture needs a critical space, a forum for people to reach out to one another—not to defeat, and much less to eliminate one another, because university and totalitarianism are incompatible. In order for culture to thrive, university spaces are essential as spaces for reflection, research, and critical thinking—the structures that we must establish to fight intolerance, lies, and violence.

In the university, everyone can be right, but nobody has the power to be right by force, and nobody has the force to insist upon one single way of perceiving what is or is not right.

In the university, we learn, in the end, that our thoughts and our actions can bring us together; sciences and humanities; univocal logic and plurivocal poetics. Planted in the soil and under the roof of a university these plants can coexist, complement one another, and bear fruit together.

The university is a stage—no doubt the most important one—in an educational process that begins in primary school and continues on in the perpetual school we all attend: that is, the education of life. I repeat: there is no such thing as progress without knowledge and there is no such thing as knowledge without education. As such, education, in a most explicit manner, should be the first item on the agendas of all the nations of the world, from the most to the least developed.

We must, of course, accept the fact that culture predates the nation and its institutions. Culture, no matter how minimal and rudimentary it may be, precedes the various forms of social organization on which it now makes demands. Ever since the dawn of time, various different types of cooperation and divisions of labor have evolved along with the development of skills, the dissemination of knowledge, and the conflicts that erupt as the result of friction between languages, customs, and territories, between the generosity of the mother that loves all her children equally and the paternal need that separates them, assigns firstborn privileges, divides land, inherits property, ascribes power, and establishes the obligation to defend, preserve, increase the family resources, and banish the Other—the Devil, the natural disaster, the adversarial god, and Death, which are seen as the original crime, divine murder.

In the course of this process, various ways of being emerge—ways of eating, walking, sitting, loving, communicating, dressing, singing, dancing. Ways of dreaming, as well. Day by day, all these elements come to comprise a culture, creating what Ortega y Gasset referred to as a constellation of questions to which we respond with a constellation of answers. This is the process of culture: questions and answers. The Spanish philosopher takes this even further: the fact that many answers are possible is a clue, telling us that many cultures have existed and continue to exist. The one thing that has never existed is an absolute culture: that is, one culture that provides a satisfactory answer to all questions. For this reason, culture and university rotate around the same axis, for both aspire to have roots and fly at the same time, to touch the local ground and ascend to the universal firmament.

Let us take root, then, in our Mexican and Latin American ground, as a starting point.

And let us be honest: our extraordinary Latin American cultural continuity has still not found, fully and completely, a comparable political and economic continuity.

A nation, Isaiah Berlin reminds us, is constituted by the wounds it has suffered. Wounded by her own hand as well as by the rest of the world—through conquest, colony, revolutions, imperialism. Latin America, despite its many calamities, has managed to create nations that, more or less, continue to maintain the borders established during the period of independence, borders that go back as far as the days of colonial administration: we are not the Balkans. Let us lose neither our individual national unity nor our shared Spanish-American fraternity as we work toward achieving, eventually, a position on the international stage that is open, generous, and without chauvinism and xenophobia.

The basis for all this is the consolidation of both national and cultural identity. If a nation is anchored in its culture, it is strong. If it simply brandishes an ideology, it is weak. My question, then, is this: can education be the bridge between the cultural abundance and political and economic paucity of Latin America? No, it is not a question of ascribing a cure-all quality to education as we did with religion (resign yourselves), independence-era constitutions (legislate yourselves), nation-states in the first half of the twentieth century (nationalize yourselves), or private enterprise in the second half of the twentieth century (privatize yourselves). It is a question, rather, of giving both the public and the private sector their respective roles as well as very specific functions in the educational process—and not by demonizing one or the other, but by holding both sectors accountable to the social needs of the collective in question and embodied by the third sector, civil society.

Classic wisdom tells us that true unity emerges from diversity. Contemporary experience tells us that by respecting our various differences we will create strong nations, and by denying them, weak nations. Historical memory confirms for us, in the end, that the origin of today's great nations lies in the mixture of races and cultures. No Latin American education can avoid addressing the continent's national and regional particularities. And we can be certain that a respectable, unified whole will emerge from such respected diversity.

Education, all over the world, needs public programs in order to survive. Without them, the explosion of demand may lead to a substandard market of low-quality education for the population at large and high profits for enterprising businessmen. We must defend public education. But public education requires cooperation from the private sector. If the private sector does not support public education, it will marginalize its potential consumers: for production to grow, education must grow and improve as well, and only when both these goals have been met can the standard of living go up. This is true all over the world.

I hasten to add that this effort also requires the support of the third sector, which represents a substantial mass of a country's human capital. Sometimes, where bureaucracy is blind, civil society is able to identify the problems of the lost village, the working mother, the urban neighborhood where Buñuel's *olvidados,* or forgotten ones, dwell: in the Brazilian *favela,* the Argentinian *villa miseria,* the Mexican *ciudad perdida,* the Venezuelan *chabola* . . . in short, the slum.

I believe that education must be a public effort, supported by the private sector and kick-started by the social sector. And its foundation is schooling: no man or woman under sixteen years of age should lack a desk and a chair. The goal is lifelong education; no citizen should ever stop learning. Learning, in our modern age, is a never-ending process: the more educated people are, the more education they will need throughout the course of their lives. The challenge—the challenge of education—is to offer knowledge that is directly connected to professional goals. Vocational education to meet the needs of villages, neighborhoods, outlying areas. Education for health. Education for savings. The social collectives of our respective countries demand this. Ultimately, we are talking about education for democracy—specifically, the democracy of the new Latin America. We must encourage citizens' initiatives, civic involvement, local solutions to local problems, all within a legal framework that guarantees the division of powers, transparency in elections, and accountability of the authorities.

Nobody can lose knowledge if it is shared.

Cultures influence one another.

Cultures perish in isolation and flourish in communication.

The university, as its very name suggests, is called to mediate between cultures, challenging prejudices, pushing our limits, increasing our capacity to give and receive, and broadening our ability to understand all that is foreign to us.

In the university we can embrace the culture of the Other so that the Others may embrace our own.

Experience

"Non sunt multiplicanda entia praeter necessitatem" ("Entities should not be multiplied without necessity"). At the height of the Middle Ages, William of Occam (1280–1349) made this statement, known as "Occam's razor," possibly the most radical defense of man's worldly experience as one that is complementary to time, space, and even the metaphysical heaven. Time and space are not independent of experience. The sky (God) supports the presence of human matter, neither condemning nor contradicting it. For this reason, Occam tends to be viewed as the distant but definitive father of scientific experience. Without Occam, neither Copernicus nor Galileo would have dared to divorce reason from faith, the experience of science from the experience of God, to the degree of his more radical descendants, the Occamists, who not only separated Church and State but regarded with suspicion—and even condemnation—a God that had deceived us.

I use this brief explanation as a way of establishing humanistic knowledge and ethics as the root of all experience (and that includes divine experience). I should mention, however, that this does not ascribe absolute or—much less—divine powers to human experience. To believe that would be to succumb to the sin of pride and expose oneself to the tragic consequences of defeat, disillusion, and deception. Experience is human, and it is necessary. But is it free or is it predetermined? How is it free and how is it predetermined? These questions reveal our existence because they pull together, in one fell swoop, all that constitutes the manner in which we live our lives.

Experience is desire, eagerness, or a project to be realized—either in and of itself, in the world, in my inner self or "I," or in other people. It encompasses a great deal. Does it harvest too little? Who does not believe experience to be supremely valuable, almost synonymous with life itself: the experience of love, of friendship, of work, of creation, of power, of joy? But experience also means pride, shame, ambition, fear. And pleasure. And hope.

Damaging experiences force us to ask ourselves if we must get to the root of what caused the experiences in order for our wounds to heal. Positive experiences allow us to maintain the hope that good things will happen again, that there will always be something else.

Nevertheless, experience itself—good or bad—makes sure to remind us that, time and again, we will fail to rise to the opportunity of the day. We will turn our backs on those who need our attention, we will not even listen to ourselves. Time and again, what we thought to be permanent will prove to be fleeting. Time and again, what we imagined to be repeatable will never occur again.

This is because experience, like Galileo's earth, moves; it changes from one place to another and its most profound force is desire. Borges describes the object of desire as simply another desire. The son of a dreamer does not know that he himself is being dreamed; the father's fear is that his chimerical scion will discover that he is not really a man but rather a projection of the dream—the desire—of another man. This baffling situation is concluded when the father discovers that he too has been dreamed by someone else. That is, desired by someone else. In Balzac, as I mentioned earlier, the object of desire is a fetish—the body of a woman and the skin of a wild ass, both of which fulfill the desire of their owner.

Balzac in *The Wild Ass's Skin,* Freud in *The Interpretation of Dreams,* Borges in *The Circular Ruins.* All offer resounding testimony of the relationship between experience and displacement.

To displace: to move. Displacement: abandonment of the place. Movement, relocation, change, mutation, transfer: money circulates, the hero rises to greatness, the adventurer travels, the conquistador pushes onward and his ships displace tons of water and will and passions and dreams. Displacement: the distortion of the visual image through the inversion of its normal coordinates. Left and right, above and below, occidental disorientation and Deep South and Far West and rudderless North, or rather new, Freudian, disorientation and displacement as dream-activity, the dream-work that is comparable to that of the novel: omission, modification, reorganization of material, substitution for satisfaction, change of the object of desire, the sublimation of perception, the identification and nomination of things, the disguise of the erotic dream projected as a social dream, the masquerade of condensed social reality in the abbreviation of a love-dream. Exorcism of the nightmare. Triumph of the replaced allusion. Translation from immediacy to mediacy. Forms of movement of surface but also of depth: trips around my room, trips to the center of the earth, the trips made by Ulysses and Phileas Fogg, but also the trips of Proust's narrator and Kafka's insect: displacements toward the lighthouse, the magic mountain, but also behind Alice's looking glass and into the garden of forking paths.

Occam asks us to look beyond the notion of movement as the mere reappearance of something that has moved to a new place. Borges, Balzac, and Freud, on the other hand, offer us proof of experiences that require displacement, movement from one place to another (spiritual or physical), but always through a transformation, a metamorphosis. Of what? Of experience in destiny.

To say it is easy, whereas to do it is more than difficult (though it is that, certainly) but complex. Transforming experience into destiny implies, for one thing, desire. But desire, in turn, opens up like a fan of possibility. It is the desire to be happy. A desire that the Enlightenment consecrated as a right, most explicitly in the founding laws of the United States: the pursuit of happiness. And while there are philosophies that see happiness as nothing more than the sister of passivity, the Faustian culture of the Western world, imposing and imperious, suggests that we act so that we may be happy. The experience of action is the condition required for arriving at happiness. But that action is going to encounter a multitude of obstacles. Comparable to Ulysses's voyage, the odyssey of the search for happiness will navigate perilously through Scylla and Charybdis, hear the siren song, frolic in the arms of Calypso, run the risk of transforming the thing it searches for into its opposite: the angel into the pig. We will see and be seen by the fearsome eye of the giant Cyclops. And we will return home to confront the suitors, the usurpers of all that we consider to be ours.

Active experience will encounter evil. And the bad thing about evil is that it knows goodness. Good, because of its innate goodness, exists within the innocence of only knowing itself. Evil has a better chance of winning, then, because it knows both good and evil. The experience of good is caught by surprise by evil, just like the cowboys caught by the Indians in the canyons and gorges of the Old West. Our dilemma is that in order to conquer evil, good must know evil. Know it without exercising it. Is this a demand fit only for saints? Or do we have ways of knowing evil without exercising it?

As a Faustian, Western male, I have a difficult time understanding and practicing the Eastern philosophies that know how to conquer evil passively. The malignant history of the age I live in leads me actively to oppose any and all assaults on liberty and life. But I am not unaware of the fact that the energy expended to achieve goodness is comparable to the energy expended to achieve evil. For the disciplined creator—and that could mean artist, politician, entrepreneur, worker, professional—it takes as much energy and experience to achieve good as it does to lose it entirely. And those of us who have witnessed drug addiction at close quarters know that it is an endeavor that demands as much energy, will, and cunning as does painting a mural, administering a company, or performing a quintuple bypass.

The temple of ethics is erected so that human experience may be, though difficult, exceptionally constructive. As far as I can see, this requires a high degree of attention that surpasses our own selves, our own interests, and focuses its concerns on the needs of others, linking our internal subjectivity to the world's objectivity through the one thing that the self and the world share: community. The *nos-otros,* the "we," us with others. And if this is a variant of the Kantian imperative, so be it. Kant may very well be the last thinker able to be fully moral before history (Nietzsche) proved that history was only very rarely in harmony with either goodness or happiness.

Given that we remain decrepit, ruined prisoners of the last great cultural revolution, which was Romanticism, this kind of skepticism has led us to believe fervently in the experience of passion, to the degree that we cannot conceive of experience without passion. *Corazón apasionado* (impassioned heart), as the old Mexican song goes. Passion means recognizing, respecting, and emulating the greatness of human emotion, to the degree of believing that passions themselves are what constitute the human soul. The experience of passion attempts to conceive of itself as a kind of free obedience to valid existential impulses. In my novel *The Years with Laura Díaz,* I describe a passion that encompasses the surrender and reserve necessary for passionate ecstasy to be truly consummated.

At the entrance to the house, he was reserved, discreet. . . . On the second floor he was surrendered, open, as if the exclusion had been the sole thing that had placed him exposed to the elements, with no reserve whatsoever for the time of love. He couldn't resist the idea of that combination, a complete manner of being a man, serene and passionate, open and secret, discreet when dressed, indiscreet when nude. . . . There he was, finally, as he always had been or invented right then, but revealing an eternal desire. . . .

To have desires and to know how to sustain them, correct them, abandon them . . . what is the path of this experiential ideal? It is precisely that very delicate balance between the moment that is active and the moment that is patient. All we need to do is observe (not imagine, but rather observe and confirm through the images and news we see on a daily basis) the manner in which passion degenerates into violence. This is what leads us to advocate a kind of balance that does not condemn passion (which is, after all, the source of such great satisfaction) but emerges from patience—not the patience of Job but rather the patience of resistance: the moral courage of Socrates, of Bruno, of Galileo, of Akhmatova and Mandelstam, of Edith Stein and Simone Weil, of all the humiliated and vilified souls of the City of Man, of all the patient pilgrims making their way to the City of God.

The concept of waiting is inextricably linked to attention. It is not resignation. It is not the terrible impatience of the Catholic confessional, where we ruin our experiences by revealing them to a man who can be just as perverted as the instructions the Church gave its confessors in the Spanish colonies ("Little girl, have you ever looked at yourself naked in a mirror? Have you ever desired your father's member?"); as indifferent as the sleepy parish priests who dispense Our Fathers and Hail Marys; or as solicitous—this is also true—as the exceptional priest who invokes the voice of confession to separate it from parlor fodder and make it the object of communion—of, I repeat, a shared attention.

The heart of all experience, more than anything, is the simple awareness that all experience is limited. And not only because we, like Pascal, are gripped by the vertigo of infinite spaces, but because death (if not life) and the gaze of the night (if not the blindness of the day) tell us that experience is limited and the universe, infinite. This is proven to us by the fact that no experience, no matter how good or valuable it may be, is ever completely fulfilled. The artist, who need not possess the chisel of Michelangelo to ensure the imperfection of his work, knows this. If the work of art were perfect, it would be divine, impenetrable, holy. Death will tell us the same thing about experience. Socrates and Greta Garbo are dead. The philosopher will never dialogue again, nor will any more of his thoughts emerge beyond the ones established by Plato. All the rest (which does not mean the "lesser")—memory, humor, prudence, hope, physical and psychical reality—have left us forever. Greta Garbo has always looked at us and will always gaze upon us as Queen Christina, from the prow of the ship that delivers her far from love and toward impassioned memory. But Greta Gustafsson will never make another movie. Yes, a passionate heart, but one that conceals a sadness within. And he who is born into misfortune embarks upon a life of pain and suffering, right from the cradle, the Mexican song continues.

Reckless courage is what a person needs to be able to endure a limitless experience, one that is exposed to all kinds of risk. Goethe, typically, asked us to search for the infinite within our own selves: "And if you do not find it in yourself and in your thoughts, there will be no mercy for you." But there is an awareness of the limits, one that the young, romantic author of *The Sorrows of Young Werther* skillfully balanced with the morality and aesthetics of *Wilhelm Meister*. Everything has a limit and the real challenge to our liberty lies in the question: do we dare to exceed those limits or do we not? The answer is yet another challenge. If we wish to broaden the area of our experience, we must understand the limitations of that experience. Not the political, psychological, or ethical limitations, but rather the limitations inherent to all experiences simply because of their nature as experiences.

Each person possesses his own personal device for gauging those limitations. Einstein did not exceed his own limitations. Hitler did.

A character from the novel *The Years with Laura Díaz* expresses a desire to be in a place where he feels exposed to danger and at the same time protected, not because he wants to banish the feeling of being in danger but because he does not want to let himself be fooled by the illusion of his own power. How many people do we know who take extraordinary pains to appear strong for those around them precisely because they are all too aware of their interior weaknesses? Who will win that duel with weakness by making themselves strong on the inside, so that the world does not deceive them with false strength, crumbs of power, or insulting pity? Stoic resistance should be taken seriously because, as Marcus Aurelius tells us, we are never given more than we can endure. And he adds: "Time is a sort of river of passing events, and strong is its current; no sooner is a thing brought to sight than it is swept by and another takes its place, and this too will be swept away. . . ."

To understand this quotation you do not need great moral courage, but to experience it you most certainly do. "Was it for this . . . ?" asks Wordsworth at the beginning of *The Prelude,* one of the greatest poems of all time. And he answers with yet another question: "For this . . . ?" Behind both questions, the fabric of our experience is being woven like a second skin, made up of the abilities that we gradually acquire as humans. The ability to be with others, and the experience of solitude as well. Forms that detach from our personal experiences and take on lives of their own, leaving testimony behind, perhaps fleeting, perhaps permanent, of our passage. And of our passion. Lights that progressively illuminate our path. And the nagging question: what are the names of those beacons that light the way for us? The skin of experience. With scars that sometimes heal and sometimes do not. The voice of experience. Sometimes we listen to it, sometimes we do not. Experience: danger and yearning. Experience and de-sire: an ardent or serene anticipation of something that has yet to happen, without losing sight of those things that already have happened.

We are on earth because this is where we were born and this is where we will die. But we are also in the world, which is not quite the same thing. In *El naranja* (*The Orange Tree*), the women to whom I give voices in my description of the walls of Numan-tia are besieged by death and famine, and they watch as the over-whelmed world—though not the earth—disappears. The earth remains while the world disappears. It makes no difference. The world (construction) dies, but the earth (instruction) is trans-formed. Why? Because the word says so. Because we do not lose sight of the experience of the word. The world shows us that we are human beings, subject to its experience. The Earth hides us for a brief moment, only to give us back the power to recreate the world. "We disappear from the world. We return to Earth. From there we will emerge to frighten everyone." In other words, we will speak.

Calderón de la Barca poses the defining question of experi-ence in *La vida es sueño* (*Life Is a Dream*), the greatest work of Spanish drama: "The greatest crime of man is that of having been born." Segismundo, the protagonist of the play, compares himself to Nature who, having less soul than he, has more freedom. Segismundo feels this absence of freedom as a deficiency, as if he hasn't fully been born: "Before being born, you died." But isn't it a greater crime not to have been born at all? Calderón liberates us to the intimate beat of dreams. Dreaming as compensation for all that experience has denied us. We dream in both forward-time and backward-time. We desire in both directions. No, it is better to have been born. And each of us must examine the reasons why it was worth coming into the world at all, and ask ourselves tire-lessly and without hope of an answer the great questions of expe-rience:

How are freedom and destiny related?

To what extent can each one of us personally shape our own experience?

What part of our experience is change and what part permanence?

To what degree does experience depend upon necessity, coincidence, liberty?

And why do we identify with the ignorance of what we are: the union of body and soul? And still continue to be precisely the thing we do not understand?

F

Family

I do not know anything of my own genealogy beyond my great-grandparents. On my mother's side, my great-grandfather Teodoro Rivas emigrated from Santander to Sonora during the second half of the nineteenth century and settled down in the beautiful city that is a bountiful garden amid the deserts of the Mexican north: Álamos (a city of silver ghosts, Indians made of smoke, and calendars of saints and crosses), where he eventually became the director of the treasury of Sonora. I know very little of his descendants, because my maternal grandmother, Emilia Rivas Gil, was chary when it came to dispensing family information; it was as if she was trying to concentrate and protect a circle devastated by pain and death. She was married to Manuel Macías Gutiérrez and they spent their idyllic early days in the port of Mazatlán, where my mother was born next to the Paseo de las Olas Altas (the Boulevard of the Tall Waves). The photographs from the turn of the twentieth century speak volumes: my grandmother is a small, dark woman with an aquiline nose and black eyes, penetrating and resolute. My grandfather is a tall, white-skinned man, very dapper, very elegant, all careful attention to detail and grooming in every aspect: the waxed moustache, the discreet gaze, the elegant frock coat and cravat. Encircling them like a bouquet of white flowers are his four daughters, all dressed in white. Three of them (María Emilia, Carmen, and Sélika) have dreamy expressions on their faces, while my mother, Berta, has the same resolute look as her mother. Before long, those luminous white clothes would be exchanged for funeral garb. Sélika died of scarlet fever at the age of ten.

And my handsome grandfather—so manly, so distinguished—fatally and mysteriously contracted the most feared of diseases: leprosy. His young wife and three daughters were forced to witness, with a pain that admitted neither pity nor rejection, the harrowing deterioration of their husband and father. I see them in the photographs taken after my grandfather's death, all of them dressed in black, with bandannas tied around their temples and their long black hair straightened. An honest, capable merchant, my grandfather left no fortune behind. I met his brothers and my aunts, his nieces. They were all identical. The old men were tall, pale as ghosts, and with the parchment skin of old people, while all the young girls had skin like wax. One of them, who had an imposing physical presence, was a nun. My widowed grandmother was forced to support her three daughters. As a girl she had been friends with Álvaro Obregón, in Sonora. When Obregón became president, he appointed my grandmother inspector of schools, and the minister of education, José Vasconcelos, gave her an active role in the remarkable literacy campaign that, in 1921, confronted the grim fact that 90 percent of all Mexicans were illiterate.

Once her three daughters were married, my grandmother was able to retire and accept the loving support of the Fuentes, Romandía, and Juárez families. The relationships Emilia maintained with her sons-in-law were often every bit as tormented as one would have expected, considering her strong character. When it came to her daughters, her attitude was consistently leonine, for she was the eternal guardian of her pride. And with her grandchildren she became a focal point of happiness, jokes, reminiscences. She was a link to a past that was growing more and more remote but that she, with great humor, returned to us intact: the days of Porfirio Díaz, the revolution, Mazatlán, the poem by Enrique González Martínez inscribed in her autograph book, her forgotten predilection for the piano, her peculiar insistence upon watching movies in black-and-white, and then dreaming of them in Technicolor. . . .

Similar in temperament, though far more severe in character, my other grandmother, Emilia Boettiger, was the descendant of German immigrants who hailed from the city of Darmstadt in the Rhineland. My great-grandfather Philip Boettiger, a fervent supporter of Ferdinand Lasalle, left Germany when Lasalle joined forces with the Iron Chancellor Otto von Bismarck under the misguided conviction that only an alliance between the Prussian aristocracy—the Junkers—and the proletarian socialists could save the country from the unseemly avarice and presumptuousness of the bourgeois arrivistes. In reality, the socialist Lasalle was an elegant revolutionary driven by the profound disgust he felt for the vulgar manners and boorish ways of his rival, Karl Marx. In any event, the Boettiger brothers set sail for the Americas and arrived at the port of New Orleans. There, their paths diverged. The older brother went to the North, to Chicago, where he became a prosperous businessman whose grandson married Anna, the daughter of President Franklin D. Roosevelt. My great-grandfather went to Veracruz, and on arrival fell in love with the town and lagoon of Catemaco. He went on to establish a prosperous coffee business there, had three daughters (my grandmother Emilia and my great-aunts María and Luisa), integrated his little mulatto daughter, Ana (born to another woman), into the family, and forbade his family to speak German. He wanted to be Mexican, to leave the Old World behind.

My paternal grandfather, Rafael Fuentes Vélez, was the son of Carlos Fuentes Benítez, a businessman who had emigrated from the Canary Islands and who entered into matrimony with a beautiful *criolla* woman, Clotilde Vélez, who would one day be assaulted on the Camino Real. A bandit asked her to hand over her rings and when she refused to give them up, she lost them in the barbaric slice of a machete. My grandfather grew up in the port of Veracruz and met my grandmother at the Candelaria festivals in Tlacotalpan. He was forty years old; she was seventeen. The photographs reveal a short man with an aquiline nose and penetrating eyes beneath a pair of extraordinarily arched brows, like twin circumflex accents, that made him appear as though he were perennially angry, even diabolical. My grandmother Emilia, on the other hand, was like a Gothic statue: tall, thin, severe, and blessed with a profile that was perfect and straight, bestowing a noble, eternal symmetry upon her face.

They had three sons: the eldest, Carlos Fuentes Boettiger, made a name for himself very early on as a poet. Tall, blond, and slender, he was the favored disciple of the poet Salvador Díaz Mirón. At the age of twenty-one he went to study in Mexico City, never to return, for he fell victim to one of the typhoid epidemics that in those days swept through Mexico, backward, unhealthy, and chaotic country that it was. But the family enjoyed many years of happiness, first in Veracruz, where my grandfather was the manager of the National Bank of Mexico, and later on in Jalapa where he held the same post and watched his health slowly deteriorate, having succumbed to a progressive paralysis that would eventually leave him mute, confined to a wheelchair with no discernible expression on his face—like old Villefort in *The Count of Monte Cristo*—other than that afforded by his monstrous eyebrows. Through my father I learned that this ancient man, whom I did get to know, had been a voracious reader in Spanish, French, Italian, and English. From my grandfather Rafael I still have some beautiful old editions of Dante, Swift, and Walter Scott, printed in the nineteenth century in such a tiny typeface that they must have required a magnifying glass to read. My father used to tell me how every month my grandfather took him by the hand to the port, in anticipation of the mail boat from Liverpool and Le Havre that arrived at Veracruz with the illustrated magazines—*The London Illustrated News, La Vie Parisienne*—and novels that were in vogue at the time: by Pierre Benoît, Alphonse Daudet, Pierre Loti.

Having lost all hope of her husband's health improving, my determined grandmother Emilia Boettiger moved to Mexico City, where she established a guesthouse high up on the corner of Mérida and Álvaro Obregón that was frequented by many Veracruz residents passing through the capital. They followed the exodus of many families who, spurred on by the devastations of the revolutionary movement, had come to Mexico City in droves from the provinces. A woman of extraordinary energy and will, my grandmother Emilia took care of her incapacitated husband, reigned over a *jarocha* kitchen of delicious Veracruz cuisine such as the beef dish known as *manchamanteles,* the rice and black beans known as *moros y cristianos,* fried plantains, *ropa vieja,* and octopus in its ink. My aunt Emilia, completely dominated by her mother's forceful will, assisted her in her tasks, feeling herself to be responsible, until the day she died, for looking after her parents even more than for looking after herself. Just like in the novels of the day, she sacrificed her own happiness in order to fulfill her filial duties.

My father, Rafael Fuentes Boettiger, on the other hand, left behind the province of his childhood and youth in order to focus his energies on a vocation that had inspired him ever since he had first visited the port with my grandfather to watch the mail boats come into town. A precocious reader from a very early age, he would stage dramatic readings, assuming D'Artagnan's role in the adaptation of *The Three Musketeers* he would perform in the massive gymnasium of Veracruz's bank. At thirteen, as a cadet in the Jalapa preparatory military academy, he departed for Veracruz to take part in the defense of the port that had been invaded by U.S. marines. He did not get far, though—the occupation came to an end soon afterward. Nor did he get very far when, at the age of nineteen, he decided to join Fernando Soler and Sagra del Río's theater company and surreptitiously escaped Jalapa one day. My grandfather was waiting for him at Córdoba station and dragged him off the train by his ear.

As a young lawyer and instructor in the law department at Veracruz University, my father entered the Mexican Foreign Ministry at the age of twenty-five as a lawyer for the Mexican and American Mixed Claims Commission, which had been created to address the grievances of U.S. citizens affected by the wartime activity along the northern Mexican border. He met my mother on a tram, one of those old yellow relics that in those days wove through the streets of Mexico City. They were married and left the country when my father was appointed to his first diplomatic post, in Panama, where I was born nine months later on November 11, 1928.

We were a happy family, if, to someone like Tolstoy, perhaps not a terrifically interesting one. But who cares about being interesting if unhappiness is the price you have to pay? My sister Berta was born in Mexico in 1932 and we spent our childhood in the Mexican embassies in Washington, D.C., Santiago de Chile, and Buenos Aires. This itinerant, mutant diplomatic life—"gypsies in tuxedos," as my father called us—clearly brought us together, but so did the mutual respect and constant affection that were the essence of our life together. The great Mexican writer Alfonso Reyes had this to say about my father: "He was an essential man, no froth." That frothless man arrived at the Mexican embassy in Rio de Janeiro one day and found Reyes attending to his administrative tasks, deciphering cables and filing news clips. "I'll look after the office, Don Alfonso," my father said to him. "You concentrate on your writing." It was in the company of another great ambassador, Francisco Castillo Nájera, the Cárdenas government's envoy in Washington, that my father honed his rigorous work ethic and close attention to detail—two qualities for which he became renowned during his years as the chief of protocol for the Ministry of Foreign Affairs, and then at embassies in Panama, the Hague, Rome, and Lisbon. Leaving diplomacy and entering retirement killed him. Back in Mexico, he yearned for his driver, his reports, his daily diplomatic agenda, all the essential elements of his life, and slowly faded away, disconcerted, wearing a poignant expression of absence and nostalgia.

I owe my basic literary education to him. His encouragement and his tacit homage to his dead brother's unrealized potential touched me deeply even as a small child. He was a man of good humor, tenderness, punctuality: a good example. My mother, at his side, lived a never-ending, real-life love story with him. The very day he died, my father did two things: he tried on a new suit and he sexually harassed my mother. She had always represented the dignity and formality of the home, the sense of security that beneath the travelling, the forced adaptations to new schools, learning new languages and new customs, there lay a principle of seriousness, rectitude, and even impatience with ambitious, arriviste, or intriguing people. Yet she did not lack a sense of humor, either. She was an excellent poker player, and I remember watching her as she trounced the revolution-era generals who, to their chagrin, had bet against her during the games they played at embassy dinners. And to the day of her death, achy but every bit herself at the age of ninety-four, she confessed to me: "I have one disappointment in life. I would have liked to pilot a plane."

What she piloted marvelously was our family Buick every summer en route from Washington to Mexico, enduring the heat, the racial discrimination in Texas ("No dogs or Mexicans allowed"), and the curves at Tamazunchale. This practical skill more than compensated for my father's dreamier, somewhat dispassionate disposition. My mother was the one who ran the family home, put together the schedules, had clean clothes ready at all times, and did the sums on the car, the schools, the apartment. She thought about the future, always much more than my father, who was disciplined and punctual to a fault but also—and bravo to him—a dreamer, a tender soul, a man utterly without material ambition. He could be emphatic and intolerant, and he certainly

Carlos Fuentes

was with me: I still wince with pain at the memory of the spank-
ings he gave me. And that was how he was with every display of
tardiness, lack of discipline, or rudeness. That was how he was
with arrogant or corrupt Mexican politicians. I still remember his
head-on confrontation with Gonzalo N. Santos, the political boss
of San Luis Potosí, over a question of disrespect. I remember his
decision to resign from the City Hall of the Mexican capital during the administration of Abelardo Rodríguez, horrified at the
offers of *mordidas* (graft) and violations of Mexican law. He had
lasted two months in the job. I think he will spend eternity in
heaven.

Faulkner

Freedom already exists. Such is the implicit postulate in all the legislation of progress. The businessman, the worker, the child, the woman, the individual, the sum total of humanity—are we not all free, given that the Law claims this to be true? If freedom already exists, pace Rousseau and via the democratic revolutions of France and the United States, nothing is tragic. From Dostoevsky to Kafka, however, tragic writers tell us that this is not so. True freedom consists in the minimal possibility of making reality meaningful, and making the world realistic is always a task just beyond our reach. Freedom is not handed over to us. We must make it, and we make it by searching for it. Not even the somber (though ever-smiling) Machiavelli would have dared claim otherwise: "God does not want to do everything, so as not to take free will from us, and that part of His glory that falls to us."

We had to reach the twentieth century to consecrate totalitarianism and nihilism simultaneously, so that, in Kafkaesque legislation, the world would have a final meaning, defined by the Law. As a result, it is useless to seek another meaning for reality. Do you insist, Herr K? If so, you will be eliminated insofar as the Law is concerned. The Enlightenment comes to an end with Kafka: you have the obligation to be happy, or else you run the risk of turning into an insect.

The most absurd aspect of freedom and the Law in Kafka reminds us, with extraordinary power, that the true meeting point between society and the human being requires a tragic vision—that is, a vision of conflict and reconciliation, which is opposed to the Manichaean vision that has governed modern history, the vision of sin and extermination. When a religion reclaims a historical basis, Nietzsche suggests, it does so to justify the dogmatism "beneath the severe gaze . . . of orthodoxy." You must be guilty so that I may be innocent. In Aeschylus's *Prometheus Bound,* the chorus exclaims: "All that exists is at once just and unjust." Who embodies these realities in a more disturbing fashion than Ivan Karamazov when he crosses the threshold, fully resolved to remain on the side of Justice and against Truth, when Truth and Justice do not coincide?

This is the immoral decision that the tragic hero does not have to make. Tragedy does not sacrifice Truth to Justice or Justice to Truth because in the realm of tragedy, the forces in conflict with one another are equally legitimate, identically moral in the deepest sense: when defeated, they are able to bring value to defeat. Value, not sin. And one of the dimensions of value without sin, even when it is ignored and at times violated, is the value of the Other. This is the value that William Faulkner identifies so magnificently: the restoration of the community divided—not by history (in this case, the military and economic might of the North) but because men and women, long before the Civil War, had already divided their souls.

The literature of the United States reveals the constant tension between the optimism of foundation and the pessimism of the critical eye. Consecrated by the Constitution and the laws of North American democracy, this optimism becomes the credo of the country's social and economic life: "Nothing succeeds like success."

Progressive optimism transforms into the mask of imperial expansion. From the thirteen English colonies along the Atlantic, the United States expanded westward (French Louisiana), through the territories of the Gulf of Mexico (Texas), all the way to the Pacific (California) and the Caribbean (Spanish Florida, Cuba, Puerto Rico, and as far as Panama in Central America). All this in the name of the "manifest destiny" of a country designated by God to be, like ancient Rome, *caput mundis* (capital of the world).

The vitality of North American literature, to a large degree, lies in the critical opposition of its writers. Aside from the sugary literature of the *Pollyanna* ilk, "the happy girl," novelists and short story writers beginning with Hawthorne and followed by Poe, Melville, Henry James, and Mark Twain in the nineteenth century, then by Dreiser, Sinclair Lewis, Frank Norris, Fitzgerald, and Dos Passos in the twentieth, portray the other side of the coin. The nightmares of the American Dream, the ghosts by day and the prayers by night, the brutality of upward mobility, the mediocrity of the middle class, the disillusion of success, the emptiness of fame, are constant critical themes in the narrative of the United States.

William Faulkner places the roundest, most miraculous, brilliant, and somber crown upon this critical process, because he goes beyond criticism and achieves tragedy. This and so much more. Franz Kafka and Samuel Beckett are, perhaps, the two other tragic writers of the past century. They are few, but that is natural. "The death of tragedy" declared by Nietzsche may well date back, as the German philosopher himself believed, to Socratic reasoning. But what seems irrefutable to me is that, primarily, Christianity is unable to coexist with tragedy if it is to promise eternal salvation.

Stripped of religious vestments, lay progress—beginning especially with Condorcet and the French Revolution—renounces God but not happiness. If, as Condorcet believed, the ascendant line of the human being toward happiness is certain, then the tragic conscience remains excluded from the successive progressive visions of Saint-Simon, Comte, and Marx.

If transforming experience into destiny is a necessary trait of the tragic, it casts a shadow upon the philosophy of progress and the salvation of souls. Not to believe in the Devil is to give him every opportunity, wrote André Gide. And the Western world, by expelling tragedy from its history, allowed crime to take its place. Instead of the inevitable, happy progress heralded by the Enlightenment and its successor, the Industrial Revolution, the twentieth century became the century of historical horror, unpunished crimes, masked tragedy. Kafka and Beckett offer the greatest European cultural testimony to this fact. In Kafka, the traditional hero wakes up one day to find that he has become an insect, but an insect that knows he is an insect and thinks, "There is a chasm between me and the world," but the chasm manifests itself as filled with power. We have known the void that a usurping power creates and fills, but, even when we are aware of the lie, we remain dumbfounded, helpless observers of the farce that hides it. God is dead and it wasn't the enlightened atheists who killed him—it was a gang of tramps who, despite the existing evidence, are nevertheless waiting for Godot.

The Faulknerian tragedy enters this painful search for a world in which, risen from darkness, we can look with clarity upon the consequences of our "rebellious freedom," as Büchner called it in *Danton's Death*. Faulkner, of course, is writing from the most optimistic and forward-thinking of societies, the United States of America, where "nothing succeeds like success." This makes the United States an eccentric country, given that the majority of the world's nations have experienced immediate and disastrous encounters with failure.

Faulkner rejects the foundational optimism of the American Dream and tells his countrymen: we too can fail. We too can bear the cross of tragedy. This cross is called racism. The North did not defeat the South. The South had already defeated itself by enslaving, humiliating, hunting down, and murdering the Other, the man, the woman, and the child who are "different" from white power. But the pain of tragedy can redeem us if, in the end, we can recognize the humanity we share with others.

The Faulknerian tragedy is inscribed within a defined space—Yoknapatawpha County, which translated from the Chickasaw means "a land divided"—and based upon family roots that sink deep into the land: the aristocratic Sartorises and Compsons, the social-climbing Snopes. Very often, however, the tragedy is touched off by the stranger, the "intruder in the dust" who arrives in Mississippi with another image, one that seems threatening because he or she is different, and that could apply as easily to Charles Bon in *Absalom, Absalom!* as to Lena Grove in *Light in August*—the foreigner from outside who shows us the foreigner from within: the black man, Joe Christmas. Whether they fan out into great family trees or are set in great historical epochs, Faulkner's novels are the novels of a land—the South—but history, geography, society, and families find resolution and significance through two tragic elements: individual destiny and collective testimony. The serenity of Lena Grove, the bitter sexuality of Joanna Burden, and the inevitable fate of Joe Christmas are individual characters within the great collective chorus of Faulknerian tragedy. In the center of this chorus, one woman fights back and lives to tell of it: Miss Rosa Coldfield. Outside of the chorus, a descendant survives to remember: Quentin Compson.

Among all these people—protagonists and scene, chorus and choryphaeus—the Faulknerian tragedy, beyond the history of the South, like Sophoclean tragedy, beyond the history of ancient Greece, becomes an integral part of the times we live in, an opportunity to transform experience into destiny. In the end, the center of the Faulknerian tragedy may very well be time. Its prodigious breadth, its incomparable receptivity, is patent in Quentin's observation that the present began ten thousand years ago and the future is happening now. Joe Christmas defines his tragic fatality, his prison on earth, when he says, "I have been further in these seven days than in all the thirty years. But I have never got outside that circle. I have never broken out of the ring of what I have already done and cannot ever undo."

It is in this temporal tension between our way of living, understanding and suffering with the past, present, and future that the tragic modernity of William Faulkner achieves true narrative greatness.

Faulkner identifies his tragic theme: the restoration of the community divided, not by history but by men and women who have already divided both their land and their souls. Faulkner merges all the time periods of his characters into one narrative present. Because for the author of *Absalom, Absalom!,* the unity of all times is the only possible answer to such division. What Faulkner proposes is the affirmation of the collective "I am" against the forces of separation. His novels acquire the form of "the ode, the elegy, the epitaph borne from a bitter, implacable reserve that refuses to yield to defeat."

Freedom

Whether we consider freedom to be absolute free will, or circumscribed by heritage, nature, inevitability, or chance, the mere mention of the word is already an act of hope. Perhaps those who lack freedom understand its value better than anyone. Those who take it for granted are those who risk losing it. And those who fight for it must be aware of the dangers implicit in the struggle to obtain it. In the midst of the French Revolution, Saint-Just had this to say about the battles for revolutionary freedom: fighting for freedom against tyranny is an epic struggle; fighting between revolutionaries is tragic. The battle for freedom has often spawned the most extreme forms of oppression that nevertheless manage to claim legitimacy by invoking their revolutionary origins. Revolutions legitimize. But once freedom is attained—call it revolution, call it independence—how can it be preserved, sustained, improved? The most pragmatic and precise formula for answering this question may very well be the one suggested by James Madison in *The Federalist:*

If men were angels, no government would be necessary. If angels were to govern men, neither external nor internal controls on government would be necessary. [But] In framing a government which is to be administered by men over men . . . you must first enable the government to control the governed; and in the next place oblige it to control itself.

Elections, revocations, impeachments, administrative trials, weights and balances, division of powers, fiscal accountability of the executive branch: the democratic governments of the world have discovered multiple ways of expanding upon Madison's formula so that citizens and institutions may hold governments responsible for controlling themselves and thus, among other things, maintain control over the populace.

Political freedom takes these goals into account and recognizes their limitations. But freedom is both a private and a public issue. Moreover, freedom conceives of itself as an institution in the first person singular. Preserving intrinsic personal values is a kind of freedom that falls within the rubric of the individual. Yet, the moment it steps outside the domain of the individual, freedom understands that no man is free on his own. And so we may say that freedom initially exercises itself in the first person singular, but can only be sustained in the three conditions of the plural. My freedom is "I," plus "we," plus the plural "you," plus "them." *Tensions will inevitably arise between my free "I" and the world around me: they can be antagonistic but are always creative, for if freedom is a possibility for me, it is only true freedom if it is also a possibility for others.*

I underscore the word *possibility* because the obstacles facing liberty are far too numerous and complicated to assure us that "being free" will be immediately accessible to us. For example, people can act freely though against their own best interests, out of masochism perhaps, but more often than not out of ignorance or flawed judgment. Freedom can be freedom for evil. Necessity fuels it but also limits and thwarts it. Nature invokes it but also expels it. It often comes wrapped in the cloak of the unpredictable. And the sum total of all these obstacles and contradictions may lead us, not without good reason, to look upon freedom as nothing more than a moral fact or an obligation. Manuel Azaña expressed this very well: freedom may not necessarily make men happy, but at the very least it will make them men.

Voltaire's Pangloss tells us that we live in the best of all possible worlds, Beckett's Winnie, that we live in the worst of all possible worlds.

In between these two visions, Socrates proposes that we live the life of the city and that we seek freedom in the city and in dialogue even if the city will ultimately deny us both dialogue and life itself, as was the case with Socrates himself. True critical wisdom consists of mending the rift between the creative interior life and the mundane exterior life both through personal knowledge (know thyself) and urban knowledge (know others), because that breach between interior and exterior freedom is altogether real and tangible, even if it does occasionally manifest itself as a precipice, a kind of void. Albert O. Hirschman, in a marvelous book, *Exits and Entrances,* observes this process of "entrances and exits" with stunning clarity.

We constantly enter and exit freedom. The extreme dilemma is twofold: on the one hand we don't want to remain locked away in our individual freedoms, for they can become a solipsistic seclusion that transforms the outside world into mere illusion. Yet on the other hand, we cannot abide the dire absence of liberty that is represented by life under a dictatorship. Freedom, in reality, is the freedom to move, not without conflicts but rather in a creative sense, between the individual and the world, between the "I" and the "Other." Freedom consistently fills the gap between interior and exterior action, the abyss between interior and exterior reality, the void between determinism and free will.

An endless task; not that of Camus's Sisyphus but of Milton's unfinished man. Can man not "finish" but rather advance, and create himself with freedom? St. Augustine, in his celebrated dispute with Pelagius, denies any freedom that does not occur through the Church—that is, the Institution. Pelagius, a millennium before Martin Luther, grants the individual the freedom to save himself outside of the ecclesiastic institutions. But that kind of freedom also implies that one must work creatively within the institutional framework, not out of inevitability or obligation but out of one's own free will. That this will, like a kind of DNA in serpentine mutation, comprises heritage, biology, education, culture, language, religion, politics, and morality only makes the notion of freedom more human, and also more complex. There is no such thing as simple freedom.

How is freedom to be measured? By the margin of free will that existing institutions grant the individual? Or is it the reverse, by the margin of authority that our free will grants existing institutions? Whatever, freedom consists of believing in it, fighting for it. Freedom is the quest for freedom. We will never fully achieve it. Death warns us that there are limits to all personal freedoms. History warns us that the institutions that, at some moment or other in time, take it upon themselves to define freedom, eventually wane and transform into something else themselves. But between life and death, between the beauty and the horror of the world, the quest for freedom is what makes us, no matter what the circumstance, free.

Friendship

What we do not have, we find in our friends. I believe in this gift and have cultivated it since childhood. In this sense, I am no different from most other human beings. Friendship is the first great link connecting the home to the outside world. Whether a happy or unhappy place, the home is the classroom where we learn basic wisdom, and friendship is the test of this wisdom. What we receive from our family, we confirm in friendship. The variations, differences, or similarities between our family and our friends will determine the contradictory paths our lives will take. And while we may love our home, we all inevitably reach for that unstable, restless moment of departure (even if we love it, even if we still remain in it). This departure from home can only be compensated by friendship. But it is more than that: without outside friendship, our internal foundations would crumble. Friendship does not challenge the family's domain that rules the early years of life; on the contrary, friendship confirms it, supports it, makes it last. Friendship plants the seed for feelings that can only grow outside the home. Locked up inside the family domain, these feelings will dry up like plants without water. When we open the doors of the home, we discover forms of love that bring the home and the outside world together. These are called friendships.

Precisely because I believe in the value of friendship as a kind of initiation into life, as well as for the wisdom it imparts, I am struck by the philosophical cynicism that hovers over it like a dark cloud. Oscar Wilde uses his fearsome talent for paradox to declare that Bernard Shaw has not a single enemy in the world, but none of his friends like him either. For Byron, sadly, friendship is love without wings. And while friendship may blossom into love, love rarely blossoms into friendship. Friends, as conventional wisdom goes, should be welcomed with joy and dispatched with haste. And if the friend is a guest, after three days, like a dead fish, he will begin to emit a most foul stench.

I think there is more pain in lost friendships than in cynicism. The emotions confessed and shared. The illusion, confirmed by our friends, that we possess a shared wisdom. The strong backbone of hope that can only grow out of a childhood lived among friends. The joy of the gang, the posse, the brotherhood, *la banda, l'équipe, la patocha.* The bonds of unity. The complicity of childhood friendship, the pride of being young and, if one is young and already wise, the admonishing voice of youth when the friendship is an old one. We learn to govern the pride of youth. The day will come when we are no longer young, and when it does we will need our friends more than ever.

The era of youth opens the experience of friendship, and my "disk" remembers the names, the faces, the words, and the actions of my schoolmates. But the things I remember do not win out against those I have forgotten. How can I not celebrate the fact that, sixty years later, I am still in contact with my very first childhood friends. I had the kind of nomadic childhood that comes from being born into a family of diplomats whose constant pilgrimage resists any kind of sustained affection. Yet I still write to Hans Berliner, a German-Jewish boy who arrived at my elementary school in Washington after fleeing the Nazi terror and became the object of childish cruelty that lashes out against all that is different. He was dark-skinned and tall for his age, and like all European children in those days, wore short trousers. To the American children, he wasn't "regular"—or, in other words, he wasn't indistinguishable from them. For my part, I lost hold of my initial popularity when President Cárdenas nationalized Mexico's oil wealth in 1938. For the first but not the only time in my life, I was suddenly suspected of being a Communist. Exclusion united us, Hans and myself, and we remain close to this day. Geography would soon separate us, but as an adolescent in Santiago de Chile I soon found my gang, my team, my *chorcha,* my *patocha* among the boys who preferred reading and debate to the rough, mud-caked sports of the Grange, our English school in the foothills of the Andes, governed by English captains convinced that the Battle of Waterloo had been won on the playing fields of Eton. I still remember all the names, all the faces—Page, Saavedra, Quesnay, Marín Stipec—but most of all I remember Roberto Torretti, my intellectual and literary companion. We wrote our first novel together. It ended up getting lost in one of Roberto's mother's old trunks, but to this day Torretti and I continue to write letters, meeting and talking in Oaxaca and Puerto Rico, as well as corresponding between Mexico and Santiago. He is an extraordinary philosopher, and our friendship always takes me back to those early years in that English school, to the play-acted adventures of two musketeers in the Mexican embassy palazzo, and it brings back other memories as well, some more distant and others more painful. That was where I met José Donoso, older than me, the future crowning glory of Chilean letters. I don't know if he knew me. And in a previous school, I discovered the pain of having a close friend die at the age of twelve; it was my first experience of facing the death of someone my own age, and it left me shattered. I was equally devastated, however, by the fate of another little boy who was the object of ridicule and abuse because of his physical deformities. I dared to defend him, and came to discover another dimension of friendship: solidarity. After the coup staged by the atrocious Pinochet, that boy, who had since become a man, was tortured in the death camps in southern Chile, and while that fact intensifies the horror I feel when confronted with such human cruelty, it also intensifies the tenderness and compassion I feel for the true reality of friendship.

This is because all of us, to a greater or lesser degree, have betrayed or been betrayed by friendship. Gangs break up and close childhood friends can become the most indifferent, alienated ghosts in adulthood. And there is nothing quite so easily betrayed as friendship. If we were to make a list of all our lost friends, the footnotes would speak of indifference, hatred, rivalry, but also different epochs and epic distances. They would speak of deaths. Why did we abandon friends? Why did they abandon us? When you really think about it, there is very little friendship in the world. Most especially among equals. William Blake expressed it in these incomparable words: "Thy friendship oft has made my heart to ache: Do be my enemy for friendship's sake." Because while friendship, at its core, is a matter of disposition, generosity, willingness to spend time with others, it is also, at the very same time, a secret and insinuating rejection of that same intimacy when it is felt as dependency. Wordsworth speaks of the vernal hours of life during which we live in a kind of paradox that flings us down the path of fate yet at the same time shelters us from its accidents. Accidents, at times, of humor. Sargent went so far as to say that each time he painted a portrait he lost a friend. And George Canning, the legendary British foreign secretary, added a diplomatic twist to friendship—"Save me from the Candid Friend," he implored. This is true: in both diplomacy and politics, to trust friendship is to take a great risk. In power, we find a concentration of laws that have the most definitive ability to destroy friendship. Betrayal. Remorse. Desertion. The field of dead bodies left behind by the use of abuse. The abandoned trenches left behind by the indifference of force. And always, the temptation of cruel humor. Malraux to Genet: "*Que pensez-vous vraiment de moi?"* ("What do you really think of me?") Genet to Malraux: *"Je ne vous aime assez pour vous le dire."* ("I don't like you enough to tell you.")

These are not useless lessons. The most barren of lands blossom forth suddenly to show us that, insofar as friendship is concerned, one must occasionally allow room for the wisdom of the Proverbs and admit that the wounds of a friend can be faithful ones. And with a friend we can dare to tell him why we do not love him. The enemy, on the other hand, should never be given that satisfaction. But the terrible thing about the loss of friendship is abandoning all those days to which the friend gave meaning. To lose a friend, then, is quite literally to lose time. Excessive expectations, jealousy of someone else's victories. It is time for a return to friendship but with the knowledge that friendship demands cultivation on a daily basis if it is to bear its marvelous fruits. To establish bonds and enjoy shared affinities. To give each other the gift of serenity. To call for a joyous mutual discipline so as to maintain the friendship. To discover with friends the power of the world and the joy of spending time together. To laugh with friends. To experience friendship as a permanent invitation to accept and to be accepted. And to challenge oneself to try to achieve perfection in friendship and protect it from anything that may attempt to undermine it. To live in the company of friends in such a way that there is never an occasion to feel shame the day after, or to speak ill of those not present. To defend friendship against jealousy, envy, fear. And to agree to disagree: differences should enhance friendship and mutual respect. In an intelligent relationship between friends, there is no place for ambition, intolerance, pettiness. Friendship is dignified modesty, it is imagination and it is generosity. And sometimes—why not?—it is also the exact opposite. Pride. Passivity. Emotional avarice.

I say "passivity" and I am reminded that while dialogue is one of the great joys of friendship, so is silence. This is something I learned through my friendship with Luis Buñuel. At first, whenever he fell silent in the course of our normally animated conversation, I would feel that his lapses were my fault, and I perceived them as reproaches. Eventually I realized that knowing how to be together without saying a word was, ultimately, a superior level of friendship. It was respect. It was reverence. It was reflection as opposed to mere chitchat. We are not, suddenly, parrots. But we will be, if momentarily, philosophers. . . . After all, weren't Seneca and the bullfighter Manolete, both from Córdoba, both stoics?

This experience of friendship as reflexive, respectful silence leads me to an inevitable edge in which the borderline between being alone and being with friends is what separates our lives. If friendship is the nexus between the life of community and the life of the self, then the life of the self needs to reclaim solitude from friendship. This is natural: for our inner selves, we demand the passion, intelligence, or love that we recognize in the gaze of a friend. But affection and gestures that invite closeness have a limit: me. I return to myself, to my own despair but also to my own power. I remember with great nostalgia the dawn of childhood, shared among friends. How difficult it is to maintain friendships as adults! I relive the moments of rifts with an inevitable sense of pain. The hours are not the same. The paths have taken odd turns. But I cannot avoid the charity that the self, sooner or later, asks of Fortune. After all, didn't we already know, from the very beginning of the friendship, that one day it would end? Haven't we always known that with intimate anxiety, almost with shame, we carried with us an imperfection that we would never be able to share with anyone, not even our closest and most trusted confidant?

And so, paradoxically, we offer the world our imperfection and society our shame—all in the hope that another kind of friendship, that of belonging to life in the community, will redeem us. The artist, by definition, learns very early on to endure solitude for the sake of his artistic creation. But in a broader sense, friendship is what forces us not only to recognize our limits but to realize that we share those limits. We are friends in the community: we need one another. With good reason Thoreau once said that he had but three chairs in his house: one for solitude; the second for friendship; the third for society. Knowing how to be alone is the essential and life-enhancing counterpoint to friendship. So is death. Just as I loyally remember my friends from the remotest reaches of my childhood, I also dedicate an unflinching memory to those old friends, long gone, who were also my teachers at some earlier point in my life. My generation recalls, with Latin *verecundia,* two great teachers of our youth. Alfonso Reyes of Mexico and Manuel Pedroso of Spain. Two wise men who were also friends. Their intellectual lessons were inseparable from their fraternal ones. They never expected, as false teachers do, idolatry without contradiction. They hoped for and sought the reconquest of youth from old age and in exchange offered us the conquest of fraternal knowledge and experience. With Reyes, small and rotund, and with Pedroso, tall and angular, we discovered over and over again that friendship means enduring through old age—or through time itself. That there is always something else to learn in the world. That friendship is reaped because it is sown. That nobody makes friends without making enemies, but that no enemy can ever attain the transcendence of a friend. That friendship is a form of discretion: it does not admit the cruel speeches that speak so ill of the person who utters them, nor the gossip that turns everything it touches to rubbish. (As La Rochefoucauld said, it is more shameful to mistrust friends than to deceive them.) Friendship, to be intimate, should show us the path of respect and distance, even if it tells us to love and detest the very same things.

In this way, the stages of life come to be measured by the degrees of close affinities we maintain from one age to the next. We forget about friends that are distant in time. We slowly let go of childhood friends who did not grow at the same pace as we did. We court younger friends to acquire the vitality that grows increasingly elusive to us in biological terms. We search for lifelong friends and yet now we have nothing to say to them. We witness the decline of old, beloved friends we no longer recognize or who may no longer recognize us. But when age creates distances, it is only because it is waiting for us. Once again, the bright lights of early youth shine in the twilight hour. In the middle of a distant fog, perhaps, we remember the complicity, we discover together all that exists, we reconquer youth, and become once again *banda, cuatiza, chorcha, patocha, barra,* posse, gang. Once again we reap passions and vanquish rebellions. And with nostalgia, we look upon the ancient hours of friendship as if they never really existed at all. . . .

G

Globalization

In the course of my lifetime, four political and socioeconomic themes have captured the world's attention. From 1928 to 1939, it was revolution, fascism, and economic crisis. For Piers Brendon, of Cambridge University, it was the age of the "dark valley." Eleven years in which stupidity and evil fought for qualifiable supremacy. Evil was personified by the ascendant totalitarianism of the day: fascism in Italy, national socialism in Germany, militarism in Japan, Stalinism in Russia. The stupidity, blind cowardice, and elegant caution of the European democracies, France and England. The testing ground, as well as the battleground, was the terrible Spanish Civil War, the arena of all the bravery and all the cowardice, all the glory and all the misery of what Eric Hobsbawm has called "the shortest century." From this terrible decade the United States of America was the country that came out best. Faced, as was the rest of the world, with economic depression, inflation, unemployment, and capitalism in crisis, Franklin D. Roosevelt's New Deal did not have to appeal to Stalinist or Hitlerian totalitarianism. It summoned human capital, democratic imagination, the social dynamic.

The second topic that mesmerized us was World War II. It has been called the only good and necessary war. Of that there is no doubt. Never before has evil emerged in such a horrifying and specific incarnation as that of the Nazi regime. Fighting this evil absolved of all sin any alliance with a "minor" evil— Stalin—but did impose an almost absolute faith in the goodness of liberty, which the Allied struggle represented. The evils of Western capitalism and Soviet totalitarianism were obfuscated by the absolute evil of the Holocaust, the concentration camps, the slavery imposed upon France, Belgium, Holland, Denmark, Norway, the Balkans, Greece. . . . Even the crimes of the Stalinist purges seemed to have been momentarily erased by the siege of Leningrad and the glory of Stalingrad.

The euphoria of the Allied victory quickly degenerated into the third topic, the long and terrible era of the Cold War. Almost half a century of unyielding Manichaeism—the good guys are here, the bad guys are over there. The total subjection of Central Europe to the Soviet dictatorship. The symmetrical reflection of the intolerance and witch hunts of the McCarthy era in the United States. And if the United States, in the end, finally rose up against "indecent" McCarthyism (as army counsel Joseph Welch called it in the Army-McCarthy hearings, 1954), it nevertheless subjected its backyard neighbor, Latin America, to a repressive, regressive demonization that, marrying U.S. imperialism with Latin American militarism, went against all economic reform and social democracy in the name of anti-Communist paranoia.

The wars of Central America began in Guatemala in 1954, and only ended thanks to the diplomatic efforts of the Contadora Group of peace mediators and the initiatives of Óscar Arias, president of Costa Rica in the 1980s. From John Foster Dulles ("The United States doesn't have friends, it has interests") to Ronald Reagan, who claimed that the Sandinistas could make it to Harlingen, Texas, from Managua, Nicaragua, in a matter of two days, Spanish America had to suffer the deaths of 300,000 Central Americans and the torture, disappearance, and death of thousands of Argentinians, Uruguayans, Chileans, and Brazilians. This is the abominable arithmetic of the Cold War in Latin America, whose wounds have still not entirely healed. The memory of the horrors is alive. I have known Chilean women raped in front of their children and husbands, in the dungeons of that savior of Christianity, Augusto Pinochet. I have known Argentinian mothers who will never again see their children who were "disappeared" by the ruthless military officers operating under the command of Jorge Videla. I have seen the terror that blanches the faces of the men and women of the Southern Cone upon the mere mention of the so-called "Angel of Death," the winsome blond Captain Astiz whose special predilection was throwing live nuns from airplanes into the River Plate, or of Contreras, the Chilean general who assassinated Orlando Letelier on the streets of Washington, D.C., in 1976, Carlos Prats on the streets of Buenos Aires in 1974, and Bernardo Leighton on the streets of Rome. Ariel Dorfman bears full testimony to the truth in his dramatic work *Death and the Maiden.* In the jail cells of the DINA in Santiago de Chile, the dictator's thugs entertained themselves by inserting live rats into the vaginas of their female prisoners.

The shortest century, from Sarajevo, 1914, to Sarajevo, 1994. How very long, in comparison, the nineteenth century seems, stretching from the French Revolution all the way to the First World War. How long it was in cultural terms, as well—in literature it went from Goethe through to Joyce; in painting, from Ingres and Delacroix to Matisse and Braque; in philosophy, from Schopenhauer and Kant to Husserl and Heidegger. And how very short was the century that began and ended with Picasso.

The last topic of the twentieth century extends into the twenty-first, and it is called globalization. Having lived through the four eras, I can now state that globalization is the name of a power system. Just like the Holy Spirit, it has no boundaries. Just like Mount Everest, it is there. And just like the Law of Gravity, its evidence is irrefutable. But like the Latin god Janus, it has two faces. The good face is that of technical and scientific progress—

the most rapid in all of history. Free trade, the postulate of economic freedom since the days of the Prussian *Zollverein* that set the stage for the unification of Germany. Productive offshore investments. The accessibility to and dissemination of information that leaves many emperors, who once covered themselves with the vine leaves of the Asian, African, and Latin American jungles, with no clothes. The universalization of the concept of human rights and the invalidity of statutes of limitations for crimes against humanity such as those of Pinochet, the Chilean murderer and torturer, the source of all criminal order during his dictatorship.

But Janus has another, less attractive, side. The sheer speed of technological progress leaves behind—perhaps forever—those countries that are unable to keep up with the pace. Free trade increases the advantages to be gained by massive, competitive corporations (which are very few) and crushes small and medium-sized industry without which the employment, salary, and welfare levels of the great mass of people suffer, hindering support for the development of the Third World. As a consequence of this, globalization only widens the gap between rich and poor, both internationally and within each nation: 20 percent of the world consumes 90 percent of world production. And what begins to emerge is the specter of a kind of global Darwinism, as Óscar Arias called it. Speculative investments prevail over productive investments: 80 percent of the 6 billion dollars that circulate daily in the world markets is speculation capital. The crises of globalization, for this reason, are not business or information or technological crises: they are crises of the international financial system, brought on by the loss of social control over the economy and the weakening of political power in the face of cresohedonic power.

In this union of Croesus (money) and Hedone (pleasure) global culture becomes a fashion show, a giant screen, a stereophonic boom, an existence made of glossy, four-color paper. It transforms us into what C. Wright Mills called "cheerful robots," and it condemns us, as the title of Neil Postman's celebrated book goes, to "amusing ourselves to death." In the meantime, millions of human beings die without having smiled once in their entire lives. A massive transfer from rural to urban life will, in the twenty-first century, bring about the eradication of one of the oldest forms of life, the agrarian life. All we will have is city life. And the widespread crises of urban civilization that go with its uncontrollable pandemics, homeless people, crumbling infrastructures, discrimination against sexual minorities, women, and immigrants. Begging in the streets. Crime.

Are there any answers to this crisis? What role is to be played in the twenty-first century by the left-wing ideology in which I was educated, whose ideals I assimilated, whose crises I witnessed and criticized? Can the political world resume control over the anarchy of the markets? Does the state have a role in the globalized world? There are. It can. It does. The Friedmanite antistate discourse of the Reagan-Thatcher years proved itself to be hypocritical and insufficient in time. The state, though declared obsolete, was certainly strong enough to save insolvent banks and fraudulent financiers and to coddle arms industries. In 2001 we realized that there is no such thing as a stable democracy without stable government. Far from reducing the role of the state, globalization has in fact broadened the areas that fall under public jurisdiction. What has been reduced is the proprietary state. And what is most necessary is a state that can regulate and establish standards. There is no developed nation in the world where this is not the case. And it is even more important in countries of weak economic agents, such as Latin America.

We have all witnessed the noxious effects of a globalization that eludes all national and international political control and promotes a speculative system that, according to one of its wisest protagonists, George Soros, has reached its limit. If this trend continues unchecked, Soros says, the world will be swept into catastrophe. The globalization crises—in the Philippines, Malaysia, Brazil, Russia, Argentina—can be attributed to the perverse fact that financial capital is overvalued and human capital under-valued.

The social collective existing within the entity that (for lack of a more appropriate term) we continue to call "the nation" has, then, a mission: that of rediscovering values such as work, health, education, and savings. In other words, that of recovering the central role of human capital.

In today's world, 9 billion U.S. dollars would suffice to address the basic educational needs in developing countries; in today's world, the same amount is spent on cosmetics in the United States alone. Is this tolerable?

In today's world, an initial investment of 13 billion U.S. dollars would suffice to resolve the problems of water, health, and food in the poorest countries; the same amount is spent on ice-cream consumption in Europe alone. Is this acceptable?

No, according to many people, including Federico Mayor, ex-director general of UNESCO, and James Wolfensohn, director of the World Bank, who find it "unacceptable that a world that spends approximately 800 billion U.S. dollars a year on weapons cannot find the money needed—an estimated 6 billion U.S. dollars per year—to put every child in school." A mere 1 percent decrease in military spending worldwide would be sufficient to put every child in the world in front of a blackboard.

All these facts and statistics should motivate the international community to give the global age a human face.

Nevertheless, in the end, we find ourselves back on our home turf and there are problems that cannot wait around for a new international enlightenment that may arrive on the scene either too late or not at all.

Charity begins at home, and the first thing that we must ask ourselves, as Latin Americans, is this: what resources do we have to establish the foundations for a progress that, beginning with the local village, will allow us eventually to become active agents and not passive victims of rapid-fire global movement in the twenty-first century?

Globalization is not a panacea for Latin America.

We will not be an exception to the fact that is becoming clearer and clearer with every passing day. If the locality is weak, the globality won't work.

In other words: effective participation in the global arena can only begin with sound governing in the local arena.

And local government needs strong, robust private and public sectors that are conscious of their respective responsibilities. The goal is "to clean one's own house, build a stable economy . . . and a solid state, one that is able to offer security in every area," as Héctor Águilar Camín states in his book *México: la ceniza y la semilla* (*Mexico: The Ash and the Seed*).

Globalization will be judged. And the judgment will be a negative one if globalization comes to mean more unemployment, fewer social services, the loss of sovereignty, the disintegration of international law, and political cynicism. And now that the democratic flags have disappeared from sight, the same ones that were so furiously waved during the Cold War to defend the free world against Communism, the free world congratulates itself for the fact that instead of totalitarian Communist governments and military dictatorships, the world is filled with efficient, authoritarian capitalist governments (like that of China) which, according to the current global logic, are always preferable to failed neoliberalist systems which in reality are crony capitalism (like that of Russia).

Globalization has the power to render the world a highly undesirable place, dominated by the logic of speculation, disregard for the human being, disdain for social capital, mockery of what still remains of many deeply scarred national sovereignties, obliteration of international order, and the consecration of authoritarian capitalism as the fastest track to security without the need for very much accountability.

But the challenge is there. Everest will not move. How can we climb it, then? How can we take the negative trends of globalization and turn them into positive ones?

Can we take advantage of the opportunities offered by globalization to create growth, prosperity, and justice?

What I am trying to say here is this: perhaps globalization is inevitable, but that doesn't mean it has to be inevitably negative.

It means that globalization should be subject to control, its social consequences evaluated and judged.

Will it be possible to socialize the global economy?

Yes, I think it will, no matter how difficult and demanding the effort may be.

Yes, as long as new forms of international economic relationships can be held accountable to the core activities of civil society, democratic control, and cultural realities.

Yes, as long as civil society is able to offer alternatives to a supposed single-model system.

Yes, as long as civil society rejects the idea that things are a foregone conclusion, a *fait accompli,* and instead strives constantly to reenvision social conditions, reminding the power structures that we live in contingency with one another, and connecting globalism to concrete and variable social actions within—for lack of new terminology—the entities we continue to refer to as "nations."

Globalization in and of itself is not a panacea.

It calls for a base of active civil societies, diversified cultures that stand up to the encroaching global culture of unadulterated entertainment, uniform, exclusionary, and vapid.

It calls for public and private sectors that are aware of their respective responsibilities: private initiatives need a government that is strong—not big, just strong. And this can be possible with a tax base and a social policy that works in favor of a private sector that, for its part, needs an educated, healthy workforce that can be consumers as well. "Poverty doesn't create a market," says Carlos Slim, a lucid Mexican businessman. "The best investment of all is to do away with poverty."

It calls for a democratic framework that can give the now-weakened notion of sovereignty back its true political meaning. The only sovereign nation on the international stage is one that is sovereign on the national stage as well. One that respects the cultural and political rights of a population that it conceives of as a complex, qualitative whole, not merely a number: citizens, not inhabitants.

I invoke the words of Juan Bautista Alberdi of Argentina in the nineteenth century: to govern is to populate. Yes, this is true, but as his contemporary Domingo F. Sarmiento would add, to populate is to educate, and only an educated citizenry can govern for the good of its country and the world.

That base is the only solid, creative one from which the processes of globalization may be transformed into opportunities for growth, prosperity, and justice. And its key lies in the active identification of civil society, democracy, and culture as inseparable repositories of a new twenty-first-century sovereignty and a renewed commitment to that daily plebiscite that, as Renan said, constitutes what we define as "nation."

Good national governments can only emerge when both the public and the private sectors are conscious of their obligations to the local communities: that should be their first priority, in the interest of becoming a positive, active player in the global community.

To this end, there must be an intermediary between these two sectors, one which can play the role of bridge, supplementary instance, and political supervisor: the third sector.

As we navigate the waters of globalism, we cannot throw the public and private sectors overboard, nor the societies in which they operate. Without these three elements, globalization could well become a kind of helpless *Titanic* facing the unexpected icebergs of a world history fraught with peril, thunderstorms, displacements, financial and economic surprises, revivals of old prejudices, and opposition from older cultures. History is far from becoming a thing of the past; it is, in fact, more alive, more contentious, more defiant than ever.

Why? Because the vices of the global village have been matched by the resurgence of the vices of the local village. Tribalism. Reductive, chauvinistic nationalism. Xenophobia. Racial and cultural prejudices. Religious fundamentalism. Fratricidal wars.

This is far from the first era of "globalization." The first one took place, overwhelmingly, during the age of discovery, the days of the circumnavigation of the globe and the creation of the *jus gentium,* the notion of international law as the answer to the global processes of conquest, colonization, and mercantile rivalry.

Rather contentiously, this first era of globalization was also manifested by the "first wave" of the agrofeudal world (Toffler) and its transition to the "second wave" of rapid industrialization that supplanted the agrarian, manual-labor world and sparked the rebellion of the Luddites, who destroyed the machines that robbed artisans and manual laborers of their jobs.

Today, the neo-Luddite sentiment that the former president of Mexico Ernesto Zedillo regards as "globaliphobia" is simply another manifestation of this old attitude of opposing the unstoppable: the new techno-information economy that favors quality over quantity, as manifested in vast global alliances for improved production, distribution, and optimization of profits.

The fact that this revolution will provoke disgruntlement, pain, and injustice is as true in today's world as it was in the nineteenth century.

The fact that the new economy will not suddenly disappear when confronted with outward displays of protest is as true in today's world as it was in the nineteenth century.

As I said earlier, the new global economy, just like Mount Everest, is there. It isn't going to budge. The question, then, is this: how do we climb it?

The Christ of Corcovado is there. That doesn't mean we should blow it up because the world isn't perfect. We should embrace it so that the world can become less imperfect.

There are already 2 billion computers in the world. Increasingly, telephones connect to computers, voices and data multiply, and communication from one person to another person is transformed into communication from one person to many.

Even guerrilla warriors, as Subcomandante Marcos has demonstrated in Chiapas, will fight their revolutions on the Internet.

The fact is novel and stunning: Bill Clinton, in his address entitled "The Struggle for the Soul of the Twenty-first Century," offers an astonishing bit of information: when he assumed the presidency of the United States in 1993, there were only fifty sites on the World Wide Web. By the time he left the White House eight years later, "the number was 350 million and rising."

Can new technologies and computers solve the basic problems of the overwhelming number of people who live in poverty, in Latin America and all over the world?

Not by themselves, no.

But to the extent that technological innovations can be used more widely to accelerate and improve the education of people in certain geographical areas and of certain social classes, people who may now be able to receive training without having to walk three hours to a school, people who cannot even afford to pay the few and poorly compensated teachers they have available to them—then the answer is yes.

To the extent that technology and information may reach people in the most eroded and barren dead zones of Latin America, and teach them how to save their land, water, and forests, and how to modernize and optimize their agricultural endeavor, then the answer is yes.

To the extent that technology and information can become the vehicles of a basic solution to poverty—that is, the promotion of the micro-credit—then the answer is yes.

To the extent that technology and information can multiply the income of small-scale producers through the identification of markets, then the answer is yes.

To the extent that information and technology can empower

citizens with the strength they need to rebuild political and social regulators of the economy, then the answer is yes.

To the extent that information and technology give every individual the cultural tools he or she needs for learning, producing, influencing, then the answer is yes.

To the extent that information and technology can allow citizens to acquire their own character, identify their own interests, and embrace culture, then the answer is yes.

To the extent that information and technology can help the state and politics reclaim their indispensable central role in society, then the answer is yes.

Globalization and politics. As the Mexican political analyst Federico Reyes Heroles so aptly put it, "In our Latin America . . . the economic agents do not have the capacity to replace the state . . . Let us dismiss the state as benefactor but strengthen the state as regulator."

Reyes Heroles reminds us that there is no such thing as a stable democracy without a stable state. This is true in all the strong democracies of all the strong economies of the Northern Hemisphere. Far from reducing the state, globalization and open markets broaden the scope of public jurisdiction and reaffirm the redistributive function of the state via the taxation system.

The Latin American state continues to be a critical factor for the implementation of policies concerning health, education, and nutrition. The state cannot abandon its function as money-gatherer, nor can it renounce its commitment to spending more efficiently and directing additional resources toward social policies.

Not big government; strong government. Not recumbent politics; politics standing on its own two feet. Productive rather than speculative private enterprise. A civil society conscious of the fact that social rights depend upon social action and organization. The third sector as a conduit for social intelligence: What is my identity? What are my interests? What are my challenges?

In no way am I attempting to cover up the evils of global economy. The ever-widening gap between rich and poor. The decline of traditional occupations. Rapacious urbanization. The plundering of our natural resources. The disintegration of social structures. The vulgarity of commercial culture.

There are, however, two modes of policy I reject: that of the ostrich which buries its head in the sand, and that of the bull which bursts into the china shop, simply to destroy everything in sight.

Categorical denial will not put an end to the globalization process. The question, then, is how can we take advantage of it?

Once the virtues have been ascertained, the rough spots smoothed over, the opposing arguments exhausted, resistance re-inforced, and the realities of the jungle and the global zoo legis-lated for and held accountable to political will, what might be the new topics of debate in the next forty, fifty years, when I am no longer here? I venture to offer three. The protection of the envi-ronment. The rights of women. And the defense of the personal sphere against public encroachment, as well as the defense of the public sphere against private avarice.

The merits of globalization will amount to empty urns if they are not filled with the elixir of local government. I am talking about policies for economic growth, welfare, labor, infrastruc-ture, education, health, and nutrition that can be enacted on a local level. Policies whose goal is to activate the "virtuous cycle" of a healthy internal market that, in turn, could come to be an ac-tive contributor to a robust but also fairer global marketplace, truly global insofar as it would include more and more men and women who find themselves in the process of achieving very real improvement in their lives. Exclusion cannot be the price we pay for achieving greater efficiency.

Only with this kind of local government as a starting point, I believe, can we aspire to an international order that is both inno-vative and sound. The more the national state enacts, cooperates with, and protects national measures to resolve the galaxy of problems that I have mentioned here, the more authority it will have to propose international laws governing the environment, family policy, feminism, education, health, child care, immigration and labor regulations, financing for developing areas, and international jurisdiction to combat organized crime.

First and foremost, effective local government: political will. And rapidly following, international alliances bolstered by local politics and vice versa. Two-way streets, true, but if the national community does not create its own instruments for solving problems locally, international aid may very well end up in a bottomless pit where, as we all know, corruption is the most insatiable of monsters.

Globalization only favors human development if, at the same time, national and international public institutions grow stronger, so that the multitude of nonpolitical actors who currently rob elected officials of their power and hand it over to nonelected people can be made to adhere to the law.

The decisions that work against legality in the global realm are those decisions that ignore environmental protection treaties, multilateral disarmament treaties, and most of all, the tremendous effort being made to unite globalism and criminal justice.

To proclaim an axis of evil is a simplistic way of fighting terrorism by identifying it with two or three poorly chosen countries. Terrorism knows no country. That is both its advantage and its danger. Terrorism has no flag. No face. One day it surfaces in Afghanistan, another day in the Basque Country, a third day in Oklahoma, and the following day on the streets of Belfast. The tragedy of September 11, 2001, horrified everyone and confirmed for all of us that terrorism is a universal fact. It must be fought with tenacity wherever it manifests itself, but without demonizing entire nations or cultures. We cannot fall into the preposterous trap of attributing terrorism to a historical hatred of the United States, to the corruption or inefficiency of certain Islamic governments, and much less to the clash of cultures. No: we most certainly should agree that the deepest sources of conflict in our world are instability, illegality, poverty, exclusion, and, in general terms, the absence of a new legality for a new reality.

For this reason it is so important to begin building, step by step, the foundations of an international legal body for the global age. Let us not open, as did Virgil in Hell, an ivory gate to send false illusions into the world. Far more preferable is the patience of Job, for whom the waters did ultimately erode the rocks but also allowed the tree to sprout anew.

Nevertheless, what we see on the streets of Seattle, Prague, and Genoa is impatience—an impatience that bit by bit helps us to move toward understanding that globalization should not be simplistically demonized but rather transformed into a tool for the public good, for increasing benefit and welfare.

In an extraordinary speech given before the French National Assembly, the then president of Brazil, Fernando Henrique Cardoso, offered guidelines to meet this challenge. The international economic system should create funds to fight poverty, hunger, and sickness in the neediest countries. The debts of the poorest countries in Africa and Latin America should be reduced or cancelled altogether. A new international contract should be drawn up between states, so that the people can be better served. Solidarity should be, in a word, globalized. Rather than a few predominant states and markets, a new international contract between free nations should be drafted and implemented.

President Cardoso does not only propose an ideal—and in any event, a goal cannot be worthy of human action if it does not rest upon ideals worthy of our human condition—he shows us that we are living in a world of mutant reality and uncertain legality, just as was the case in Western cultures as the transition was made from the secure, consecrated order of the Middle Ages to the uncertainty of the brave new world of the Renaissance—an uncertainty that is expressed most eloquently in the tragedies of William Shakespeare and the novels of Miguel de Cervantes.

Today, one of the many challenges of our new century is that of envisioning the new legality.

Shakespeare and Cervantes, yes, but Vitoria and Bodin, Las Casas and Grotius as well.

From this, our Latin America, from these fertile, beautiful, aching, trampled lands that have been shot down by themselves and by those who covet either their poverty or their beauty—I don't know which—we ask, today, to globalize not only the fact but the right to make rights out of commerce and health, education and environment, work and security.

Let the North, for its own benefit, understand how to distribute profits and reduce burdens in the global era.

Let the South, instead of reading its register of complaints, its *cahier de doléances,* over and over again, learn to clean its own house first, before demanding from the world those things that we do not give ourselves: the sovereignty of internal freedom, democracy, and human rights, the legitimacy of a justice system that eradicates corruption, impunity, and the culture of illegality in our own land.

Only then, by using that as a point of departure, can we create a legitimate globalism of shared rights and obligations in accordance with the conviction that globality isn't worth a damn if it doesn't have a working locality behind it.

God

"Nietzsche said: 'God is dead.'"

"God was patient and one day whispered, from a mental hospital in Weimar: 'Nietzsche is dead.'"

"Was the voice of Nietzsche human, perhaps too human? Because his words convey a tremendous contradiction. If God is dead, that must mean that at some point, God lived."

"But then, when exactly did God begin to live? Which came first, God or the Universe? The egg or the chicken? If we admit the Universe is infinite, God must be more infinite than the infinite, and that notion is patently absurd."

"Let us imagine, then, that God and the Universe have existed together, always."

"To me, that seems to defeat Reason but, on the other hand, it does contribute to Faith. Science and Technology are reconciled. Neither God nor the Universe has beginning or end. On the other hand, if we accept the big bang theory, was this seminal explosion the work of a divine fiat?"

"Do you mean to say that God inhabited the Universe before the big bang and then, one day, for a little fun, ordered an expansive, universal explosion, knowing that everything would end, not in some kind of final explosion but in one final sob? That is, 'Not with a bang but a whimper.' Because the God that knows all, knew everything, including T. S. Eliot's ' The Waste Land.' "

"Excuse me, but I seriously doubt that God reads literature. Why would He if He knew everything beforehand?"

"That is precisely what I am arguing with you. Let's take it step by step. Let's suppose that before God there was darkness. Let's agree—after all, the Bible says so—that when God appeared, light emerged. But what came before God? What is that darkness that preceded the divine words 'Let there be light.' Can we even conceive of it?"

"I would tell you that if we admit to the existence of God, we should also admit that God subjugated Nothingness."

"But if He were Everything, could there have even been a Nothingness? Do God and Nothingness coexist like absurd twins or, rather, are we simply confusing Nothingness with the absence of the world and mankind?"

"You are moving dangerously close to an argument that will leave us bereft of all arguments: that God is a creature of Man, not vice versa. But if God only exists because Man has imagined, thought of, or desired Him, then God does not exist in and of Himself."

"Although he may very well have the greatest existence possible, that of being the product of human desire and imagination."

"That is not what we are disputing right now. We are trying to envision a solitary God who, for some reason that escapes us, decided to create a being in His image and likeness: Man."

"What for? If God is God, He needs neither the world nor man. He exists in and of Himself. He is enough for Himself. Why would he create something that is unnecessary? That is the core of the matter."

"Perhaps God created the world because He felt lonely and one fine day experienced the horror of the void."

"And so then are we creatures of a baroque God that reacts, as did Góngora and Bernini, to the *horror vacuii*?"

"Let me suggest another image instead: a God that spends all of Eternity thinking about what would have happened had He not created the world."

"I can also imagine a God that spends Eternity not worrying the least little bit about doing us the favor of creating us and introducing, incidentally, an intruder in His Creation."

"The fact is there was a divine fiat, and Man and the World were created. We can argue as to whether God created us, but we cannot argue that we are here, that we live, that we exist and that we die. The issue really should be whether our existence bears a relationship with God or not. Are we or are we not His creatures and if we are, what is our position in His creative plan?"

"Well, for starters, the Bible presents us with a God that is a mere organizer of things. The sea and its little fishes are here, the land is there, although without cocoa or coffee or tomatoes or corn or potatoes. The animals are all in their place and set up in pairs, just as the tale of Noah describes. But in the Creation there are no buffaloes or iguanas or quetzals. Very well. God as the overseer of a vast, pre-American zoo. Manager of the largest pre-Columbian aquarium. Author of Eolus, the god and master of storms and the movement of the heavens."

"But not of Ehecatl, the Aztec god of the wind, the American Eolus . . ."

"Hold on—we will get to that in a moment. Let me continue; you keep interrupting me."

"Am I like the Devil?"

"No, my friend. Not even the Devil's advocate. As I was saying . . ."

"As you were saying . . ."

"The essential fact of human creation is that God created us in His image and likeness. The point of contention is clear and immediate. If He made us in His image and likeness and if, moreover, He knew everything beforehand, why then did He create us in the image and likeness of Evil? Why did He include the Devil in our image and likeness? Did the image of God, from the very beginning, encompass the image of the Devil?"

"Listen, I think Adam sniffed this part out from the very first moment. Milton offers a profound bit of intuition in *Paradise Lost*. Adam lashes out at Creation and rebukes God, asking Him, 'Why couldn't you have let me remain as clay? Why did you turn me into a man?' "

"Just imagine, as a response, that God had His temptations as well in the Garden of Eden. The temptation of living side by side for all eternity with His creations, Adam and Eve, like a father who spoils and is spoiled by his children. And then imagine that Adam and Eve, wiser than God, commit sin and expel themselves from Paradise, only to expel God at the same time. At God's side for centuries of centuries, would Adam and Eve have been humans? They would never have had sexual relations or descendants. And they would have frustrated God's design. He who is Immortal cannot live surrounded by Immortals. He is Unique. God fooled Himself inventing Paradise and Adam and Eve did Him a favor by divesting Him of this illusion."

" 'Did I request thee, Maker, from my Clay / to mould me Man, did I sollicite thee / From darkness to promote me?' Did Adam perceive the burden of existence as something so terrible that he would have preferred, as Milton says, to remain as clay in the darkness?"

"The advancement toward the light: one of the loveliest definitions of Creation, of all creation. But light only exists in contrast to darkness. Perhaps God regretted the Creation because He could not bear Adam's immortality?"

"Are you trying to say that God is co-responsible for the horrors of humankind?"

"I am trying to say that perfect Good only lasts for a second whereas Evil will forever occupy the space of the subverted Eden."

"Allow me to make a distinction. Evil knows itself to be Evil but it also knows Goodness, and this is precisely its advantage. Perfect, absolute, total Goodness does not know Evil and precisely because of this can fall victim to Evil."

"God, after the Fall, turns himself into the referee in these issues."

"No. In the end, He gives the Church that power. But we will discuss that topic later, with Jesus, in person. For the moment, I only wish to suggest that if the world is born out of God's essence, Evil is inconceivable. And if Evil is born from Goodness, then we live in a world of the absurd. From there, this is what follows: First, burden the creatures of God, Adam and Eve, with an Evil that God could never have envisioned as part of a creative plan. Second, remind us that the Devil also belongs to Eternity. And third, console us by demonstrating that human liberty is a gift from God, practiced by Adam and Eve, that serves as an example of the infinite Divine goodness."

"Are you saying that God is able to endure Evil if Evil is an act of liberty?"

"No, I am only suggesting that perhaps God negotiated with the Devil hoping that the eventual triumph of liberty in favor of goodness would give Him back the chips He lent the Devil to explain the existence of Evil."

"But that would make God, whether He liked it or not, the Devil's associate. Because, I repeat, Evil is capable of knowing both Evil and Goodness. Goodness, however, cannot conceive of anything beyond itself, including that which denies it. That is both the strength as well as the weakness of Goodness."

"And I say to you that of course God knows both Good and Evil; but He knows them as a unit. In Man, Good and Evil are separated. And we have neither the might nor the right to unite them because that would make us God and God would no longer stand for that."

" 'No longer.' Do you add that condition to insinuate that, after the Fall from grace, God robs Man of the power to see Good and Evil as one discrete unit? That God wants to reserve that exclusive right for Himself?"

"No. At this level it is not God who intervenes, but History."

"Which begins in the garden with Adam and Eve."

"No. I believe that history begins with Cain. Abel is the promise of Paradise recovered, if you will, to continue with the Miltonian allusions. Cain, not Abel, is the second father and his patriarchy is based on crime. If God, *malgré* Nietzsche, has not died, it is because Cain's crime makes it unbearable for us to experience history as crime, as fratricide, as injustice. We turn our eyes to God so that He may redress the fratricidal crime of Cain, civil war—not the nonexistent crime of Adam and Eve, givers of life and pleasure."

"Is Cain the second coming of Evil, no longer as part of the Creation but as part of History?"

"I am not sure. Perhaps the World, after the Fall, is no longer God's responsibility and becomes the poisonous garden of a Devil that is the gleeful spectator of human suffering. The world becomes the theater of the Devil disguised as God, an exclusive God—that is, one who excludes, who takes away."

"Is the God who deprives, then, the Devil?"

"Only if God, secretly, privately, feels satisfied, smug. Instead of destroying a world that has betrayed Him from head to toe, why does God give the World a second chance? Noah's chance, that of escaping the deluge."

"Because I believe that if Man ceases to exist, God will die without him. Not with him, please understand me. Without him."

"If the World comes to an end, God is rendered impossible?"

"For Himself, perhaps not. For human beings, yes. And the reason for that is that before killing God, men will have all killed one another first."

"In that case God is the greatest human invention of all, because He frees us from the other great human invention, History."

"Don't you think that perhaps instead God might grow accustomed to the idea that Man commits acts of Evil because Man was created in the image and likeness of God and God, too, is both Good and Evil?"

"Such an idea would test the limits of Faith and would inevitably prove Origen's point: the grace of God is so great that in the end, it is capable of forgiving the Devil. Because if God is not capable of forgiving Beelzebub, then He would be an insincere and crippled God."

"Origen ended up castrating himself to prove his faith, never imagining that the Emperor Decius would do him the favor of castrating his entire life for him."

"Origen puts the limits of Faith to the test. But Faith can only be limitless because it consists of believing the unbelievable. 'It is true because it is absurd.' That is how Tertullian defined Faith."

"Does God also consider it absurd to believe in Him?"

"He couldn't answer because then He would be saying that Tertullian was right. God is God because He never allows himself to be seen. That is why He demands Faith."

"Even though He speaks through the voices of children, saints, and lunatics."

"Probably. But a visible, everyday God sitting in on literary circles in cafés would not be God."

"He would be Christ."

"But that is another story entirely."

"Take a look under 'C' in this book."

"Thank you."

"So now tell me one thing, which person is superior: the one who believes or the one who doesn't?"

"For me, doubt does not weaken God, and it strengthens us. There are theologians, like Hans Kung, for whom the modern world and all its comforts are responsible for the loss of faith. For many people, believing in God has become an anachronism. Just as before Copernicus, people believed that the sun revolved around the earth."

"Does doubt strengthen us as individuals or believers?"

"In your novel *La campaña* (*The Campaign*), you place these words in the mouth of the guerrilla priest Father Anselmo Quintana:

". . . you can't fool Him. Little games don't work with Him. God is the Supreme Being who knows everything, even what we imagine about Him, and he gets ahead of us and imagines us first; and if we go around thinking that believing in Him or not is something that depends on us, He gets ahead of us yet again and finds a way of telling us that He will go on believing in us no matter what, even if we abandon Him and deny Him. . . . Jesus said to me, 'Anselmo, my son, don't be a comfortable Christian; raise hell for the Church, because the Church loves peaceful Christians. I, on the other hand, love pissed-off Christians like you; you gain nothing by being a Catholic without problems, a simple believer, a man of faith who doesn't even realize that faith is absurd and that is why it is called faith and not reason . . . Please . . . always be a problem . . . Don't let them pass through your soul without paying for the right at the spiritual customs house; don't hand your faith over to any ruler, any secular state, any philosophy, any military or economic power without also giving them your mess, your complications, your exceptions, your goddamned imagination. . . .' "

"That is a call to faith as freedom and as responsibility. How is it lived out with the triumph of Man that Georg Büchner proclaims in *Danton's Death:* 'No longer will it be possible to accuse God, because God does not exist. Rebellious freedom has occupied all the space of the world'?"

"We must ask ourselves what we have done with our rebellious freedom . . ."

"We have created science, we have penetrated the secrets of matter, we have improved the living conditions of millions of people, we have eradicated sicknesses that formerly ravaged the human race, we have prolonged human existence, cleared our consciences . . ."

"But we have also tortured and killed millions of people in wars fought for political and economic supremacy, motivated by irrational impulses and hatred, prejudice, the cynicism of industrial militarism, the ambition of superpowers, the misery of the helpless. . . . Don't we have the right to question aloud, 'God, what have we done with our rebellious freedom?' "

"The terrifying silence of the infinite cosmic void will answer you. Do you give in?"

"No. I prefer to continue doubting, asking questions, debating with you, with me, with the three of us . . ."

"Always three, as in the poem by José Gorostiza, 'Muerte sin fin' (Death without end). You and I, laid siege by our own epidermis, full of ourselves. Who is the third person? Is it one of us? Is it God? Is it the Other?"

"Let us suppose it is God. And once again, we doubt and we question. Is God co-responsible for the errors of humankind? Does God need to take human failure and turn it into proof of His power? Does He need our failure to test himself? Is God co-responsible for the human horrors that our freedom has bestowed upon us, along with the glory that freedom has also bestowed upon us? Does God know the results of the game before it is played out, or doesn't He? Is God the great croupier—William Blake's great 'old Nobodaddy aloft'—who knows each and every spin of the roulette game before they are played out?"

"Yes, let's imagine that God knows the future. But does God know what He will think in the future?"

"Are you trying to say that our freedom may affect the image that God has of Himself and the manner in which He will act?"

"I will answer you with another question. Can a person love God without knowing Him? Yes, the mystic and the saint will tell us. Can a person know God without loving Him? Yes, the artist tells us. I offer you the example of St. John of the Cross. The verb of God is unknown. The verb of Man is known. The creation of God through words is Man's great honor. We will never know when, where, or why God created Man. On the other hand, we do know that St. John of the Cross created God: '*Oh llama del amor viva / que tiernamente hieres / de mi alma en el más profundo centro.*' (Oh, living flame of love / gently you wound / my soul at its deepest core.) He also created a world without God: '*En mí yo no vivo ya / y sin Dios vivir no puedo / pues sin Él y sin mí quedo / este vivir, ¿qué será?*' (No longer do I live in me / and without God I cannot live / to Him or me I cannot give / myself, so what can living be?)★ Neither St. Thomas nor St. Anselm gave greater proof of God's existence than St. John of the Cross."

"Do you think God found out? It strikes me that God mustn't like literature very much, because literature robs God of both Heaven and Hell. That is why God never writes. He hires his ghostwriter to do it for Him. God never writes. He only speaks. He is an orator. A hummingbird."

"Well then, we should listen to the voices that speak on God's behalf . . ."

"For example?"

"St. John of the Cross, once again. '*Vivo sin vivir en mí / y de tal manera espero / que muero porque no muero.*' (I live yet do not live in me / and wait as my life goes by / and die because I do not die.)"

"Lovely but funereal. Something a bit more lively, perhaps."

"Simone Weil. 'God did not create anything except love itself, and the means to love.' As such, Weil reasons, God exists because my love is no illusion. This is why Simone Weil feels in control of her free judgment to believe in God. Her acceptance or rejection of God depends on her freedom."

"Pascal goes further than that, when he places these words in the mouth of God: 'Thou wouldst not seek Me, if thou hadst not found Me.' "

★St. John of the Cross, "Verses of the Soul That Pines to See God."

"But he follows that with a warning that is almost a commandment: '*Console toi.*' Console yourself. And I rebel against the notion of consolation."

"Didn't you say you believed in rebellious faith, inconsolable faith?"

"The glory of God is that of human creation. Let us accept this on the condition that this creation neither punishes nor rewards us. It simply identifies us."

"Admit it, we live in a wounded world."

"Only the action of humans will be able to close the world's open wounds one day."

"What you mean then, is that creation is unfinished."

"Yes. And this is the fissure through which God inevitably finds His way into the world. If God created us in His image and likeness, does God contain human evil? I answer yes. We are also the reflection of the bad or incomplete side of God. We strive to make God 'complete.' "

"We strive to make God complete. You know, I feel that you approach faith from the perspective that not believing in God—given that we strive to complete God—diminishes our own possibilities as humans. That not believing in God would be closing off our own horizons as humans. Is it cowardice not to believe in God?"

"Take as an example that God is both object and subject at the same time. His condition as a living being is subjective. But objectively speaking, for you and for me, He is—and can only be—the mirror of the soul. The work, then, of humans."

"Don't you believe in eternal life?"

"If it exists, when we arrive there we will receive a new agenda that will be unknown until that very moment. We don't know the agenda of Heaven."

"New instructions?"

"That's right. If there is such a thing as eternal life, let us leave the details up to God."

"Today we cremate dead bodies. How can we attest to the resurrection of the flesh that proclaims the credo?"

"Think, my friend, of the equivalence of the body rather than its resurrection. Think of the renewal of the soul rather than of survival."

"In conclusion, do you believe in God?"

"In conclusion, does God believe in me?"

"Listen, I think I will stick with Pascal's wager. I believe in God, because if God exists, I come out winning, and if He doesn't exist, I don't lose a thing."

H

Happiness

Happiness, *felicidad, bonheur, felicitá*. Few words inspire, so universally, such conceptual abundance and at the same time such ambiguity. Happiness has never been absent from Western thought. Eudaemonism to the ancients, the notion in the Latin distinguishes between happiness as external fortune on the one hand and internal fact on the other. For Socrates, happiness is an interior phenomenon that is identified with virtue. Aristotle, as one might expect, transforms happiness into an external action that operates according to reason. For hedonists, happiness is pleasure and pleasure is happiness. The Epicureans are more specific: we take pleasure in external life, but if we want to be happy let us not succumb to its charms. Democritus identifies happiness with serenity (*ataraxia*) and serenity with stability and the expulsion of desire, fear, and physical pain.

The English utilitarians (Hobbes, Bentham, Mill) give happiness its more modern, straightforward, and, arguably, dogmatic meaning. What is useful is good. However, we generally (and erroneously, I believe) consider the French Revolution to be responsible for the consecration of the brand of happiness that has prevailed from the eighteenth century onward in the West and all its peripheral societies. The founding laws of the United States of America declare this as its citizens' right—if not the right to happiness itself, then its less presumptuous equivalent, the pursuit of happiness. This enlightened right rapidly fused with a kind of Puritanism that rendered happiness the great aspiration of the United States, but also turned the nation into the Manichaean bearer of happiness as good versus evil. In our own times, we have witnessed the supreme example of this concept: the United States as the self-proclaimed axis of good (and thus the axis of happiness) pitted against the axis of evil (and thus the source of all misery). One side defines itself through the good-happy synonymy and all nonadherents to this belief are relegated to the evil-unhappy synonymy.

The current situation on the international stage illustrates yet again—as if the horrors of the twentieth century did not suffice—the ambiguity of happiness. One need look no further than the films of Leni Riefenstahl or the newsreels of Soviet congresses and public rallies to see a vision of "happiness" amidst a sea of smiling, sun-kissed faces. Andrei Blinov, hack writer of Socialist realism (also known as Zhdanovism), published a novel entitled *Happiness Cannot Be Sought Alone.* What he meant, of course, is that happiness requires the cooperation of the faithful, disciplined multitudes who are unable to conceive of happiness of their own accord, without the direction of Party and Chief.

But it is true that individual happiness must be incorporated into the social sphere, whether you call that phenomenon solidarity, or even pity. The philosophers of the Enlightenment had a profound understanding of the significance of this dimension of happiness. The great Spanish historian Carmen Iglesias addresses the issue directly in her book *Razón y sentimiento en el siglo XVIII* (*Reason and Emotion in the 18th Century*). With Montesquieu in mind, Iglesias poses the following question: How can we reconcile individual freedom with "social happiness"—without which individual happiness is incomprehensible, at least in the eighteenth century? Montesquieu would no doubt invoke "an institutional articulation that protects the freedom of the individual and reconciles it with a certain prosperity of the State, as a guarantee of the material well-being of the citizens or social happiness."

Condorcet is the thinker who examines Montesquieu's balancing act between personal and social happiness and transforms it into myth—a dangerous myth on all counts, for it is one that unites happiness and progress, and regards progress to be something inevitable, fatal, and ascendant. We are condemned to achieve progress and the degree to which we achieve it will determine our degree of happiness. And so Condorcet tells us we had better be happy, whether we like it or not, because the laws of progress are ascendant and inexorable. It was Nietzsche who had to remind us, with his characteristic critical pessimism, that happiness and history rarely coincide. Rousseau, to whom Amado Nervo could have dedicated the verse he dedicated to Kempis—"Jean-Jacques, what evil for me you have wrought / with that book you wrote"—proposes a social contract, let us not forget, that is based upon a pessimistic vision of the disintegration of the modern world, which renders each and every individual an unhappy being. But then, were we *ever* happy? In the state of nature, the philosopher tells us, happiness is as fleeting as a bolt of lightning. Beyond his perspectives as a philosopher-politician, however, Rousseau is also, without a doubt, the father of Romanticism and the exaltation of happiness in the erotic realm, the pleasure of the senses, the recklessness of a Byron, the suicide of a Werther. . . .

Romanticism, however, is more than just a seminal literary school. It also gives rise to a dangerous political theory that champions the recovery of a lost totality as a method for achieving happiness. Karl Marx will call this alienation. But the praxis of the two extremes (that is, right and left) will call it totalitarianism. Adorno warned us of this in advance: "A liberated human race will never be a totality." The retrograde fantasies of a return to some kind of happy past (the Golden Age myth) serve as the foundation for the elaboration of futuristic fantasies about "the happy identity of subject and object."

The great tragedy of the modern age has been the loss of tragedy as it existed in antiquity. What I mean is that the alienation brought on by inevitable, ascendant progress as a condition of happiness has led us to the perplexing paralysis of Panurge's sheep when history proved to us how very easily happiness could be sacrificed on behalf of totalitarian political systems that promised total happiness, though only in exchange for total submission.

I see two paths—equally difficult, perhaps impassable—that we may embark upon to arrive at a new concept of happiness for our times. The more arduous one calls for a restoration of the tragic spirit. The tragic perception harbors no illusions regarding the evil that men are capable of inflicting upon one another. The tragic hero transgresses. But, as Anaximander reminds us, he purges his excesses in accordance with "the laws of time." Tragedy is the "law of time" that the Mediterranean thinker identified to redeem the fallen hero and reestablish the order of the city through catharsis, the manifestation of which resolves the conflict between freedom and inevitability, and thus grants us, through an understanding of ourselves and of those around us, the measure of happiness that is our due.

The more accessible path is one that affirms identity without undermining diversity, that ensures the preservation of identity while still defending the respect that diversity deserves. It is all too easy to point out, ad nauseam, the various modern-day obstacles strewn across the path of this equilibrium between diversity and identity: political obstacles, social obstacles, personal obstacles, informational and educational obstacles, et cetera. Yet can we conceive of a reality that does not encompass both the personal gratifications that associate "happiness" with creativity, eroticism, filial love, bed and board, home and hearth, those little things that are as much our true "nation," as José Emilio Pacheco describes in his great poem "Alta Traición" (High Treason), as are the social or collective gratifications of good government, administrative integrity, public security, the right to dissent, and the faculty to elect?

Yet we must not fool ourselves either. In the personal sphere alone, can we conceive of a happiness that is unsullied, sooner or later, by the death of a beloved, a fissure in a romantic relationship, a fidelity betrayed, a friendship broken?

Precisely for this reason, happiness is an ambiguous, critical, and at times disguised word whose true nature can only be revealed by the light of love.

History

Latin American, Euro-Latin, and, I suppose, Franco-African and Franco-Asian children learned their Universal History out of the little green books by Messrs. Malet and Isaac that neatly compartmentalized history into the Middle Ages, the Modern Age, and the Contemporary Age. The first segment began with the consolidation of Christianity after the fall of Rome. The second age was up for grabs—it began either with the discovery of the Americas or the fall of Constantinople, and the third began, of course, with the French Revolution in 1789.

It was a history of the Western world, for the Western world. Nevertheless, far more significant times and spaces were hidden behind the catalogue of dates and events. The life force of the hierarchical medieval system, organized vertically and grounded in faith, was rooted in the political tensions between the spiritual and temporal powers of the day. After a time, this tension— which was absent in the Russian and Byzantine realms—would give way to democracy. The Renaissance put an end to feudal fractionalism and saw the birth of the nation-state, fueled by a mercantile tradition and ravaged by many religious wars. Non-

European peoples were granted admission into this Universal History, but only as the result of foreign conquest, and only insofar as they allowed themselves to be colonized—that is, "civilized," or in other words (and without quotes), exploited. This was the age of divine right and absolute monarchy, which would eventually be undermined by the emergence of the industrial and mercantile bourgeoisie whose cries of emancipation led the French and American revolutions. The Contemporary Age, finally, was presented as a nineteenth century of material development that, at the beginning of the twentieth century, promised to be synonymous with progress, freedom, and happiness: the dream of modernity, the triumph of Condorcet's optimism.

In this sense, the millenarian framework possessed a space: the entire world, colonized by the West, but only one time, specifically that of Western history as a measure of all that was exclusively human: Hume, Herder, Locke. And can there be any doubt that a Western millennium written by Dante, Cervantes, and Shakespeare, sung by Bach, Mozart, and Beethoven, built by Brunelleschi, Fisher von Erlach, and Christopher Wren, painted by Rembrandt, Velázquez, and Goya, contemplated by Thomas Aquinas, Spinoza, and Pascal, sculpted by Bernini, Michelangelo, and Rodin, novelized by Dickens, Balzac, and Tolstoy, versified by Goethe, Leopardi, and Baudelaire, filmed by Eisenstein, Griffith, and Buñuel, and explained by Kepler, Galileo, and Newton is one that has granted glory not only to the West but to all of humankind?

"How is it possible to be Persian?" Montesquieu asked himself ironically during an Enlightenment that nonetheless (and despite Vico) left the nonwhite, non-European majority of humankind shrouded in shadows? The conquest or reconquest of the historical presence of the marginalized peoples of Asia, Africa, and Latin America is one of the essential realities of this millennium. As it turns out, there wasn't just one history. There were many histories. There wasn't just one culture. There were many cultures.

To arrive at the end of the millennium with this understanding is one of the triumphs of that millennium.

On the other hand, the age that comes to a close will also bear the mark of Cain, the violence of man versus man. Hobbes's *homo homini lupus* sullied the great scientific and artistic conquests of the millennium. Intolerance manifested itself from the Catholic and Protestant tribunals and continued on through the tribunals of Vishinsky and McCarthy. Amidst all this, increasingly painful pages of a universal history of violence were written during the conquest of America, the Thirty Years War, the persecution and expulsion of Europe's Arab and Jewish minorities, the European colonial assault on black Africa, India, and China. But they were also written during times of economic expansion thanks to forced labor, child labor, racially motivated slavery, and the marginalization of the female gender.

Man's capacity to inflict pain on his brethren culminated in our own moribund twentieth century. Never before in all of history have so many human beings died in so cruel a manner. Add up the millions of dead in the two world wars, plus the subsequent colonial wars—Algeria, Vietnam, the Congo, Rhodesia, Central America—to those who were victims of internal terror regimes, such as Adolf Hitler's order to exterminate Jews, Catholics, Communists, Gypsies, slaves, and homosexuals; those who perished in Joseph Stalin's prisons as he systematically exterminated first his own comrades and later millions of citizens; and then, on a more modest though no less painful scale, the victims of the military dictatorships of Latin America, fostered and coddled by the United States under various administrations.

The most extraordinary aspect of this inventory is that the millennium that boasts the most significant technological and scientific advancement in history is also the most politically and morally retrograde in all of history. Attila, Nero, and Torquemada were not as cruel as Himmler, Beria, and Pinochet. But nor did they have Einstein or Freud to match up against. The tragedy of the millennium as it drew to a close is that we had every kind of resource imaginable for achieving happiness, yet we violated them all by employing the very worst methods that only served to achieve misery. Fleming, Salk, Watson and Crick, Pauling, Marie Curie: all the great benefactors of the century that so recently came to a close must live forevermore alongside the specter of the criminals of history who had neither the need nor the justification for killing so many millions of people.

Violence in classical tragedy was always depicted as part of humanity's ethical battle: we are tragic because we are not perfect. The tyrannies of the twentieth century turned tragedy into crime, the tragic crime of contemporary history. The monsters of the political realm denied history the opportunity for redemption through self-knowledge. The victim of the Gulag, of Auschwitz, or an Argentine prison was denied the tragic recognition and simply became a statistic of violence—victim number 9, 9 thousand, or 9 million. . . . The profound importance of certain writers of the past century—and I think particularly of Franz Kafka, William Faulkner, Primo Levi, and Jorge Semprún—lies in their ability to restore tragic dignity to the victims of criminal history.

Criminal or tragic, when the Cold War ended in 1989, we were told that history too had ended. Given the growing violence in the Balkan states and Chechnya, in Algeria and sub-Saharan Africa, as well as in the Holy Land, the notion of violence as normal and not an exceptional or unusual condition of urban life should have served to deter us from any excessive celebrations on the last day of December 1999 or the first day of January 2000. Neither the greatest nor the most wretched of human conditions cares about calendars. On more luminous days, we will create communication and art, we will achieve startling medical breakthroughs and we will delve into those parts of the infinite universe—without beginning, without end—that remain elusive to us today. We will create friendship and love. But on darker nights, we will allow one third of the human race to die of hunger, we will deny half the children on the planet the right to go to school, and we will prevent women—half the human race—from gaining equal access to employment. We will continue to exploit the natural environment as if our arrogant rapaciousness were trying to prevent the air, water, and forests from outlasting us.

A millennium in which history was no longer one single history—that of the Western world—but incorporated many histories and many cultures. Will the new one be better? This is the question asked of me by my great friend Jean Daniel, and I answer him with these words:

Dear Jean Daniel,
The twentieth century has embraced, to an equal degree, both the promise of a perfectible humanity and the promise of a freedom that, to be truly coherent, would have to include the freedom to do Evil. Century of Einstein and Fleming, and also of Hitler and Stalin. Century of Joyce and Picasso, and also of Auschwitz and the Gulag. Century of scientific light, and also of political darkness. The universality of technology, and also of violence. Progress heretofore unequaled, even in its inequality. Never before in the history of Man has there existed so wide a gulf between the progress of the scientific-technical realm and the barbarity of the moral-political realm. Does the twenty-first century promise something better? We have the right to be skeptical. Or at the very least to define pessimism as a wise man once did: well-informed optimism.

I

Ibero-America

I believe in Ibero-America, Spanish America. For me the Atlantic is not an abyss but a bridge. The waters of the Mediterranean flow from the Bosphorus and Andalucía to the Antilles and the Gulf of Mexico. Ocean of encounters. The first encounter was a collision. The America desired was an America destroyed. The European dream of a new Golden Age perished in the mine, at the hacienda, on the slave ship. Great civilizations crumbled and fell. The conquest of America was a catastrophe. But catastrophe, says María Zambrano, is only catastrophic if it does not allow for redemption. All of us were born out of the catastrophe of conquest. The majority of us are *mestizos,* mixed-breeds, children of the encounter. The majority of us speak Spanish and Portuguese. And even when we are atheists, we are Catholic. But our Christianity is syncretic, for it sustains, transforms, and deforms the great traditions of the constructive indigenous cultures of Chichén Itzá, Teotihuacán, Mayapán, and Machu Picchu. Indigenous societies with political regimes that were authoritarian, occasionally cruel, exploitative . . . and isolated. But at the heart of each one a battle was being waged between the darkness of sacrifice and war (Huitzilopochtli) and the principle of light and creation (Quetzalcoatl). Who would have won out, the son of Coatlicue or the son of the Plumed Serpent? We will never know. The indigenous cultures of America are cultures interrupted, conscious of their fragility—"In vain have we come, passing through the land. At least some flowers, at least some song . . . !"—and condemned to surrender out of pure surprise. Prophecies are fulfilled. The Other arrives. We are not alone in the world.

The conquest of America did not give rise to justice but rather, to the universal struggle for justice. Spain is the only colonial power that questions itself about the justice or injustice of its acts. This debate, initiated by the friars Antonio de Montesinos and Bartolomé de las Casas, paved the way for the concept of human rights as universal rights, as proclaimed by Fathers Vitoria and Suárez of Salamanca in the sixteenth century. And out of the racial and cultural interchange a syncretic religious culture would emerge (the idols behind the altars, Holy Mary, mother of both God and the Indians, Jesus Christ, the astonishing God who sacrifices himself rather than asking for sacrifice). A culture that is at times a culture of astonishment, irony, patience, memory, and sometimes resentment. At other times it is a culture of the most generous humility, and the most original and urgent creativity: Kondori, the Indian architect of Peru; Aleijadinho, the mulatto sculptor from Brazil; Sor Juana, the *mestiza* poet of Mexico. If the Baroque signifies a "horror of the void," then all the souls in Spanish America filled it. It was different from the European Baroque, the sensual sublimation of the Counter-Reformation. The American Baroque is the art of the Counter-Conquest. It fills the gaping voids of the New World utopia.

Spanish American nationalities emerged both with the colonial regime and against it. The king of Spain was far away; he never even set foot on his vast American dominions—King Juan Carlos I, in fact, is the first Spanish monarch ever to actually visit America. The Laws of the Indies granted protection to the native peoples, but distance and isolation aided the establishment of rural authorities, the great country estates, the exploitation of labor. In Brazil and the Caribbean, the enslaved black population served to replace the decimated indigenous population. The faraway Habsburgs allowed the elite *criollos,* those born in America but of European descent, to do as they wished. The Bourbons, however, were reformers who were rather too close for comfort, rather too obtrusive, and made the *criollos* bow to the wishes of the Spanish metropolis. And so the *criollo* elite, from Buenos Aires and Santiago de Chile to Caracas and Mexico, rose up in simultaneous rebellion in 1810. We had heroes: Bolívar, Hidalgo, San Martín. We had statues.

That was the hour of our independence, of dreams and of constitutions that were "made for angels not men," as Victor Hugo put it. The protective shield of the monarchy, benevolent in the case of the Austrian monarchs, meddlesome in the case of the Bourbons, imploded. Through these rough moments, we created instantaneous democracies, Nescafé republics, desperately trustful of the illogical imitation of France, England, and the United States, fatally condemned to exacerbate the differences between the "real" country and the "legal" country. The result was a pendular movement that went from dictatorship to anarchy: an age of national and local tyrants, an era caught between civilization and barbarity, as the Argentine Domingo Sarmiento declared in his book about the most fearsome of the gaucho tyrants, Facundo Quiroga, a man capable of splitting his own son's head open with a hatchet.

Building some semblance of a nation-state with a firm legal foundation was a task undertaken by statesmen who were debatable then and continue to be debated to this day, such as Diego Portales in Chile, Sarmiento and Bartolomé Mitre in Argentina, and Benito Juárez in Mexico. Juárez is saved by his vital statistics: Zapotec Indian, illiterate until the age of twelve, liberal lawyer, reformist president, a patriot who stood up to the French invasion and the phantom crown of Maximilian of Austria and Carlota of Belgium. But the work had yet to be completed. Liberal reforms and democracy seemed to consecrate the notion of development but not justice, and they perpetuated inequality. In Mexico, after Juárez, came Porfirio Díaz and his thirty years of peace without freedom. Argentina established the foundations of an oligarchic prosperity based on its commercial dependence on Europe. It was effectively a British colony until 1940. Chile, on the other hand, achieved more significant advances in terms of civic, labor, and political struggle. Colombia fooled itself into thinking it was the Athens of America: liberals and conservatives took turns occupying the seat of power, but somehow never achieved the power actually to change anything, and with this they sowed the horrors of perpetual war. And in 1898, Puerto Rico and Cuba, the last vestiges of the Spanish colony, became colonies of the United States, and Central America and the Caribbean became Washington's "backyard."

The simultaneous defeat of both Spain and Spanish America in 1898 in Caribbean waters should have served to warn us as to the dangers of resentment and isolation. It should have opened our eyes to that "community of Hispanic nations," the Spanish American commonwealth that the minister Aranda proposed to Charles III to avoid the dismemberment of Spanish America in the eighteenth century. What began to emerge during the twentieth century, however, was an awareness of Spanish America's cultural continuity. The Mexican revolution revealed the totality of the country's past, previously hidden by the cardboard façade of Porfirio Díaz's purported progress. And the country's past turned out to be its present: its culture. Instead of a superficial imitation of the European model ("Guatemala, the Paris of Central America," proclaimed a triumphant arch at the entrance to the city), we had both internal catastrophes (dictatorships, injustice, latent wealth, fragile prosperity, chronic poverty) as well as external ones (the two world wars, the Holocaust and the Gulag, the Latin American belief that violence was not our privilege but rather a universal condition of history that the Germany of Bach and Goethe could not escape), that spawned a kind of Spanish

American culture that was at once more modern and nevertheless even more deeply rooted in tradition. The Afro-American
tradition of Alejo Carpentier and Wilfredo Lam, Edouard Glis-
sant and Jorge Amado. The Indo-American tradition of Miguel
Ángel Asturias, Rufino Tamayo, and José María Arguedas. The
Euro-American tradition of Jorge Luis Borges, Alfonso Reyes,
and Roberto Matta. And then there were those who united root
and firmament, the two greatest Latin American poets of the
twentieth century: Pablo Neruda of Chile and César Vallejo of
Peru. The former epic and the latter tragic. We saw how tradition
could nourish creation and creation nourish tradition: the music
of Carlos Chávez and Heitor Villa-Lobos, the architecture of
Oscar Niemeyer and Luis Barragán, the painting of Orozco,
Frida Kahlo, Portinari, and Soto, the films of Emilio Fernández
and Nelson Pereira dos Santos, but also the science of Ignacio
Chávez and Bernardo Houssay, the popular art fed by "high culture" as well as itself, the spoken word as delivered by Cantinflas
in Mexico, Sandrini in Argentina, and Verdejo in Chile, tangos
by Discépolo and boleros by Lara, and the voices of Gardel,
Lucha Reyes, Celia Cruz.

Perhaps this Indo-Afro-Spanish American assimilation was
exactly what we needed in order to be able to build a bridge
across the Atlantic, fill the chasm of resentment and grievance so
that we might see ourselves in our other half, the part of us that
is Spain. But for Ibero-America, Spanish America, Spain is so
much more than Spain. It is the Mediterranean reborn in the
Caribbean, in the Gulf, in the American Atlantic and Pacific.
Spain is Greek philosophy and Roman law. Spain is the Spain of
the three cultures, Christian, Muslim, and Jewish, all of which
had their place at the court of Alfonso the Learned before some
of them were violently expelled by the blind dogma of Isabel and
Ferdinand, the Catholic monarchs. Spain is the great example of
a culture strengthened by adversity. This is the Spain of the Jewish *converso* Fernando de Rojas and *La Celestina,* the first great
urban novel that toppled the walls of the medieval city so that

sex, money, love, and death might circulate freely. It is also the Spain of Cervantes and Velázquez, the two great creators—*Don Quixote, Las Meninas*—of a reality based on the imagination. Reality as a creation of the imagination, not a servile reflection of convention: Quevedo and Góngora. The Spain of Goya, the most bitter, sharp, and biting criticism of modernity's beatitudes: be careful, the sleep of reason produces monsters; be very careful, Saturn devours his own children. . . .

Spain was something more than the "black legend" invented by "perfidious Albion," two concurrent but rival themes. It was the Spain of the first European parliaments (León, in 1188, was the first in Europe; Catalonia, in 1217; Castile, in 1265), of municipal liberties and rebel communities crushed by royal absolutism in 1521 (the Castilian community flags fell in Villalar, the banners of Cuauhtemoc fell in Tenochtitlán). It was the Spain of the Liberal Constitution of Cádiz in 1812, the Spain of the "child republic" (as María Zambrano called it), murdered by fascism in 1939. It was the pilgrim Spain that reactivated and at times set the standard for the cultural modernity of a Latin America in exile. It was the Spain of internal resistance against Franco. It was the Spain that had the tremendous political talent to join forces, reconcile ideologies, and strengthen an exemplary European democracy in the last thirty years of the twentieth century.

It is the Spain that, along with the Spanish Americans of the New World, speaks the second most widely spoken language in the West and the fourth most prevalent language in the world: Spanish, or Castilian, the language of 500 million men and women. The differences are right there. Nationalism and regionalism create shadows here, shed light there, and scatter complexity everywhere. But the language unites. Thirty-seven million people speak Spanish in the United States.

We are the Territory of La Mancha. Stained, impure, *mestizos,* forcibly open to communication, migration, and confidence in our own contributions to the world. We are the squires of Don Quixote.

J

Jealousy

Jealousy kills love but not desire. This is the true punishment of passion betrayed. We despise the woman who broke the pact of love, but continue to desire her because her betrayal was evidence of her own passions. For jealousy to exist, the romantic relationship cannot end with indifference. The lover who abandons us must have the intelligence to insult us, debase us, assault us savagely so that we cannot forget her in resignation. So that we continue desiring her with jealousy, the perverted name we give to our erotic will.

Norman Mailer describes jealousy as a kind of museum full of pictures that the jealous man guards like a curator. To me, jealousy is like a life within the life we normally live. We can take a plane, return to our home city or one we do not know, call our friends and sometimes even forgive our enemies, but during all that time we are living another life, a life that obeys its own laws, that is separate from us even though it lives within us. That life inside our life is jealousy and it manifests itself physically. As the popular Mexican expression goes, *nos hace circo la barriga,* that is, it makes the stomach churn. A ferocious, bitter wave of bile that churns, rising and falling from the heart to the stomach and then from the stomach to a crippled, useless member that has suddenly been rendered a casualty of war. It makes you want to hang a medal around the poor penis. And after that, a funeral wreath. The crescendo of jealousy, however, neither celebrates nor stops for very long in any one part of the body. Like a poisonous liquid it courses through the body, not to destroy it but to plague it, squeezing tightly so that its most vile juices rise up to the head and affix themselves, like the hard, green scales of a snake, upon our tongue, our breath, our gaze. . . .

Jealousy makes us feel expelled from life, as if a loved one has died. Of course, when someone dies, we are allowed to exhibit the pain we feel. The pain of jealousy, however, must be concealed, dark and venomous, to avoid pity and ridicule. Exposed jealousy exposes us to the laughter of others. It is a journey back to adolescence, that blighted age when everything we do in the public sphere—walking, talking, looking—can be the object of someone else's laughter. Both adolescence and jealousy separate us from life and prevent us from truly living.

K

Kafka

"Have you read Kafka?" Milan Kundera asks me.

"Of course," I reply. "To me, he is the essential writer of the twentieth century."

Kundera smiles scornfully. "Have you read him in German?" he asks.

"No."

"Then you have not read Kafka."

Milan Kundera's reflection on the untranslatable excellence of Kafka's German does concede, at least in the case of the Spanish, one notable and worthy exception. The translation of Miguel Sáenz (Franz Kafka, *Obras completas,* Galaxia Gutenberg/Círculo de Lectores, Barcelona) is so very splendid that I sincerely doubt it would affect the irony of my friend Milan.

Kafka, the fundamental writer of the terrible twentieth century. Without Kafka, we could never understand the age we live in.

With moral and intellectual courage, Pietro Citati dares to think the unthinkable: that Kafka's Josef K, of *The Trial,* is in fact guilty. That the apparent victim is possibly the guilty party.

Citati does not ignore Kafka's various biographical layers: his relationship with his father, with Judaism, with the bourgeois professional life of Prague, his native city, the "little mother with claws." After all is said and done, Citati tells us, Gregor Samsa would still rather be a sacrificed son than a free insect. He is an Isaac whose sacrifice, in *The Metamorphosis,* is not aborted by the Angel of God.

In his novel *El daño* (*The Damage*), the Mexican writer Sealtiel Alatriste offers a Kafka intimately connected to his mother, who sacrifices her own musical vocation in favor of her son's literary genius.

And while Citati's suggestion that the victim is guilty may seem scandalous at first, it nevertheless becomes luminously rigorous when he forces us to realize that power is virtual and that the victim of power exerts a force that otherwise would not exist.

We dress the emperor with no clothes.

We turn the ghost of power into the body of power.

All Kafka does is demonstrate the imbalance that exists between real power and the myth of power. And from here emerges the question: if power can make its own fiction reality, how can culture make its own reality convincing? Is subjectivity enough?

According to the Chilean philosopher Martin Hopenhayn, Kafka's *Diaries* give his novels a subjective resonance that they would otherwise lack. There is no interiority in Kafka's fiction. The *Diaries,* on the other hand, are the interior appeal to external passions. This is a vexing complementarity, as when the protagonists of the novels are heroes of reason. They suffer because they have been marginalized by reason. But they do not understand the "reasons" that marginalize them. Their "rationalism," then, consists of losing themselves in an undifferentiated system and perceiving themselves as outsiders in the formalization processes of social interaction.

From here we can appreciate Kafka's extraordinary construction and staging of the relationship between the individual and power—without doubt the most lucid, the most disturbing, and the most contemporary that has been written in the last hundred years.

According to Hopenhayn, the individual in Kafka's world is a parasite who wishes he wasn't but who, to his own chagrin, exposes the world of parasites that the system requires in order to exercise its power. The Kafkaesque "hero" only wishes to be embraced by power. But by subjecting himself to it, he unwittingly scratches at its mask. He reveals the arbitrary basis upon which power rests thanks to his clumsiness, not his intelligence. In Kafka, the emperor's clothes are not removed by some critic or other of the emperor. The nakedness of power is brought to light through the inability of its subjects to decipher the strategies employed by the power system.

Kafka's literary power boils down to one fact: his fiction describes a kind of power that makes its own fiction convincing. In both *The Trial* and *The Castle,* Kafka describes a void in the power structure that presents itself as something perfectly filled. We are aware of the lie that has usurped the power system, but even knowing that it is a lie, we are shocked as we witness the spectacle that carries out the charade. In Kafka, power exercises its might through pure virtuality. The authorities in *The Castle* always remain intact because they are only potentialities. As a consequence, the victim of power (e.g., Josef K, Land Surveyor K) imagines a power system that is proportional to the force of its absence. The rule of the rule of power is the uncertainty felt with respect to its enforcement.

When he died in 1924, Franz Kafka had no way of knowing, with the precision of the chronological historian, that ten years later his infernal visions of power would become a historical reality of power. But as they arrived by night—without reason, without excuses—to arrest their victims, the gestapo and the NKVD were arresting Franz Kafka. Is there anything more Kafkaesque than when Comrade Commissar I. V. Kovalev arrived at Minsk in

1937 to assume his duties, only to find himself in an office that had been emptied totally because his predecessor and all his underlings had been executed as traitors to Stalin?

Kovalev, as fate would have it, took the desk of the next victim: himself. Mikhail Koltsov, the *Izvestia* correspondent during the Spanish Civil War, declared in an equally Kafkaesque manner that if Stalin declared him, Koltsov, to be a traitor, he would believe it, even if it were untrue. And in fact Koltsov was imprisoned and executed as part of the quota of arrests that the secret police were forced to make in order to satisfy their dictator, even though they knew that they themselves, the executioners, would be the next victims of Stalinist paranoia.

Yet Kafka is not a political analyst. He is a writer. This means that, unlike what can happen in the realm of political history, in the realm of personal history and imagination entire dramas of doubts, blindness, ambivalence, and mute acts of heroism can be played out in the space of a room, an office, or a bed, complementing the exercise of power.

Gregor Samsa, in *The Metamorphosis,* becomes a bug to escape not only from his father but also from his manager, his business, bureaucracy (as Félix Guattari and Gilles Deleuze suggest in their study entitled *Kafka: Toward a Minor Literature*). Hopenhayn very astutely notes that Samsa the bug is not entirely a bug. He continues to think. The conscience uses the body as a screen while imprisoning it at the same time. And if there is some irony there, we can attribute it to the fact that the very essence of irony is to take us out of context and create a schism between ourselves and the world. The void then becomes the nexus between us and the world. This means that irony, as Hopenhayn brilliantly concludes, is metamorphosis in and of itself. The law is mad but it is the law. And an inexhaustible litany of obligations is what precludes Samsa, Josef K, and the Land Surveyor from fulfilling their obligations. For this reason they will be punished.

If Franz Kafka gave a face to the horrors brought about by power in the twentieth century, he may very well be a prophet of power in the twenty-first century as well. Power was made visible—too visible—in Hitler's Auschwitz and Stalin's Gulag. Today, power has learned how to become invisible, relying as never before on the premise that the victim himself will grant power all the power it needs.

L

Left

So what about the Left? Does it have a *raison d'être* after all its miserable failures, opportunism, betrayals, and passivity throughout the twentieth century? I want to remember its victories as well here, because I believe in them too—I believe in the fight against fascism in Europe, in the United States, in Latin America. And the fight against the left-wing dictatorships too: the democracy of the Left manifested itself in figures as diverse as the poet Osip Mandelstam in Russia, the journalist Carlos Franqui in Cuba, writers like Milan Kundera, Gyorgy Konrad, and Leszek Kolakowski in Central Europe. . . .

What about its situation today? The Berlin Wall fell. The Soviet Union disintegrated. Social injustice, however, did not crumble. Man's exploitation of his fellow man did not decrease.

Two reductionist theories of economy and society petered out as the past century and millennium came to a close. One was the so-called "real socialism," which was neither real nor socialism, but rather the totalitarian and dogmatic façade of an economy that enjoyed neither liberty nor efficiency and died when the Berlin Wall came down in 1989. It was replaced by another dogma, one that espoused unbridled market freedom and was set in motion by Ronald Reagan's administration in the United States and Margaret Thatcher's in Great Britain. Ostensibly surrendered to the divine hand of the market, the economic forces concentrated at the very top were supposed to render benefits that would trickle down to the masses. Things didn't work out quite as predicted in that case either. The concentration at the top stayed at the top, and as John Kenneth Galbraith astutely (as always) pointed out, the absence of government became a brutal presence whenever it tried to increase military spending or save duplicitous or insolvent banks. In the end, the post-Communist right wing widened the gap between rich and poor, making the poor even more vulnerable, concentrating wealth and confirming the neo-Darwinist philosophy expressed by Reagan, that the poor are poor because they are lazy.

The leadership of center-left movements in European countries represents, most certainly, a reaction against both these dogmatic philosophies. But they have all lived through the inescapable reality of economic globalization and, unlike the Thatcherite and Reaganite Right, they deplore not globalization itself but rather lawless globalization, the kind that is left to its own speculative whimsy, superior to all national or international regulatory efforts.

If there is one thing that unifies the New European Left, it is its determination to subject globalization to law and politics. "Global Darwinism" will only generate instability, financial crisis, and increasing levels of inequality. The mission of the New Left is to control globalization and regulate, by democratic means, the conflicts that arise from globalization. This does not mean that the Left is afraid of globalization. On the contrary: the Left sees the processes of globalization as a new historical territory in which to act.

Globalization allows the Left to call attention to the ever-widening gulf between economic space and political control. In other words, we have an economy that is swift and a political world that is slow to adapt to this reality. Under these conditions democratic control becomes complicated, but that is precisely why the Left must fight the market's wild distortions with respect to the allocation of resources, and balance it by instituting policies aimed at social solidarity, environmental protection, the creation of public resources, and giving politics priority as the foremost instrument for rational decision making.

Globalization puts a tremendous amount of influence in the hands of nonpolitical agents and robs elected powers of their power in favor of nonelected powers. The danger is no longer that of the "philanthropic ogre," the rapacious State so criticized by Octavio Paz, but rather the "unbridled ogre," the market that comes to be regarded as sacred when, in the words of Milos Forman, "we leave the zoo and enter the jungle." The marketplace and the political realm should support each other mutually. Such is the desideratum of the New Left. "We live in a market economy, not a market society." This, Lionel Jospin's catchphrase, is central to the philosophy of the New Left. But precisely because new inequalities have emerged alongside the old ones, the Left reaffirms the value of equality and, far from fearing globalization, sees a new historical territory in which the Left may act. Norberto Bobbio continues to insist that equality is the central theme for defining leftist politics: equal values and equal opportunities for each and every individual. Globalization, far from limiting the concept of equality, should reevaluate it within a far broader spectrum, without deterministic dogmas and with as concrete policies as can be conceived—in starting with educational opportunity in all its contemporary incarnations: primary, advanced, and from now on, lifelong education.

Those who oppose innovation lead the workforce to failure. The New Left cannot be a neo-Luddite movement—it must espouse more opportunities for work through contractual agreements that take into account the flexibility not only of the corporate world but of its workforce as well. Capitalist Fordism and Soviet Stakhanovism are dead. The Left must move beyond zero-unemployment policies and define itself through the notion of satisfactory employment—that may then help to spur employment by fomenting more temporary positions, of limited duration and greater mobility, which, to return to the basic premise of the project, requires a system capable of providing continuous education and training. Under Jospin's guidance, the French government has been the quickest to realize that in the modern economy, work output is multiplied and salaries improved when fewer hours are distributed over a greater number of occupations.

More growth and more equality. This calls for concrete measures: modernization of the economy's regulatory infrastructure, fiscal reforms, financial market reforms, and reforms in the banking and corporate sectors. This calls for a constant flow of social negotiation to combat inflation and raise the workforce's net income. The DS (Democratic Left) in Italy has made a point of demonstrating how, between 1996 and 1998, the Italian Left managed to raise the real income of the workforce by 3 percent without inflation, whereas the previous technocratic administrations allowed salaries to decline considerably.

The Left can safely say that globalization is neither a monster nor a value in and of itself. And there is no real need to ascribe any kind of value to globalization; what we do need is the assurance that it can be held accountable to responsible, publicly elected political powers. As Massimo D'Alema insists, what we need is a supranational political entity that can govern globalization. Properly governed, globalism is an opportunity for everyone. Without government, it will degenerate into anarchy and inequality for everyone. Today, globalism and irresponsibility fraternize far too much. The Left must insist upon the need for an international political code empowered to "regulate expansion and ensure that it is compatible with the values of democracy, individual and collective liberty, and the fair distribution of wealth."

As the former Italian prime minister said, the future of the Left will be determined by its capacity to generate ideas and transform itself. The Left knows that the future cannot be planned for by sacrificing lasting values of equality (not "egalitarianism" or "leveling") or liberty at whim, with values that free us from need. Capitalism proposes the reasons for the economy. But democracy proposes the values of political consensus. In order to achieve a compromise between these two elements, the Left represents the political forum in which the weakest members of society and the market may fight and negotiate their victories.

This challenge is clearly a difficult one. Another, more radical wing of the Italian Left argues that global capitalism has stopped trying to achieve consensus and exists in constant contradiction with its own democracy and its own human rights declarations. The rights of man do not exist. Rights of the market exist.

In the end, this radical critique does not exclude the goals of political primacy and the regulation of globalism proposed by the reformist Left. To think otherwise is to reward the status quo and even encourage disillusion in the face of the supposedly inevitable. As a counterpoint, Walter Veltroni and the democracy of the Left in Italy offer a series of guidelines to help distinguish Right from Left, just as Bobbio asks of us, and gives the Left a plan that promises more growth and more equality.

I cannot overlook, however, my friend Rossana Rosanda's very commendable stance: it is better to have more doubts than reasonable certainties. That, perhaps, is also part of a New Left that throws off the terrible shackles of the dogmatisms that, time and again, have led to the Left's fragmentation, lack of viable proposals and, in the end, failures. Painful as it is, the case of the Mexican Left illustrates this point particularly well.

In the wake of the democratic elections of July 2, 2000, which heralded the end of seventy-one-year, single-party rule by the Partido Revolucionario Institucional (Institutional Revolutionary Party), party life in Mexico revealed its anachronistic inadequacies. The PRI lived through its symbiosis with the President of the Republic. The PRI without a president is like an egg without salt: like a chicken with its head cut off running mad through a farmyard surrounded by nopales. The PRD (Partido de la Revolución Democrática, or Democratic Revolution Party) represented the leftist opposition to the PRI but, just like the PRI, has shown signs of internal debilitation. The PRD's protests against the PRI have lost their meaning, for both are now opposition parties. But the PRD's proposals are too similar to those of the old nationalist Left, hungry for a macro-state, the kind that was big in terms of size but small in terms of effectiveness. Less willing to capitalize on the advantages of the modern world and more inclined to categorically condemn them as part of a conspiracy against the nation, the Mexican Left has looked forgivingly upon foreign dictatorships that claim to champion left-wing causes. In this respect, the Mexican Left needs reforms that can steer it toward the path of social democracy. There is one faction of the old PRI that is beyond redemption: the so-called dinosaurs who are unable to give up their decrepit practices of electoral fraud. Yet there is another group of a more social democratic slant that continues to uphold the best traditions of the Mexican Revolution while adapting them to a country that is wide open to the world, to a critical modernism, and to the opportunities of building a globalism and a modernism based on locality.

I am writing this in 2001. The Center-Right represented by President Vicente Fox's PAN (Partido de Acción Nacional, or National Action Party) is in power. Faced with this, the only viable source of opposition is that of a Center-Left social democracy.

The transition to democracy in Spain has proven to be a great example of the shift from dictatorship—far harsher than that of the PRI—to democratic statehood. Four decades of civil war and dictatorship under Franco presented Spain with a series of obligations that its political actors were able to fulfill thanks to their desire to serve both their country and democracy in general, rather than their own partisan interests. King Juan Carlos was a superb mediator between all the various political groups, a beacon of political balance. The post-Franco Left did not gain control of the government until 1982, with Felipe González, an exceptional politician. For thirteen years, González and his socialist party in power at the time confronted and resolved the great dilemma of the post-Franco era, that of enabling the political structures to tackle social and economic development, adjusting the three powers—political, economic, and social—to a Europe that was preparing to leave behind both Manichaean Cold War simplifications as well as the defeated formulas of the so-called "real socialism" to the east of the Elbe River.

Felipe González's administration encouraged the growth of the internal Spanish market, yet always paired this with socially oriented policies for increasing employment, salaries, production, and health care, and proved that the modern Left could satisfy the demands for both growth as well as justice, whereas the recalcitrant Right was only interested in restoring antiquated privileges and patently ignoring any and all social demands. As he stewarded Spain into the European community, González secured tremendous advantages for his country with the goal of compensating, as efficiently as possible, Spain's underdevelopment in areas such as communications and the modernization of industry and capitalization, so that his country might attain the level of progress found in the rest of Western Europe. Socialist Spain did not lose sovereignty: it gained cooperation.

Like any political enterprise, that of Felipe González and his socialist party colleagues was not perfect: it rose, it fell, and it suffered the usury of time. Nevertheless, through González and Spanish socialism, I can envision a blueprint for a democratic Left worthy of the twenty-first century, a Left that demonizes neither private enterprise nor the state, and instead ascribes both sectors their appropriate functions and obligations. These sectors, in turn, can be sustained by the vigor and plurality of civil society, partisan life, and the effective, conscientious exercise of democratic processes.

Latin America, where the ravages of excessive state control on the one hand and a ruthless market on the other have demonstrated their respective inabilities to tackle the frightening level of indigence and inequality in a continent where 200 million out of 400 million souls are mired in poverty, has the right to hope that a post-Soviet democratic Left may be able to give people back their power within a framework in which social issues are the priority: health, education, housing, work, salaries, infrastructure, women's rights, care for the elderly, respect for sexual minorities, freedom of expression, protection for ethnic groups, the fight against crime, citizens' security. A less ideological and more thematic Left.

The nostalgic Left that looks back on what no longer exists cannot be the constructive movement that it needs to be. But the Left in power must always admit the existence of the other Left, the one that is not in power, the one that resists power, until (and even when) the Left occupies the seat of power. This is the Left's great challenge in the twenty-first century: to learn to oppose itself so that it will never again fall into the dogma, chicanery, and tyranny that soiled it so badly during the twentieth century.

M

Mexico

The next morning we arrived at the broad causeway . . .
[which led] to Mexico, and we stood there, marveled at
what we saw, and we said it was like those things of enchantment described in the book of Amadís . . . some of our soldiers even asked if what they saw was not a dream. . . .

BERNAL DÍAZ DEL CASTILLO,
THE TRUE STORY OF THE CONQUEST OF MEXICO

The conquistador's dream—his awe—rapidly turned into the
nightmare of the indigenous world. Of that enchanting thing that
was once Tenochtitlán, not a single stone remained in the end.
The dreamer became the destroyer. Despite all that, however, let
us not forget that the conquistador was also a man of desire: a
complex desire made of fame and gold, space and energy, imagination and faith.

There is no such thing as innocent desire because desire implies not only possessing the object of our desire but transforming it as well. Discovery leads to conquest: we love the world so
that we can change it. Bernal Díaz's melancholy is that of a pil-

grim who finds himself facing a paradise he must immediately destroy. Awe will give way to pain and the only way Bernal Díaz can save both is through memory. He is the first Mexican writer, the one who initiated the Spanish-language narrative tradition of the New World.

An immense country five times the size of France, Mexico loves itself, paradoxically, through all that is small. Not because we Mexicans like to dress fleas but because we compensate for the vastness of our land and landscapes with delicate decorum, meticulous, tender attention to the tasks of daily life, from a cuisine whose preparation often requires hours and even days ("slow food") to the protracted lunch of three, four, six hours so that we may infuse the acts of community life with words, memories, fraternity, and human joy and warmth. A country of contrasts, despite the cliché, it is a community of space, a gathering place. The saddest songs and the happiest songs. The most humble of men and the most arrogant of men. The most natural, perfect courtesy alongside the most offensive vulgarity. Extremes that are painfully invisible and patently present.

"Who goes there?"

"Nobody, sir."

"Who goes there?"

"Just your father, you motherfucker."

"At your service."

"Go to hell."

"My house is your house."

"One more step and you're a dead man."

"I'm nobody."

"You don't know who you're talking to, you wretch."

"I'm the master of my own hunger."

"I earned my money, and I don't have to share it with anybody."

"Whatever you wish, sir."

"Watch it: around here, what I say goes."

"What can I do? I'm the one they left behind."

"Jalisco never loses, and when it does, it steals."

"Yesterday I may have been marvelous, but today I am not even a shadow."

"You do whatever I fucking say."

"Woman, woman divine, your poison is so sublime."

"You are to blame for all my anguish, all my sorrow . . ."

"This is a motherfucking mess."

"My heart belongs to Daddy."

"What lovely eyes you have beneath those two lovely eyebrows . . ."

"What are you looking at, fucking asshole?"

The Mexican use of language—rich, mutable, serpentine—conceals as much as it reveals. And though I may have selected from the extremes of spoken expression, from genuine humility to insufferable pride, I cannot omit that middle ground of courtesy, intelligence, and the ability to both speak and listen, which are the temperate zone between the convivial tropics and the silent mountainside. The average Mexican speaks in relatively measured tones, with a tendency, yes, toward lowering the voice. The verbal energy of the Spaniards seems downright scandalous to us.

"Why do you speak so loudly?" asks a Mexican intellectual, sitting in a café one day, of the Spanish poet León Felipe, who happens to have the bearing of a towering, thunderous Jupiter.

"*Coño,*" the poet replies, in his booming voice, "because we were the first to shout 'Land!' "

(I should mention, incidentally, that there is nothing louder than a group of gringos who, when convened in public, somehow feel the need to show off what a marvelous time they are having, with eruptions of offensively loud cackles. It's their money, they can spend it however they want to.)

Mexicans don't shout. We were shouted at—"Land!" to be precise. Precisely because of this we suffer, not from the complex of a people conquered, but from the complex of a people bewildered by the "modernity" they must confront. We always arrive late at the banquet of civilization, said Alfonso Reyes. And to a certain degree, he is right. Fernando Benítez said that Mexicans haven't managed to invent a single useful object for the modern world. We are, however, great improvisers: we reassemble things that are broken, connect cables, pirate lights, resuscitate roosters in the cockpit, and ably cook what nature granted us: we are the *chefs de cuisine* of poverty. But the minute you give us a chance—in an oil well, in a border-town assembly plant, at a modern factory in the center of the republic, at a dynamic corporation in the north, on a movie set—we prove ourselves to be the workers who learn the fastest and who take the greatest advantage of technical progress.

In our better moments, we understand that the more authentic our experience, the deeper we delve into the roots of our origins and the more we reach out toward another excellent formula expressed by Alfonso Reyes: the notion of being generously universal so as to be profitably national. We have by no means learned this lesson perfectly. In Mexico there are far too many *sospechosistas,* or suspicionists, as Daniel Cosío Villegas called them. Those who see Mexico as the eternal victim of a vast foreign conspiracy to exploit us, belittle us, humiliate us. There is plenty of evidence to prove that this is true, or at least has been true in the past. According to my childhood history book, given to me by a U.S. elementary school (and I quote directly from the text), "Mexico's backwardness is due to the insurmountable indolence of an inferior race. . . ."

But then we are succumbing to mental colonization if we are always so concerned with what foreigners think of us. And the same is true of the attitude that rejects all forms of openness and importation as a mortal danger to the national essence. After all, what does this purported national "essence" consist of if not a multiplicity of encounters between the indigenous, the European, the African? To define the national identity categorically is to transform it into a mausoleum. Modernity is inevitable but it can also mean freedom if we perceive it as opportunity. What we cannot do is condemn all that is new or all that comes from the outside as sickness, misfortune, or shipwreck. Mexico has so much modernity. For the indigenous, Tzotzil, Chamula, or Tarahumara, their culture is their modernity. They deserve respect and yes, even protection. Not adulation that perpetuates the misery, ignorance, and injustice with which they live. In the twenty-first century, will Mexico be a country that is open, that fears neither its indigenous legacy nor its *mestizo* modernity? Demographically, soon neither a purely indigenous nor a purely white Mexico will exist, and so we are far better off if we can understand the value of both.

We have a proven identity. We know what it is to be Mexican, we know how it unites us and how it divides us. We don't confuse ourselves with anyone. But we don't separate ourselves from anyone, either. The search for a national identity—the nation-narration—has left us perplexed for centuries. To think that we do not possess any identity is a pre-Copernican form of living in the universe. It gives us a pretext for not moving forward from the identity we have acquired to the diversity we have yet to conquer. That is where national identity and personal identity become a creative challenge. Let us conquer political, religious, sexual, and cultural diversity. Let us move from identity to diversity through a path of respect. Let us renounce, as Héctor Águilar Camín advises us, the cult of "the legend of the defeated" as our repository of self-admiration.

Nevertheless, we must pay the tithe of risk to achieve courage. In Mexico, risk is the facility with which we move from desperation to optimism, only to fall back into desperation—or grab on to faith, the next life preserver. The PRI dominated us because it was our mirror. Revolutionary, agrarianist, laborist, socialist, nationalist, sectorial, corporativist, developmentist, stabilizer, authoritarian, open, populist, neoliberal. In a succession of reactions to previous inadequacies or failures, we run the risk of throwing out all we have achieved, and surrender only to those things we see as most desirable. Or, more tragically, force ourselves to love only that which is born out of loss and desperation, as if we had a rosary of lost utopias to which we might add our own nostalgic experience. Juárez and Cárdenas were great men because they were men of their time who nevertheless possessed historical memory. Though we may be frightened of the world we live in (and there is plenty to be frightened of), we cannot seek refuge in the nostalgia of singular, spectacular heroicides. Let us choose, instead, to learn lessons and avoid mistakes.

In my books, I have expressed some of the more extreme Mexicanophile faith of certain compatriots, bordering on the "There is only one Mexico" vein. "One does not explain Mexico. One believes in Mexico, with fury, with passion," as Manuel Zamacona says in *La región más transparente* (*Where the Air Is Clear*).

I have also given a voice to the disillusion of many Mexicans: "Don't let yourself get carried away with enthusiasm; in Mexico disappointment is quick to punish people who have faith and take it out onto the street."

And so I return to the kingdom of small things in Mexico because they are the greatest things. The modesty of an artisan, the pride of a cook. The melancholy of a singer and the cry of a rebel. The discretion of lovers. The beauty, without exception, of all the children of Mexico. The inborn courtesy of good Mexicans. The lasting, imperishable beauty of the loveliest Mexican women. Patience, when it is wise reflection. Impatience, when it is meditated rebellion. Isolated triumphs of the landscape in the midst of an abrupt, impatient, occasionally too leafy, occasionally too sterile natural realm, unattainable in its solar heights, undesirable in its hellish depths (only in the Mictlan mythologies of Mexico is the *inframundo,* or underworld, both heaven and hell, a flowering inferno). Mexico is the heart of the battle in which the beautiful and the steadfast—art, sculpture, cities, and temples, things built for all eternity—fight the toxic progression of the ugly—garbage, the chaos of the city, the desolation of the countryside. . . .

My vision of Mexico will always be caught between the enigma of the dawn and the certainty of the dusk, and to tell the truth, I don't know which is which. Doesn't each night contain the day that preceded it, and each morning the memory of the night that gave it life? . . . For this reason the victories of the human realm are greater in Mexico. Though our reality may be extreme, we do not deny any aspect of it. Rather, we try to integrate them all into the art, the gaze, the taste, the dream, the music, the word . . . Mexico as the portrait of a creation that never rests because its work is still unfinished.*

An incomplete country, Mexico is patient and serene, yet it still harbors the rage of a hope that has been frustrated too many times. This country has waited for centuries, dreaming, for its day in history to finally arrive. Its scowl and its smile have become one. Mexico is tender fortress, cruel compassion, mortal friendship, instantaneous life. All its ages fuse into one—the past that is *ahorita*—right now—as well as the future *ahorita* and the present *ahorita*. No nostalgia, no lethargy, no illusion, no inevitability. A nation of all possible histories, Mexico only asks—with force, with tenderness, with cruelty, with compassion, with fraternity, with life, and with death—for things to happen, for once and for all, now, that *already* that is a sigh, an exclamation, an epitaph and a convocation, all at the same time: I'm coming. Enough is enough. He's already dead. Let's get together already. It is my history, not yesterday's nor tomorrow's, and I want my eternal time to come today, I want love today, paradise and inferno, life and death, today, I'm tired of all the disguises, accept me as I am, for our wounds and our scars, your tears and your smile, my flower and my dagger are inseparable. Nobody has waited as long, no-

---

*Fuentes, Carlos, *Los cinco soles de México* (*The Five Suns of Mexico*), 2000.

body has battled so fiercely against the inevitability, passivity, ignorance that others have invoked to condemn it, as this nation of survivors that should have died a natural death after all the injustice, all the lies, and all the scorn its oppressors have heaped upon its aching body, the aching body of Mexico. Through many millennia of suffering and rejection, of oppression, so many centuries of unconquerable defeat, Mexico has risen, time and again, from its own ashes. Until when? What will be the time limit of our next great hope? What shall be the intensity of our next great desire?

N

Novel

What can the novel say that cannot be said in any other manner? This is the very radical question asked by Hermann Broch. It is answered, specifically, by a constellation of novelists so extensive and so diverse that together they offer a newer, broader, and even more literal notion of the dream of *Weltliteratur,* the world literature that Goethe envisioned. If, as French critic and novelist Roger Caillois said, the first half of the nineteenth century belonged to European literature, then the second half belonged to the Russians, while the first half of the twentieth century belonged to the North Americans, and the second half to the Latin Americans. Then, at the dawn of the twenty-first century, we can speak of a universal novel that encompasses Günter Grass, Juan Goytisolo, and José Saramago in Europe; Susan Sontag, William Styron, and Philip Roth in North America; Gabriel García Márquez, Nélida Piñón, and Mario Vargas Llosa in Latin America; Kenzaburo Oe in Japan; Anita Desai in India; Naguib Mahfouz and Tahar Ben-Jeleum in North Africa; and Nadine Gordimer, J. M. Coetzee, and Athol Fugard in South Africa. Nigeria alone, from the "heart of darkness" of the shortsighted

Eurocentric conceptions, has three great narrators: Wole Soyinka, Chinua Achebe, and Ben Okri.

What is it that unifies these great novelists beyond their respective nationalities? Two things that are essential to the novel. . . . and society. Imagination and language. They answer the question of what distinguishes the novel from journalistic, scientific, political, economic, and even philosophical inquiry. They give verbal reality to that part of the world that is unwritten. And they all share the urgent fear of all authors of literature: if I don't put this word down on paper, nobody else will. If I don't utter this word, the world will fall into silence (or gossip and fury). And a word unwritten or unspoken condemns us all to die mute and discontent. Only that which is spoken is sacred; unspoken, unsacred. By saying something, the novel makes visible the invisible aspect of our reality. And it does so in a manner that is entirely unforeseeable by the realistic or psychological canons of the past. To the full (plenipotentiary) manner of Bakhtin, the novelist employs fiction like an arena in which characters appear along with language, codes of conduct, the most remote historical moments, and multiple genres, causing artificial walls to crumble, endlessly broadening the territory of human presence in history. The novel ultimately reappropriates the very thing that it is not: science, journalism, philosophy. . . .

For this reason the novel is much more than a reflection of reality; it creates a new reality, one that did not exist before (Don Quixote, Madame Bovary, Stephen Dedalus) but without which we could not imagine reality as we know it. As such, the novel creates a new kind of time for readers. The past is rescued from the museums, and the future becomes an unattainable ideological promise. In the novel, the past becomes memory and the future, desire. Yet both occur in the now, in the present time of the reader who, by reading, remembers and desires. Today, Don Quixote will go out to fight the windmills that are giants. Today, Emma Bovary will enter the pharmacy of the apothecary Homais. Today, Leopold Bloom will live through a single June day in the city of Dublin. William Faulkner put it best when he said that time was not a continuation, it was an instant: "There was no yesterday and no tomorrow, it all is this moment."

In this light, the reflection of the past appears as the prophecy of the narrative of the future. The novelist, far more punctual than the historian, always tells us that the past has not yet ended, that the past must be invented at every hour of the day if we don't want the present to slip from our grasp. The novel expresses all the things that history either did not mention, did not remember, or suddenly stopped imagining. One example of this is found in Argentina—the Latin American country with the briefest history but the greatest writers. According to an old joke, the Mexicans descended from the Aztecs, and the Argentinians from the boats. Precisely because it is a young country, with relatively recent waves of immigration, Argentina has had to invent a history for itself, a history beyond its own, a verbal history that responds to the lonely, desperate cry of all the world's cultures: please, *verbalize me*.

Borges, of course, is the most fully developed example of this "other" historicity that compensates for the lack of Mayan ruins and Incan belvederes. In the face of Argentina's two horizons—the Pampa and the Atlantic—Borges responds with the total space of "The Aleph," the total time of "The Garden of the Forking Paths," and the total book in "The Library of Babel," not to mention the uncomfortable mnemotechnics of "Funes, the Memorious."

History as absence. Nothing else inspires quite so much fear. But nothing provokes a more intense response than the creative imagination. The Argentine writer Héctor Libertella offers the ironic response to such a dilemma. Throw a bottle into the sea. Inside the bottle is the only proof that Magellan circumnavigated the earth: Pigafetta's diary. History is a bottle thrown into the sea. The novel is the manuscript found inside the bottle. The remote past meets the most immediate present when, oppressed by an abominable dictatorship, an entire nation disappears, to be preserved only in novels, such as those by Luisa Valenzuela of Argentina or Ariel Dorfman of Chile. Where, then, do the marvelous historical inventions of Tomás Eloy Martínez (*The Perón Novel* and *Santa Evita*) occur? In Argentina's necrophiliac political past? Or in an immediate future in which the author's humor enables the past to become the present—that is, presentable—and, more than anything, legible?

I would like to believe that this mode of fictionalization fills a need felt by the modern (or postmodern, if you wish) world. After all, modernity is a limitless proposition, perpetually unfinished. What has changed, perhaps, is the perception expressed by Jean Baudrillard that "the future has arrived, everything has arrived, everything is here." This is what I mean when I speak of a new geography for the novel, a geography in which the present state of literature dwells and that cannot be understood—in England, let's say—unless one is aware of the English-language novels written by authors with multiracial and multicultural faces, who belong to the old periphery of the British Empire—i.e., the Empire Writes Back.

V. S. Naipaul, an Indian from Trinidad; Breyten Breitenbach, a Dutch Boer from South Africa; but also Marie-Claire Blais, of francophone Canada, and Michael Ondaatje, a Canadian as well though via Sri Lanka. The British archipelago includes other internal and external islands: Alasdair Gray's Scotland, Bruce Chatwin's Wales, or Edna O'Brien's Ireland, all the way to Kazuo Ishiguro's Japan. There would be no North American novel to broaden the diversity of culture, race, and gender without the African American Toni Morrison, the Cuban American Cristina García, the Mexican American Sandra Cisneros, the Native American Louise Erdrich, or the Chinese American Amy Tan. They are all modern Scheherazades: each night as they tell their tales, they stave off our deaths one more day. . . .

Jean-François Lyotard tells us that the Western tradition has exhausted what he calls "the meta-narrative of liberation." But doesn't that mean, then, that the end of those "meta-narratives" of the modern Enlightenment signals the multiplication of the "multi-narratives" that have emerged out of a polycultural and multiracial universe that transcends the exclusive domain of Western modernity?

Perhaps Western modernity's "incredulity toward meta-narratives" is being displaced by the credibility being gained by the polynarratives that speak on behalf of the multiple efforts for human liberation, new desires, new moral demands, and new territories of human presence throughout the world.

This "activation of differences," as Lyotard calls it, is simply another way of saying that despite the realities of globalization, our post–Cold War world (and, if Bush Jr. gets his way, a world of white-hot peace) is not moving toward one illusory and perhaps very damaging unity but rather toward a greater, healthier, though often more contentious differentiation of its peoples. I say this as a Latin American. For much of our independent existence, we were absorbed by a nationalistic preoccupation with identity—from Sarmiento to Martínez Estrada in Argentina, from González Prada to Mariátegui in Peru, from Hostos in Puerto Rico to Rodó in Uruguay, from Fernando Ortiz to Lezama Lima in Cuba, from Henríquez Ureña in Santo Domingo to Picón Salas in Venezuela, from Reyes to Paz in Mexico, Montalvo in Ecuador, and Cardoza Aragón in Guatemala. And this did, in fact, help give us exactly that: an identity. No Mexican has any doubt as to whether he is a Mexican, no Brazilian doubts he is a Brazilian, no Argentinian doubts he is Argentinian. This reward, however, comes with a new demand: that of moving from identity to diversity. Moral, political, religious, sexual diversity. Without respect for the diversity that is based upon identity, liberty cannot exist in Latin America.

I offer the example that is closest to me, the Indo-Afro-Latin American example, to support the argument that sees the novel as a factor in cultural diversification and multiplicity in the twentieth century. We enter the world that Max Weber heralded as "a polytheism of values." Everything—communications, economics, science, and technology but also ethnic demands, revived nationalism, the return of tribes and their idols, the coexistence between exponential progress, and the resurrection of all that we thought was dead. Variety and not monotony, diversity rather than uniformity, conflict rather than tranquility will define the culture of our century.

The novel is a reintroduction of the human being in history. In the greatest of novels, the subject is introduced to his destiny, and his destiny is the sum of his experience: fatal and free. In our time, however, the novel is a kind of calling card that represents the cultures that, far from having been drowned by the tides of globalism, have dared to affirm their existence more emphatically than ever. Negative in the terms we are all familiar with (xenophobia, aggressive nationalism, cruel primitivism, the perversion of human rights in the name of tradition, or the oppression by the father, the *macho,* the clan), idiosyncrasy is positive when it affirms values that are in danger of being forgotten or eliminated and that, in and of themselves, are bulwarks against the worst tribalistic instincts.

There is no novel without history. But the novel, by introducing us to history, also allows us to search the nonhistorical path so that we may contemplate history in a clearer light, so that we may be authentically historical. To become so immersed in history that we lose our way in its labyrinths, unable to find our way out, is to become a victim of history.

Insertion of the historical being into history. Insertion of one civilization into others. This will require a keen conscience on the part of our own tradition if our goal is to extend a welcoming hand to the traditions of others. What unites all tradition if not the need for building a new creation upon it?

This is the question that new Mexican novelists like Jorge Volpi, Ignacio Padilla, and Pedro Ángel Palou resolve so brilliantly.

All novels, like all works of art, are composed simultaneously of both isolated and continuous instants. The instant is the epiphany that, with luck, every novel captures and liberates. As Joyce puts it in *A Portrait of the Artist as a Young Man,* they are delicate, fugitive moments, "lightnings of intuition" that strike "in the midst of common lives."

But they also strike us in the middle of a continuous historical event, so continuous that it has neither beginning nor ending, neither theological origin nor happy ending nor apocalyptic finale, just a declaration of the interminable multiplication of meaning that opposes the consoling unity of one single, orthodox reading of the world. "History and happiness rarely coincide," wrote Nietzsche. The novel is proof of this, and in Latin America we gain the novel of mindful warning when we lose the discourse of hope.

New novel: I speak of a still tentative but perhaps necessary step, from identity to "alternity"; from reduction to enlargement; from expulsion to inclusion; from paralysis to movement; from unity to difference; from noncontradiction to perpetual contradiction; from oblivion to memory; from the inert past to the living past; from faith in progress to criticism of the future.

These are the rhythms, the meanings of newness in narrative. . . . perhaps. But only with them, with all the works that liberate them, can we attain the magnificent potential for creating images that José Lezama Lima bestowed upon the "imaginary eras." Because if a culture is not able to create an imagination, the result will be historically indecipherable, adds the author of *Paradiso.*

The novelty of the novel tells us that humanity does not live in an icy abstraction of the separate, but in the warm pulse of an infernal variety that tells us: we have yet to be. We are in the process of becoming.

That voice questions us, arriving from far away but also from very deep within us. It is the voice of our own humanity revealed in the forgotten boundaries of the conscience. And it hails from multiple times and distant spaces. But it creates—with us, for us—a space where we can gather together and share our stories with one another.

Imagination and language, memory and desire—they are not only the living matter of the novel but the meeting place for our unfinished humanity as well. Literature teaches us that the greatest values of all are those that we share with others. We Latin American novelists share Italo Calvino's sentiments when he declares that literature is a model of values, capable of proposing stages of language, vision, imagination, and correlation of events. We see ourselves in William Gass when he shows us that the body and the soul of a novel are its language and imagination, not its good intentions: the conscience that the novel alters, not the conscience that the novel comforts. We identify with our great friend Milan Kundera when he reminds us that the novel is a perpetual redefinition of the human being as problem.

All of this implies that the novel must formulate itself as a constant conflict of all that has yet to be revealed, as a remembrance of all that has been forgotten, the voice of silence and wings of desire of all that has been overcome by injustice, indifference, prejudice, ignorance, hatred, and fear.

To achieve this, we must look at ourselves and the world around us as unfinished projects, permanently incomplete personalities, voices that have not yet uttered their last word. To achieve this, we must tirelessly articulate a tradition and uphold the possibility that we are men and women who not only exist in history but make history. As Kundera suggests, a world in the midst of rapid transformation invites us constantly to redefine ourselves as problematic, perhaps even enigmatic beings, never as the bearers of dogmatic answers or conclusive realities. Isn't this what best describes the novel? Politics can be dogmatic. The novel can only be enigmatic.

The novel earns the right to criticize the world by proving, firstly, its ability to criticize itself. The novel's criticism of the novel is what reveals the labor that goes into this art as well as the social dimension of the work. James Joyce in *Ulysses* and Julio Cortázar in *Rayuela* (*Hopscotch*) are prime examples of what I am trying to say: the novel as a criticism of itself and the manner in which it unfolds. But this is the legacy of Cervantes and the novelists of La Mancha.

The novel proposes the possibility of a verbal vision of reality that is no less real than history itself. The novel always heralds a new world, an imminent world. Because the novelist knows that after the terrible, dogmatic violence of the twentieth century, history has become a possibility; never again can it be a certainty. We think we know the world. Now, we must imagine it.

O

Odyssey

Language is the creation of time. And time, in the language of myth, is the eternal present. It is language that expresses the aspiration of being one, complete, as in the beginning: before the first sacrifice, before the first murder, before the first rape, before the first testimony of death. Everything in the cultures of the dawn is remembrance, a representation of the privileged instant before separation. Time and again, myths have attempted to illustrate this yearning for a return to that first age, that "Golden Age." The purpose of the eternal present—the myth—is to relink us (through religion) to the natural world at the moment it becomes the human world.

From Vico to Lévi-Strauss, myth and language are identified as one: the paradox that an animal sound (the "moo" of a cow) gives rise to both the word that it *is* (*mitos,* word) as well as the word that it *isn't* (*mutus,* mute). Myths are like a glass wall between the two dimensions of language. To say or not to say. To return or not to return. And while the nostalgia of language may consist of offering us a reversible structure that brings us back to the primary unit of man, the inevitability of language is that it depends upon a successive and irreversible medium: the word. The dilemma of language is right there in its very origins: how can we employ a fragmented and sequential medium to create the impression of immediate, complete presence? This is the dilemma of the first shaman, María Sabina, who is every shaman, and the last one, James Joyce, who is every writer.

History is the privileged locus of chronological time. From there emerges its fraternal parallel with the successive destiny of discourse. Each step forward taken by history and its servant, which is the word (because history is only that which survives, that which speaks or writes of history), takes us one step further away from our origins. The so-called "primitive cultures" (which are not in fact primitive, just different) reject this accelerating impulse of history. The life and passion of Christ occur, as far as Western culture is concerned, between two very specific historical moments: the reigns of Augustus and Tiberius. Transposed onto the culture of the Cora Indians of Nayarit, Mexico, Holy Week does not cele-brate the sacrifice of a historical God, Jesus, but rather the sacrifice of the original God who at the dawn of time spilled His blood so that the corn could grow. The price of the communitarian unity of mythical worlds is called isolation. The price of the individual translation of myth is called freedom, and freedom means fallibility.

As in all cultures, the culture of Greece originally manifested itself through myth: the memory of dawn, the space of the home, the living flame of genealogy. But Greece is the first civilization to travel. And by displacing itself (that is, leaving the place), it must confront all that is foreign. Through displacement, through roam-ing, through transplant, Greek culture displaces myth (moving it from its original place) and gives it two opportunities to grow and transform human life. One is the epic poem. The other is tragedy.

In the *Odyssey,* the heroes are those who travel, and the gods are those who follow them. Ethics, then, are born from a norma-tive identity between society and its literary manifestation or song. The dead are abandoned in the tombs of the Hellenic home. They are the object of anguished memory; they are the guardians of a culture that is running the risk of traveling to far-away citadels, foreign kingdoms, and islands of tempting sirens.

The gods accompany the heroes; thus the epic poem is born. But the hero is fallible; thus tragedy is born. Amid these three singular discoveries—myth, epic, and tragedy—freedom emerges as an inevitable value. Because while the hero may be able to abandon the original world of the myth, he is nevertheless unable to separate himself from the cosmos that envelops him—he is part of the natural world but he sees himself as a being that belongs to nature, given that his mission is to maintain a social and political order that *differentiates* man from nature. When the hero is able to shoulder this burden, he is an epic hero: Achilles. When he cannot endure it, or when he betrays it, he is a tragic hero: Oedipus.

Why does the tragic hero transgress? Because he is free. Why is he free? Because he is part of nature but he separates himself from nature. How does the hero know this? Through his knowledge of himself. And how does he come to know himself? Through action. Aristotle warned us that tragedy is the imitation of action. And human action not only affirms values; it disturbs and, on occasion, destroys them. The debt must be paid.

Oedipus liberates Thebes from the Sphinx. He condemns himself. Orestes kills his mother. He reestablishes the order of the city. Prometheus liberates men by granting them the divine fire of intelligence. By doing so, he condemns himself and proposes the very highest order of the tragic dilemma: would Prometheus have been freer had he not exercised his freedom, since by exercising it, he loses it? The Andalusian philosopher María Zambrano, in love with her moral sister Antigone, gives us the key to tragic illumination. Without Antigone, without her tragedy, the evolution of the city would not have continued.

And this is true because tragedy, in the end, proposes a conflict of values, not virtues. Accustomed to living in a melodramatic world that pits the good guy against the bad guy, we have lost the wisdom and generosity of the tragic world, where both parties in conflict are in the right: Antigone, by defending the value of the family; Creon, by defending the value of the city. The mission of tragic drama is to grant the community—which includes both individual and society, family and city—the right to resolve the conflict. The values do not destroy each other. But they must *wait for the representation* that allows them to reunite, so that one may resolve the other and restore both individual and collective life. Medea, mother and lover; Antigone, daughter and citizen; Prometheus, god and man. Through tragic catharsis, they reconstruct the life of the community. Tragic theater, through catharsis, allows catastrophe to be transmuted into knowledge.

The loss of tragedy, eliminated by one optimism that is supernatural (the Christian promise of eternal happiness) and another that is far too natural (the progressive promise of happiness on earth), gave us crime in its place. Not to believe in the Devil is to give him every opportunity to catch us by surprise, said André Gide. Beatifically trusting the notion that our destiny was an inevitable ascent toward perfect happiness through irreversible progress, we arrived, blind, in the land of crime: the Nazi Holocaust, the Soviet Gulag. Never can we be as we were before. The myth has slipped from our grasp. "We are too wounded," to use the words of Adorno. There is no possible epic when wars are waged from the sky, protecting soldiers from harm and killing only civilians. There is no tragedy when the Manichaean melodrama fully inundates our entire lives, our discourses, our television, movie, and computer screens, and our feelings. We know in advance who are the good guys and who are the bad guys.

Nevertheless, I find a poignant echo and a sliver of hope in between two statements: one by Franz Kafka, the greatest tragic writer of our modern times, the other by Simone Weil, the greatest Judeo-Christian witness of the concrete validity of the classic epic. "There will be much hope, but not for us," Kafka writes. And Weil, rereading the *Iliad,* concludes that the contemporary lesson to be learned from the classic poem is that "those who dreamt that might, thanks to progress, belonged henceforth to the past, have been able to see its living witness in this poem."

P

Politics

For me, politics was a second amniotic fluid. I grew up swimming in it, for between 1930 and 1960, the first thirty years of my life, the best and the worst of the *polis* paraded before my eyes. The best thing about it was the constructive, Aristotelian understanding it gave me of political challenge: politics as a worthy endeavor, one that responded to culture, tradition, individual respect, and the strength of community. Of course, as a child or adolescent I didn't think of it as such. I *felt* it because I had the good fortune to grow up in two parallel political societies: the United States of President Franklin D. Roosevelt and the Mexico of President Lázaro Cárdenas; the New Deal and the culminating moment of the Mexican Revolution. Roosevelt led his nation out of the worst depression it had ever known, through acts that reflected his trust in the human capital of the United States. He inspired faith and even enthusiasm among his citizenry, and he gave the state an active role in tackling unemployment, financial restructuring, the creation of modern infrastructures, education, and culture. He saved North American capitalism and North American capitalism neither recognized it nor thanked him for it.

Roosevelt, the aristocrat from Hyde Park, New York, was a rene-gade, a cripple, and possibly even a Jew. In Mexico, Cárdenas gave the revolution the definitive impetus it needed. Agrarian re-form liberated hundreds of thousands of rural peasants who had been tied to the earth for centuries, and if the effects of agrarian-ism were and still are debatable, one thing remains certain: the peasant was now free to go to the city and offer himself up as cheap labor for the (also debatable) process of industrialization. The nationalization of the oil business contributed cheap fuel to nascent Mexican industry. Cárdenas laid the foundations for cap-italist development in Mexico. And the Mexican bourgeoisie neither recognized this nor thanked him for it. With Cárdenas, this growth was accompanied by distributive justice. Never be-fore in Mexico's history had the distribution of wealth been as equitable as it was during his presidency. The labor and farm unions of the day fulfilled their role in defense of the worker. At their core, however, they harbored a snake: an exclusionary, anti-democratic corporativism.

Roosevelt's politics prepared the United States to enter World War II. Cárdenas's politics served to demonstrate that the fight was an ethical struggle as well. His principled foreign policy was also a pragmatic policy of generosity. Cárdenas opened Mexico's doors to a pilgrim Spain, the republican emigration that strengthened and brilliantly enlightened the cultural life of Mexico.

But while these were the bright lights of politics, the shadows that hovered over everything during those years threatened to ex-tinguish them entirely. Spain's war was the first sign of a political regime that was openly designed to serve the interests of evil. Franco disguised it as a nationalist crusade, his bishops blessed it, and his fascist and Nazi allies provided the weapons for it. Spain was a warning of what was to come. Never before in history had evil proclaimed itself as such, so openly and without any kind of aesthetic justification. Genocide, absolute tyranny, racism, exter-mination, the Holocaust, the Final Solution: it was all a foregone conclusion. Adolf Hitler decided that the Devil should finally take human form. If God had done so with his son, Jesus, Satan could do the same with his clone Adolf. Jaspers warned us in advance that Hitler's strength resided in his lack of existence: Hitler was the empty leader of the rootless masses.

The defeat of the German socialists and Communists in 1932 can be explained by the fact that the Left looked at the world through the tunnels of economic infrastructure, exactly as the Marxist bible preached. Hitler kidnapped the cultural superstructures, looked up toward the heights of Valhalla, and appealed to the Wagnerian myths, to the dreams and false illusions of the German *Volk,* to the damage and humiliation of the peace at Versailles, to his country's sense of ethnic and intellectual superiority, and to their physical need for a space to live, the *Lebensraum.* His evil and its means were always so transparent. Yet the lies Stalinism told may have been even worse, for Communism was a movement that was supposed to put a humanistic, liberating philosophy into practice. Stalin's perversion of the socialist dream—the purges, the Gulag, the abolition of the most basic rights, the leader's paranoia, and the atrocities of his torture—was worse than the fulfillment of the Hitlerian nightmare. Hitler never deceived anyone. Stalin donned the mask of Marxist humanism and cheated hundreds of thousands of honorable, devoted, though perhaps naïve Communists. Gide may have lost his faith in 1936, but Aragon hung on until the invasion of Czechoslovakia, and Neruda held out until Khrushchev's report to the Twentieth Communist Party Congress.

World War II was justified; it has been called the only good and necessary war. Our youthful solidarity enthusiastically joined forces with the fight against fascism. I spent the war years in Argentina and Chile, the latter being the first Latin American country to consciously develop into a democratic system, from a democracy of aristocrats to a democracy of political parties, the press, and social organizations. In 1941 the Frente Popular (Popular Front) was in power, with Pedro Aguirre Cerda as its president, and the prevailing spirit was one of social reform backed by a literary growth that fused words with freedoms, poetry with politics. My Chilean education necessarily contrasted quite powerfully in my mind with Argentina, where I lived during 1944. A fascist military regime, sinister precursor to Perón's populist dictatorship, deformed education (the anti-Semitic Hugo Wast was minister of education at the time) and maintained Argentina as fascism's political redoubt and, later on, a safe haven for Nazis on the run.

Politics may very well be the eagle that flies higher and achieves a broader vision of things from the "high cliff of the human dawn," as Pablo Neruda asserted in his *Canto General*. Or perhaps it is Yeats's "rough beast" of "The Second Coming" that "slouches towards Bethlehem to be born." The Cold War tried to put the eagle in a cage and cast a spell upon the serpent, replacing them with a hybrid between camel and crow, that sleepy creature of the desert so resistant to thirst, and that rapacious scavenger bird, ready to claw our eyes out. With McCarthy, the United States succumbed to an anti-Communist paranoia that led its inquisitors to emulate the very thing they were fighting against, the intolerance and cruelty of Stalinism. The resistance of the North American democratic institutions held out and, as an extension of their social struggle, set the stage for the civil rights movement and antidiscrimination laws. There was a McCarthy. There was a Martin Luther King, Jr. But if Americans can sometimes be benevolent Dr. Jekylls inside their own country, they so easily become monstrous Mr. Hydes when they leave its borders. The good-neighbor policy of coexistence with the Mexican and Chilean Left, Brazilian corporativism, or the Central American and Caribbean dictatorships ("Somoza is a son of a bitch, but he's our son of a bitch," as FDR said) turned into an anti-Communist campaign under Eisenhower and Dulles. This campaign confused Kremlin politics with many reformist movements, and ended up fighting them all: Arbenz in Guatemala and Goulart in Brazil, the seductive and comprehensible revolution led by Castro in Cuba, and the cleanly elected democratic government of Salvador Allende in Chile.

All of this fatally stunted the growth of much-needed social, economic, and political reform in Latin America, and plunged Cuba into an extralogical imitation of "real socialism" as pernicious as the extralogical imitation of the models of authoritarian capitalism in the rest of Latin America, which would become ruthless dictatorships in Chile, Argentina, and Paraguay. As a result, politics in Latin America has come to be synonymous with reconstruction but above all construction. Chile, Uruguay, and to a certain degree Argentina, can *restore* democracy. Central America and the Caribbean must *construct* it, while Mexico must transform the "perfect dictatorship" of the singularly powerful PRI president into an *imperfect* democracy with political parties, division of powers, accountability of the executive branch, activation of human capital, and improved distribution of income.

How can the challenges of democracy be met?

The world stage has undergone radical changes. The Cold War created a kind of shared jurisdiction between the United States and the Soviet Union based on the balance of nuclear terror. Ever since then, we have witnessed the weakness and, occasionally, the disappearance of traditional methods of social bonding and problem solving.

Nation and empire, state and international community, public sector, private sector, and civil society. All these traditional labels are now very clearly—sometimes paradoxically, sometimes furtively—in crisis or at least in mutation.

Why does this happen?

Because we have not been able to create a new legality for a new reality—the reality of globalization.

The modern Western world—that is, from the Renaissance onward—built itself around notions that had little relevance in the medieval realm: the nation, the state, international law, the mercantile-capitalist economy, and civil society.

What kind of relevance—moreover, what kind of reality—do these circumstances represent to our globalized, post–Cold War world? Given that Latin America finds itself situated between both of these premises, we can venture to suggest some shared ideas.

Nation and nationalism, for example, are modern terms that arose to legitimize notions of territorial, political, and cultural unity, and were necessary for the integration of the new states that emerged from the rupture of medieval Christian communities.

But what, then, provoked the emergence of nationalist ideology?

Emile Durkheim speaks of the loss of old centers of identification and adhesion.

The nation fills that loss.

Isaiah Berlin adds that all nationalism is a response to a wound inflicted by society.

The nation heals that wound.

And today, we repeat with them:

If both nationalist ideology and the very concept of the nation are in crisis, what new ideology and structures will keep society aloft? What is the great contemporary social wound, and what kind of sutures will close it? What will we call this still nameless process that will allow us to create a new legality for a new reality?

How can the national and collective centers of identification be replaced?

We would like to think that as nationalist moments become diluted, internationalist moments will fall into place.

But things haven't happened that way.

The case of Kosovo demonstrates the peril and doubt that plague the new international order.

The possibility of armed intervention in a delinquent state is provided for in the United Nations Charter. Not provided for, however, is the notion of a regional organization—NATO, in this case—assuming the right to intervene, overriding the international judicial order, sowing confusion and insecurity, and promoting a de facto right to interfere.

A new international order will not be possible if the strongest parties are allowed to intervene at whim, for that will generate dilemmas that will only jeopardize justice, security, and the very powers behind such intervention.

This does not mean that a solution is impossible.

On the contrary. The Balkan crisis calls upon all of us to introduce reforms to an international system created for and by a multitude of victorious nations at the end of World War II, whose goal was to confer greater representation and greater mobility on the various international institutions.

Once, when I was in Rome, I had a conversation with the prime minister of Italy at the time, Massimo D'Alema, who was convinced that NATO needed to take action in Kosovo. He confessed that although he had moved ahead with the conviction that he was on the side of the right, he had nevertheless been quite distressed about it and above all was aware that had action been taken a decade earlier, tragedy could have been averted through diplomatic and judicial means. "This has not been the case," D'Alema said, adding that to prevent a Kosovo from occurring again, the international system would require reforms, through the creation of—and I quote the Italian premier—"crisis prevention instruments, based not only on military means, but on political and economic resources as well."

In other words: a new legality for a new reality.

Now we find ourselves facing a situation of diluted international jurisdiction. But at the same time we find that national sovereignties, once the nemesis of people's rights, have also grown pale and weak in the face of an onslaught that was unforeseeable half a century ago.

This is called globalization, a movement in which so many men and women on the threshold of the twenty-first century have deposited both their hopes and their fears.

Globalization subjugates and almost categorically rejects the nationalist ideology upon which the modern world was founded, but it also poses some critical questions to be answered within each individual national community, the public, private, and third sectors, the business world, culture, democracy, and the state itself.

The political responses to this transition from nation-state to globalized world will not come quickly, as was the case with the nation-state and the rise of sovereignty during the transition from the Middle Ages to the Renaissance. It is worth noting that the Middle Ages did not create a vertical, unaccountable system for the Christian community. The system evolved—and evolved into what would come afterward—through a conflict between temporal and religious power. The battles between Gregory VII and Henri IV, Gregory IX and Frederick II, and Boniface VIII and Philip IV of France created a tension between the Church and the state absent in Byzantine Russia and its identification between the czar and the Church, the Caesaro-Papism that lasted until the arrival of the party-state symbiosis under Lenin and Stalin. Democracy was born out of Western medieval tension, as the temporal sphere broke free from the spiritual sphere and both found themselves obliged to accept and respect the configuration of local powers, political powers (legal systems, courts, municipalities), and social powers (corporations), all of which introduced the possibility of a sovereign nation-state as well as a new round of debates concerning this novel issue. Politics, as far as Machiavelli is concerned, is an autonomous and amoral realm. For Bodin, it cannot be separated from sovereignty, which excludes all pluralistic participation. Hobbes invokes a naturalist absolutism, and only with the advent of the Enlightenment (and before that, with English parliamentarianism) do social classes, corporations, and eventually individuals become actors on the political stage.

Are we now in the throes of a movement comparable to such political upheaval? Will we be able to establish an international order that can control the lawless jurisdictions of the market, of drug trafficking, of migration? Will we have international bodies that we can rely on to regulate these processes? Markets that will be forced to obey regulations governing social welfare and the development of the poorest nations? Decriminalization of international drug trafficking, which will deny the cartels their extravagant and illicit profits? Controlled and codified immigration policies protected by labor laws that recognize the invaluable contribution that immigrants make to the societies that receive them? Some indicators point in this direction. A universal agreement on the sanctity of human rights, a refusal to allow the statute of limitations to be used in cases of crimes against humanity, and the International Court on Human Rights can deny impunity to those who shamelessly violate these rights and help to foment a culture of international justice that could be applied to the world's markets, which would then be forced to adhere to social welfare regulations and political responsibility. The creation of the International Criminal Court (the Rome statute) will crown this effort by investing politics with a legal basis and punishing the violation of both.

All of this will strengthen the nation-state politically, just as the events of the very early twenty-first century have proven. Strong economies are only possible with strong states—not big states, simply regulatory ones. And strong states are only possible with strong societies that demand adherence to political mandates and regulations regarding transparency and accountability, societies that not only hold periodical elections, as Pierre Schori notes, but can fill the voids between elections as well: to revoke mandates, hold referenda, demand parliamentary responsibility on the part of governmental ministers, and provide for an independent public prosecutor who is empowered to bring to justice any and all abuses of power.

Politics is so much more than an election-day event. We need to increase political participation, broaden access to communications, and ensure that people understand and defend their rights. Politics must become a daily exercise of rights and vigilance.

More than ever—and despite the fact that it is unpopular to quote Hegel—politics have a thesis (law), an antithesis (ethics), and a synthesis (legality and morality). And to counterbalance Hegel, there is perhaps no one better than Burke to remind us that politics is an association, not only in an economic sense but "in all art, in all virtue, in all perfection."

The sum of my political hopes does not mean I am blind to the dangers of the proliferation of criminal jurisdictions beyond all control, or to the notion that one single superpower might jeopardize the world's will to create entities for justice, development, and environmental protection, or to the possibility that in the name of a supposed "clash of civilizations" entire cultures can be demonized.

Thanks to Judaism, thanks to Islam, late medieval Europe came to understand once again, and the Western world came to see once again. And we, their descendants, cannot subscribe to a "clash of civilizations" that negates half of our existence. History is ebb and flow; its nature is cyclical and the modern Western world would not exist were it not for the contributions of the Islamic world. As such, Islam's current technical deficit can only be overcome by generously repaying the universal debt to the communities that live by the faith of Mohammed.

Islam and Judaism have given us all so much. Can we not reciprocate, in the first place, with a commitment to peace through the generosity of negotiation? And in the second place, by acknowledging the intrinsic and predominant humanity of the Arab nations, and by refusing to imprison them behind the intolerable bars of something synonymous with terror and blatant evil?

With this in mind I offer my political concerns for the new century.

I am concerned about the ruthless exploitation of our planet's limited resources and by our assault upon air, water, and land.

I am concerned about the fact that by the year 2001 we were 6 billion men and women on this Earth: the greatest demographic leap in history, if you consider that when Christ was born the population was 300 million, and in 1900 it was 1.7 billion.

I am concerned that prejudice and exploitation, disguised as social order, continue to deny women—who account for more than half the world's population—their basic rights to work, representation, and freedom.

I am concerned that the freedom of the markets will dominate and deny the freedom of labor.

I am concerned that the global economy encourages the free movement of goods and restricts the free movement of workers.

I am concerned that an authoritarian capitalist order with no totalitarian Communist enemy to battle will impose a single and dogmatic market model upon the world.

I am concerned about the return of the worst signs of fascism: xenophobia, racial discrimination, political and religious fundamentalism, and the persecution of the migrant laborer.

I am concerned that the drugs empire has created its own jurisdiction of impunity, above all national and international legal jurisdictions.

I am concerned about the deterioration of urban civilization right across the globe, from Boston to Birmingham to Bogotá to Brazzaville to Bangkok: the homeless, the indigent who must beg for subsistence, the disregard of our elderly, uncontrollable pandemics, insecurity, crime, the decline of health and education services. . . .

I am concerned about the resurgence of senseless arms races between poor neighbors for the benefit of wealthy neighbors.

I am concerned that for the first time in history human beings have the frightening capacity to commit suicide while murdering nature, whereas before the nuclear age, nature always survived our tragic madness.

I am concerned by the rise of unilateralism, which denies multilateralism as the only possible path to international cooperation.

I am concerned by the barbaric stance of preventive war, which denies diplomacy, conciliation, and constraint as instruments of international order and promotes suspicion between neighbors, an extension of the arms race, and deception on an international scale: where were Saddam's weapons of mass destruction?

I am concerned by the diversion of the fight against terrorism to the selective overthrowing of tyrants if they happen to sit on barrels of oil.

I am concerned by the curtailment of freedom in the name of security.

I am concerned about a world without witnesses.

I am concerned about all that jeopardizes the continuity of life.

All of this is part of politics, of life in community, and of the citizenry in the *polis.*

Q

Quixote

In the figure of Don Quixote, Michel Foucault sees a symbol of the modern divorce between the word and the object. An emissary of the past, Don Quixote desperately searches for the place where the two may meet, as in the medieval order of things. The Quixotic pilgrimage is a search for similarities, and Foucault observes how Don Quixote rapidly recruits the weakest analogies: for him, everything is a latent sign that must be awakened to speak and to demonstrate the identity of words and objects: stocky peasant women are princesses, windmills are giants, inns are castles because such are the identities that words ascribe to objects *in* the books *of* Don Quixote.

But seeing as how flocks of sheep are really flocks of sheep and not armies, Don Quixote, orphan of the universe where words and objects no longer correspond, travels alone, the incarnation of the eternal dilemma of the modern novel that he inaugurates with his tale: How to achieve unity without sacrificing diversity? How to maintain the analogy damaged by impertinent humanistic curiosity as well as the difference threatened by the hunger for restored unity? How to fill the deep abyss between words and things through the divorce between analogy and difference?

Don Quixote contains both the question and the answer: the divorce between objects and words that previously corresponded cannot be fixed by a new setting or "placement" but rather by displacement. Set in his place by the static world of the knight errant, Don Quixote wants to destroy the paradox of an immobile adventure, prisoner to the old books in his library in the immutable village of La Mancha, and displace himself—that is, enter into movement. And that, in the age of antiquity, was how men distinguished themselves from gods: they displaced themselves. They moved. Don Quixote believes that he is traveling so that he may reestablish the unity of man and the faith that is his certainty, though in reality he travels only to find himself in a new physical space where everything has become a problem, beginning with the novel that Don Quixote inhabits.

The modern novel, a perpetual invitation to leave oneself and see oneself and the world as an unfinished problem, implies a kind of displacement similar to that of Don Quixote, although we may venture to say that no other novel—not even at its most experimental—has been able to propose displacements as radical as those of Cervantes. The radical displacement from purity to impurity and to the dissolution of genres, from classic narrative authority to the manifestation of multiple points of view, from the residual tradition of oral, tavern-oriented storytelling to the full Cervantine awareness that the novel is to be read by a reader and printed at a printing press, *Don Quixote* is a novel, to use the words of Claudio Guillén, that lives in "active dialogue" with itself. Its displacement of genres, authorities, and recipients of the verbal fact grant the novel an open destiny, forever unfinished, incessantly redefined: the novel is the art of displacement.

Don Quixote is the first modern novel, and its historical paradox is that it emerges from the Spanish Counter-Reformation, the Inquisition, the dogmas declaring purity of blood and

Catholic orthodoxy. In the Spain that exiled half of itself when it expelled the Jews in 1492 and the Moors in 1603, Don Quixote is a paradox of the paradox. He is a reader of chivalric tales, a man who yearns to restore the medieval values of honor, justice, and courage, and to do this he leaves his home in the Castilian plain, mounted atop a feeble nag, accompanied by a plump little squire straddling a mule.

Don Quixote is a reader. But despite the nostalgia he feels for the Middle Ages, he is a modern reader who reads his books in printed form, thanks to the genius of the German editor Gutenberg. Mad about books, Don Quixote transforms his reading into madness and, possessed by both, wishes to take the things he reads about and turn them into reality. He wants to resuscitate a lost world, an ideal world. But when he leaves his village, he stumbles upon a world that is far from ideal, a world of bandits and chain gangs, goatherds, rogues, scullery maids of easy virtue, and unscrupulous innkeepers all too willing to ridicule him, batter him, and thrash him about in a blanket.

Nevertheless, despite his battles with reality, Don Quixote insists upon seeing giants where there are only windmills and armies where there are only flocks of sheep. He sees them because he has read about them. He sees them because the things he has read have told him to see them that way. His reading is his madness. *Su lectura es su locura.*

Cervantes's genius lies in his ability to transform this fable of chivalric nostalgia into the foundational novel of critical modernism. Because while it emerges from a dogmatic world of certainty and faith, *Don Quixote* is itself the incarnation of the modern world and all its uncertainty.

Everything is uncertain in the *Quixote*. The authorship, uncertain. Who wrote the book? Cide Hamete Benengeli, the Arab scribe whose papers were translated into Spanish by an anonymous *morisco* writer? The author of the apocryphal version, Avellaneda, whose falsehoods lead Don Quixote to a printing press where he discovers that he is a character in a book? Some man named Cervantes? Somebody called De Saavedra? The adversity of the former? Or the liberty of the latter?

Uncertain name: Don Quixote is but one of the many names of a certain Alonso Quijano (or might it be Quezada, or Quixada?) who calls himself Quijote for a more epic effect, but who becomes Quijotiz for a more pastoral effect, or Azote for micomicomical effects* in the castle of the Dukes. The names constantly change. Rocinante was *Rocín antes:* literally, "Rocín, before." The idealized damsel Dulcinea is actually Aldonza, a common peasant woman. The names of the enemies change too. The enchanter Mambrino becomes the malevolent Malandrino. Even the authors of the book, already somewhat ambiguous, change names. In Sancho's version, Benengeli becomes Berenjena—that is, "aubergine."

Uncertain places: to start with, the very place from which Don Quixote emerges, "somewhere in La Mancha, in a place whose name I do not care to remember."† And yet is there any doubt that this is the decadent Spain of Philip III, the Spain of rampant corruption, aristocratic whims, cities teeming with destitute souls, the Spain of rogues and violent assaults? The Spain of Roque Gunart, the real-life attacker and contraband smuggler who makes his appearance in the novel.

Uncertainty of the genre; Cervantes inaugurates the modern novel by breaking through every genre so that they all may have room to exist in a genre of genres, the novel. The epic tale of Quixote evolves, hand in hand, with the picaresque tale of Sancho. But Cervantes also gives a voice to the *morisco* story, the romantic novel, the Byzantine narrative, comedy and drama, philosophy and the carnival, as well as the novel within the novel.

---

*"Micomicomical" is a reference to a character in *Don Quixote,* Princess Micomicona.
†All the quotations from *Don Quixote* here and subsequently in this book are taken from the translation by Edith Grossman (New York: Ecco Press, 2003).

His patent disregard for the purity of the genre is as remarkable as that of his great contemporary Shakespeare—so contemporary that they died on the same date, April 23, 1616, if not the same day, for Cervantes went by the Gregorian calendar, whereas Shakespeare lived by Julian hours. But purity was not what Shakespeare and Cervantes were after: what they cared about was poetic liberty, in its broadest possible form.

The modern uncertainty of *Don Quixote* does not, however, exclude the lasting values that modernity must save, or perpetuate, so as not to dissipate into moral ambiguity. One of these values is love, and on this point at least, Don Quixote does not delude himself. He idealizes Dulcinea but, in one surprising passage, admits that she is, in fact, Aldonza, the stocky country peasant woman. But doesn't this quality of love possess the ability to transform the beloved into something incomparable, something above and beyond the considerations of wealth or poverty, vulgarity or nobility? "And therefore," says Don Quixote, "it is enough for me to think and believe that my good Aldonza Lorenzo is beautiful and virtuous; as for her lineage, it matters little. . . . I depict her in my imagination as I wish her to be . . . Let each man say what he chooses. . . ."

The other value is honor, personal integrity, and on this point Don Quixote's arrival at the castle of the Dukes is the most revealing episode of all. Until this moment, the Knight of the Sorrowful Countenance has believed that the inns he has visited were castles and the servant girls, princesses. Now, when the Dukes offer him a real castle with genuine princesses (plus an island for Sancho to rule over), the Quixotic illusion falls apart. Reality robs him of his imagination. Love turns into something cruel: the farces of Clavileño and the Dolorous One. When Quixote's dreams become reality, Quixote can no longer imagine.

He returns to his village. He emerges from his madness, though only to die. "There are no birds today in yesterday's nests." With good reason Dostoevsky said that *Don Quixote* is "the saddest book ever written, for it is the story of an illusion lost."

Lost Illusions is the title that Balzac gives his magnificent series of Lucien de Rubempré novels, proving that Don Quixote is the founder of the modern world, bestowing upon it novels of tears and sadness, illusion and disillusion, the logic of madness, the madness of logic, the uncertainty of all things, and the certainty that all lasting reality is based firmly on the imagination.

R

Reading

Don Quixote is a reader. Or, perhaps more to the point, his reading is his madness. Possessed by the madness of reading, Don Quixote would like to take the things he has read—books of chivalry—and turn them into reality. The real world, the world of goatherds, marauders, innkeepers, servant girls of ill repute, and chain gangs, fails to meet Don Quixote's illusions, wearing out the poor *hidalgo,* bruising him and thrashing him about.

Despite the beating he has been given by the real world, Don Quixote nevertheless insists upon seeing giants where there are only windmills. He sees them because that is what his books tell him to see.

But there is one extraordinary moment when the voracious reader Don Quixote discovers that he, the reader, is also being read.

This is the very first moment in the history of literature in which a character, Don Quixote, enters a printing press in—where else?—Barcelona. He has made his way there to denounce the apocryphal version of his adventures, published by a man called Avellaneda, and to tell the world that he, the genuine Don Quixote, is not the false Don Quixote of Avellaneda's version.

Don Quixote travels through the noble city of Barcelona and comes upon a sign that reads BOOKS PRINTED HERE. He enters the printing press and watches the work as it is being carried out, and sees the printers "printing in one place, correcting in another, typesetting here, revising there," until he realizes that the book being printed is in fact his own novel, *The Ingenious Gentleman Don Quixote de la Mancha,* a book that recounts, to Sancho Panza's consternation, things that only he and his master spoke about, secrets that the printing and subsequent reading will make public, thus subjecting the protagonists of the story to the critical, democratic realm of knowledge and analysis. Scholasticism has died. Free analysis has been born.

Unlike any other literary moment either before or after, this moment in *Don Quixote* reveals the liberation that comes about from the editing, publication, and reading of a book. From this moment on, literature and, by extension, the book itself, become the repositories of a truth revealed not by God nor the power structure but by the imagination—that is, the human ability to mediate between sensation and perception and to establish a new reality that is the fruit of that mediation, a new reality that would no longer exist were it not for the verbal experience of Cervantes's *Quixote,* Pablo Neruda's *Canto General,* or Stendhal's *The Red and the Black*.

Is this intimate yet shared, secret yet public mediation between the spectator and the work of art becoming muddled in the so-called postmodern world? Are we finally witnessing the end of the era of Gutenberg and Cervantes, five centuries in which reading and literature have held fast to their cultural preeminence, and moving instead into the era of Ted Turner and Bill Gates, in which the only things worthy of our attention are those that we can see directly in front of us on a television or computer screen?

I grew up during the days of radio. In those years, when you wanted to be certain of what the announcer on XEW Radio had said about the bullfighter Manolete's great performance, you had to go to the newspapers to ascertain and confirm the facts: yes, it was true, the Monster of Córdoba had cut both ear and tail. It was true because it had been written. In today's world, the bombing of Baghdad is carried out and we watch along on our television screens. There is no need to confirm this in writing. There is no need, even, to understand it in political terms. Thanks to the ubiquitous, instantaneous nature of the image, we have a dazzling spectacle in living color. And the dead? We neither saw nor heard them.

The fate of the book and reading in our time is a dilemma for which I offer two extreme examples.

All one has to do is enter the indigenous world of Mexico to discover, with amazement, the tremendous capacity of its men and women for telling stories and recalling old legends and myths. Poor and illiterate they may be, but the Mexican Indians do not suffer cultural deprivation. Tarahumaras and Huicholes, Mazatecos and Tzotziles, they all possess an extraordinary talent for remembering and imagining dreams and nightmares, cosmic catastrophes, and sublime rebirth, as well as the infinitesimal details of everyday life.

With good reason Fernando Benítez, the great Mexican writer who extensively documented these indigenous lives, said that each time an Indian dies, a whole library dies along with him.

At the other extreme we find the frighteningly fulfilled fantasy of Ray Bradbury's *Fahrenheit 451,* in which a dictatorship—now perfect, of course—outlaws all libraries, burns books, and yet cannot prevent one last tribe of men and women from memorizing the literature of the world, until he or she actually becomes the *Odyssey, Treasure Island,* or *The Thousand and One Nights.*

We are talking about two distinct libraries here: one, of a purely oral culture, inside the head of an Indian, and another, in the memory of a postmodern, post-Communist, postcapitalist, posteverything suprayuppie. But what they both possess is the universal possibility to choose between silence and voice, memory and oblivion, movement and paralysis, life and death. The bridge between these two poles is the word, spoken or unspoken, wretched or joyous, visible or invisible, but always deciding, in each and every syllable, whether life should go on or end once and for all.

But can't we say the same thing of the visual image? Aren't analogous vital functions performed by a Goya painting, a Coyolxauqui sculpture, a Buñuel film, or an Oscar Niemeyer building? Painting, said Leonardo, is a mental thing. Is the same true of the superhighway containing so many thousands of television channels? Is the same true of the so-called modern media of visual communication that purportedly robs books of their potential readers, dig the grave of the age of Cervantes and Gutenberg, and saturate visual communication with such quantities of information that we all feel supremely well informed, never asking ourselves if the information we are receiving is at all important, and if, in fact, the truly important information is precisely what we are not receiving?

I am not arguing in favor of the book and the library as elements to supplement the possible—and obvious—shortcomings of audiovisual communication at this turn of the century and millennium. On the contrary: I would like to explore that area in which the modern media of communication may help rather than hinder the culture of the book and of reading in general. One thing is true: all you have to do is visit any family home where the television antenna has become the parish cross to confirm the universal phenomenon of the couch potato, the spectator who watches television in the most purely passive manner, very much like a prostrate, sleepy potato that is almost being raped by the succession of images observed from that supine position, images that are received without any kind of critical, creative response. This is the very opposite of what a good book, a good painting, or a good movie asks of us.

But then again, all you have to do is visit an academic center such as the Monterrey Technological Institute to realize, as well, that audiovisual information can be an extraordinary tool for extending the radius of students' knowledge, enriching the interaction between teachers and students, and counteracting the most negative aspects of the passive way in which we receive and digest images at home. We should probe and exhaust every last possibility and opportunity that audiovisual culture can offer the culture of the book, and vice versa.

In the first place, there has been an astronomical growth in the number of audiovisual "spectators" around the world, but the shrinking number of book readers does not have to be the inevitable or absolute consequence of this fact. It is not inevitable because, once again, what counts is how these media are being used. Their mere existence is not the threat. The editors of the Library of America, a collection of American classics, have proven that new technologies may be used not just to preserve but to broaden a literary legacy, by promoting the works of great writers to great numbers of people who have never heard of them—in the same way that in music, *Don Giovanni* reaches more listeners in a single day now than it did during Mozart's entire lifetime.

As such, with the support of audiovisual media, this collection of classic American literature has sold 3 million copies of its first titles, from Jefferson to Faulkner, over the past decade.

José Vasconcelos, the first education secretary of the Mexican Revolution, published a collection of universal classics, beautifully bound, sometime around 1923. Why publish Cervantes in a country with a 90 percent illiteracy rate, people asked him and criticized him in his day. But today the answer is self-evident: so that the illiterate, once they are no longer illiterate, will be able to read *Don Quixote* instead of *Superman*.

In the same vein, today's book world should operate from the premise that new media can create new readers, not steal existing ones away. For this to happen we must insist, from the very start, from the classroom and if possible from the home as well, that the audiovisual image be judged by the same criteria that literature and the plastic arts have always been judged by. Spectators need to learn how to observe critically the images they receive.

Optimists tell us that a society with such abundant audiovisual resources will eventually move toward greater specialization, less commercialization, and, as a result, the birth of a new community composed of book editors and the audiovisual public, readers and spectators, all of whom will be able to choose from an increasingly diversified array of cultural offerings.

In other words, the mass media can certainly help to create more, not fewer, readers with all of today's means for promoting, selling, and selecting books—means that are far superior to those of yesteryear. If the audiovisual dynamic can add that critical dimension I mention above, then massive promotion and high literary quality do not need to be at odds with each other.

We should not, however, turn a blind eye to the dangers—not so much the relatively minor danger presented by commercialization as promoter of fleeting trends and bad taste (something that has always existed) but rather the danger of abusing new technologies to make the inconclusive seem conclusive. In the human world, which has always been a world of necessity and chance, texts are necessary to make things intelligible—things that otherwise would lack meaning. This necessity, for example, may produce the Bible, but also *Mein Kampf.* Rudderless societies, ones in which material satisfactions leave the spirit unsatisfied, and where the unsatisfied grow tired of waiting, are the societies where the most dogmatic texts have most powerfully captured the attention and imagination of the masses. Just imagine what Hitler would have done with a television screen.

This is the danger. We live in a global village of mass communication, technical progress, and economic interdependence, but we can easily cultivate the fears and even the rebellion of the local village that does not see itself reflected in these media and which, like Tantalus, will try in vain to attain the fruits that the temptations of advertising emblazon on screens all across the planet.

An authoritarian capitalism, no longer facing a totalitarian Communist enemy, hovers as a dismal, vague threat in some parts of the world. It poses a threat not only to books and to reading, but to the free and creative use of audiovisual media. And the only way to neutralize this noxious effect is with a fully democratic order, a pluralistic political regulation of the use of these media and, above all, a political and social mandate to ensure that public education programs, public libraries, free textbooks, and the freedom for all creative expression meet the highest standards of availability, quality, and effectiveness.

Over the past century, in every Latin American country, we have all witnessed and participated in the creation of a great circle, a circle that travels from writer to editor to distributor to bookseller to the public and then back to the writer. Unlike what has happened in countries with more mercantile development but less intellectual stimulation, in Mexico and Latin America there are certain books that never disappear from the shelves. Neruda and Borges, Cortázar and García Márquez, Vallejo and Paz; they are always present in our bookshops.

They are always present because their readership is constantly being replenished, never depleted. These are young readers, between fifteen and twenty-five years old. They are men and women of the working class, middle class, or somewhere in between, carriers of the changes and the hopes of our continent.

Today, the succession of economic crises endured by Latin America since the 1980s is the greatest threat to the continuity of the reading tradition, which is a reflection of society's continuity. Various generations of young Latin Americans have discovered who they are by reading Gabriela Mistral, Juan Carlos Onetti, or Jorge Amado. A break in this circle of reading would signify a loss of identity for many young people. Let us not condemn them to leave behind libraries and bookshops only to get lost in the subterranean realm of misery, crime, and neglect.

Let us not allow a single young reader-in-waiting to waste away in the limbo of the lost city, the slum, the marginal neighborhood, or the shanty town.

The library is an invaluable institution in the panorama I describe, because it allows us to witness, close up, the verbal riches of humanity, in a civilized environment and with a protective roof over our heads.

But once there, even when we are surrounded by beauty, peace, hospitality, and even the unique aroma of the library, we must never lose sight of the fact that the perils of censorship, persecution, and intolerance can still strike out against the written word. The *fatwa* against Salman Rushdie is a case in point.

In 1920, José Vasconcelos launched a literacy campaign that met with fierce resistance from the landowning oligarchy of the day. The hacienda owners did not want workers who could read and write; they wanted submissive, ignorant, dependable laborers. Many of the teachers Vasconcelos sent to the countryside were hanged from the treetops. Others returned mutilated.

Vasconcelos's heroic literacy campaign was matched, with no contradiction whatsoever, by a parallel trend toward high culture. In 1920, as the dean of the Universidad Nacional de México (National University of Mexico), Vasconcelos ordered the printing of a collection of beautifully bound volumes of Homer and Virgil, Plato and Plotinus, Goethe and Dante—a collection of true bibliographical and artistic jewels. But for a population of illiterate, indigent, marginalized people? Yes, precisely: the publication of these classics at the university was an act of hope. It was a way of saying to the majority of Mexicans: one day you will be at the center, not the margins of society. One day you will have the resources to buy a book. One day you will be able to read and understand those things that now, in our day, all Mexicans understand.

Let the book, even as it is being commercialized, transcend commerce.

Let the book, even as it competes in the contemporary world with the abundance and ease of the information technologies, stand as something more than just a source of information.

Let the book teach us all the things pure information does not: a book teaches us to extend simultaneously our understanding of ourselves, of the objective world outside of ourselves, and of the social world where the city (the *polis*) and the human being (the person) come together.

The book shows us something that no other form of communication is able, willing, or equipped to show us: the complete integration of our faculties for understanding ourselves so that we may become fully realized people in the world, both within ourselves and with others.

The book tells us that our lives are a repertory of possibilities that transform desire into experience and experience into destiny.

The book tells us that the Other exists, that others exist as well, that our persona does not exist in and of itself but has a compelling moral obligation to pay attention to others, who are never superfluous to our lives.

The book is the education of the senses through language.

The book is tangible, olfactory, tactile, visual, an act of friendship that opens the doors of our respective homes to the love that unites us with the world, because we share the verb of the world.

The book is the intimacy of a country, the inalienable notion we create of ourselves, of our time, of our past and our remembered future, experienced throughout the ages as verbal memory and desire in the here and now.

Now, more than ever before, a writer, a book, and a library give a name to the world and a voice to the human beings in it.

Now, more than ever, a writer, a book, and a library tell us: if we do not give things names, nobody will give us one. If we do not speak, silence will impose its dark sovereignty upon us.

Revolution

As part of a survey to commemorate the start of the twenty-first century, *The New York Times* asked me the following question: in my opinion, which revolution was the greatest of the millennium?

A difficult question to answer for many reasons, the first being the ambiguity or polyvalence of the term "revolution" itself, which contains an element of rupture as well as return. The revolution of a planet refers to the manner in which a heavenly body returns to its point of origin. But the revolution of a society is the exact opposite. It refers to a rupture in the established order and a movement toward a future, hopefully a better one.

The association between the terms "revolution" and "progress" strengthens this futurizable notion. Nevertheless, the utopian element present in all revolution is much more ambivalent. Just as it yearns for a better society, revolution does not think only of the future. Revolution also dreams, perhaps subconsciously, of the past, the Golden Age, the dawn of time. In this sense, revolution could also be considered the restoration of an untainted past. This was, and very notably so, the hope of Emiliano Zapata and his dream of a peasant Arcadia in Mexico.

Nevertheless, the association between "modernity" and "revolution" has been the driving force behind the uprisings in Russia, China, and Cuba. The veil we have drawn over the past has given the past a marvelous opportunity to reappear in disguise. Revolution—whether in Petrograd, Peking, or Havana—ultimately reinforced the oldest designs of power. In Russia, Caesaro-Papism, the unification of temporal and spiritual powers, reemerged in the symbiosis between party and state. In China, the "celestial bureaucracy" of the Middle Kingdom reappeared beneath the authoritarian tunic of Maoism. And in Cuba, Castro has revived the most antiquated traditions of Hispano-Arabic *caudillismo,* the tyrannical leadership of one political chief.

Perhaps the most coherently "modern" revolutions are those of France and the United States. Nevertheless, when *The New York Times* asked me which I felt was "the greatest revolution of the millennium," I was very tempted to leave the realm of politics and consider Copernicus, Einstein, Shakespeare, Cervantes, Joyce, Piero della Francesca, Brunelleschi, Picasso, Beethoven, or Stravinsky, who may well have been greater revolutionaries than Washington or Mirabeau.

But confined to the territory of politics, I can safely state my conviction that the French Revolution was, indeed, the greatest revolution of the millennium, though I cannot help but qualify the response with Winston Churchill's famous warning that democracy "is the worst form of government except all those others that have been tried from time to time."

The American Revolution was a colonial uprising against a colonial power. The French Revolution was a social, political, and economic uprising against the *ancien régime*. It did not have to expel a colonial power. It had to destroy an internal power structure that had been sustained for centuries on the basis of tradition, legitimacy, and the paradoxical marriage between monarchic absolutism and feudal privilege. The French Revolution had to violently destroy the institutions of the *ancien régime* and replace them with new and perhaps improbable forms of self-determination and civil associations.

Both were violent revolutions. The French Terror sent 16,000 souls to the guillotine—a negligible figure, says Jules Michelet in his *History of the French Revolution,* if we compare it to the number of executions ordered by the monarchy over the course of 600 years. Nor was violence absent in the American Revolution, which was in fact profuse in its summary executions of those who remained loyal to the British throne. Jefferson and Franklin's revolution was equally unable to avoid its own brand of terror. The public health committees of the French Revolution had a precedent in the committees of safety, protection, and correspondence that were created to catch and punish the enemies of the American Revolution, or the committee for the detecting and defeating of conspiracies, established by the provincial congress of New York.

But "terror?" The indigenous people of North America—Native Americans—may have suffered more than the French aristocracy.

Both revolutions, the American and the French, confiscated private property. "Notorious conspirators," "absentists," "refugees," and "evaders" were all objects of expropriation in North America. Today they would be aided by a British disposition comparable to the Helms–Burton law.

Both revolutions forced the emigration of countless souls. Comparatively speaking, there were far more émigrés from the United States than France: the masses of boat people who fled the American Revolution in vessels bound for Newfoundland and died during the crossing.

Both revolutions were sullied by the ugly stain of inequality. They proclaimed the universal rights of man, but women were excluded from the list and denied the right to vote. Those without property were also denied suffrage. But whereas the United

States had cultivated a middle class of small property owners, the French Revolution had to be far more radical, eliminating the privileges of property, creating a new class of property owners, and establishing the political and legal instruments that such a revolution required.

The extraordinary, truly extraordinary milestone in France, as Michelet notes in his book, is the fact that throughout France people acted spontaneously, and actually anticipated all the revolutionary laws before they were enacted. Michelet calls it "the spontaneous organization of France," a singular occurrence, on such a grand scale, in the history of humanity. (The Zapatistas' spontaneous organization of the rural communities of Morelos, in 1915, as described by John Womack, would be another, if slightly more modest example.)

In 1789, despite the aforementioned limitations, almost 5 million French people became voters for the first time and took it upon themselves to form municipal committees whose first task was to replace the monarchy's impenetrable laws with transparent revolutionary legislation. By 1791, the people of France, advancing ever more rapidly than the revolutionary authorities in Paris, had created throughout the country a total of 1,200 new municipal positions and 100,000 magistrates to impart justice. Such was the impact of this movement that by the spring of 1792, France possessed a completely rehabilitated political and judicial system, an achievement accomplished through direct elections.

Thanks to this truly radical revolution, France established a new property system that became the basis for modern capitalism. The Church and the aristocracy, the remnants of the feudal system, found themselves forced to adhere to the new market system as barriers to free commerce and privilege were abolished, along with the guilds. The free market broadened the horizon of the European economy to an unprecedented degree. The prohibition, however, of the guilds' freedom of association (the Le Chapelier Law of June 14, 1791) also denied the working class their collective power and protection, and effectively handed them over to the ruthless exploitation of the Industrial Revolution.

Capitalism and democracy are the powerful legacy of the French Revolution, beyond the episodes of revolutionary terror and the contradictions of the Bonapartist interim. Napoleon marched through Europe in the name of revolution but with a bogus crown upon his head. He was defeated in Russia and Spain by patriots who preferred their nationalist shackles to the revolutionary liberties of the French. Nevertheless, Napoleon, by giving Europe its modern civil and mercantile legislation, guaranteed the future of the bourgeoisie that the great Corsican represented on such a heroic, unsustainable scale. And in Germany, it broke the back of the ghettos and liberated the Jews.

The American Revolution did not abolish slavery, the blackest spot in its legacy. A second revolution, led by Lincoln, was necessary to liberate the slaves, and then a third, the civil rights movement, completed the work that still remained to be done in our own times. The United States did not have a Napoleon. Instead, it had a "Manifest destiny" to broaden its borders—at Mexico's expense—so that it might extend across the continent from the Atlantic to the Pacific. In the United States, an enlightened colonial aristocracy made its presence felt through admirable documents such as the Constitution of Philadelphia, the Bill of Rights, and the Federalist Papers. In France, a frenzied, choleric, intuitive, and fraternal mass of people rose up and, paradoxically, focused its greatest efforts and its most solid laws on liberal development and modern capitalism. But this is a cold definition of the enthusiasm with which William Wordsworth greeted the news from France in 1789, when he affirmed what a marvelous place the world could be when one's happiness was echoed by millions.

The secular quality of a revolution is perhaps the greatest guarantee of its rigor. Russia was unable to abandon its Byzantine religious legacy with Communism and imposed it upon Western nations where the Caesaro-Papist tradition was completely alien:

that is, all of Central Europe. The Chinese Revolution was never able to shake off the legitimist, bureaucratic severity of the old Middle Kingdom, nor could the Cuban Revolution evade, from the Left, the deathly trap of the Latin American Right: the cult of the number-one leader, the providential chief.

The Mexican Revolution is full of contradictions. It emerged as a democratic political movement—elective suffrage, no reelection—led by a good, naïve man, Francisco Madero. Quite possibly his greatest achievement was to motivate a country of illiterates with one book, *La sucesión presidencial en 1910* (*The Presidential Succession in 1910*). But once he took office, Madero made the mistake of leaving the pillars of dictatorship in place— the federal army, the privileges of the great landowners—and was forced to endure the affronts, obstreporousness, and even the betrayal of a press and a congress without any kind of democratic political experience. The assassination of Madero, carried out by General Victoriano Huerta and the ambassador of the United States, Henry Lane Wilson, was what precipitated the real Mexican Revolution: the social, economic revolution.

From the Mexican night the leaders of revolution emerge. They come from the great ranches and the towns, the middle class of the provinces and the indigenous mountainside, from the haciendas in flames and the cities under siege. And they represent two clear trends: that of the peasantry and that of the bourgeoisie. Emiliano Zapata, a man of silence and mystery, looks like a ghost who was granted the privilege of brief human incarnation so that he might demand Land and Liberty. Francisco Villa is a rusty copperhead who had been to Mongolia, Andalucía, and the Rif mountains in Morocco, and with the nomadic tribes of the American north until it finally settled squarely down upon the shoulders and beneath the gold-trimmed hat, stained with blood and dust, of a man from Chihuahua who "narrows his gaze against the assault of light, with vast reserves of intuition and ferocity and generosity" (*The Old Gringo*). Both Zapata and Villa represent the tumultuous will of justice, as old as the centuries yet, unlike those centuries, incomplete. The bourgeois faction is led by Venustiano Carranza, an old dictatorship-era senator disguised as himself: long white beard; eyes hidden behind violet lenses; tall, paternal, protective, distant, self-assured. Never sit where the sun can strike you directly in the face, for that is the place of either the blinded opponent or of the supporter who has learned his place. Never sit with your back to a door or a window, for that is where murderers enter. "The old king," Fernando Benítez called him in an exceptional novel that tells how, despite everything, the old lion was assassinated by his impatient little pups, Álvaro Obregón, a young farmer from Huatabampo, and Plutarco Elías Calles, a young schoolteacher from Sonora. The eyes of Obregón smile—he is ingenious, witty, friendly. The eyes of Calles penetrate—he is a preying tiger, unsmiling.

In Mexico the bourgeois revolution led by Carranza, Obregón, and Calles defeats the peasant revolution of Zapata and Villa. But the 1917 constitution makes concessions to the peasant movement. The right to work and the division of land are elevated to a constitutional level, along with individual guarantees, which include the right to property. Society and its laws fashion themselves around the dead bodies left behind by the revolution: Saturn devours his own children until one extraordinary president, Lázaro Cárdenas, pulls together all the revolution's causes—public education, infrastructure, communications, agrarian reform—and liberates the laborer from the landowner, offering him the chance to migrate toward the city to become cheap labor for the process of industrialization that, thanks to Cárdenas's nationalization of oil, will have cheap fuel with which to operate.

All of this is accompanied by an implicit pact. The governments born of the revolution give the people education, work, and stability, but not democracy. As long as this pact remains unaltered, from 1938 to 1968, Mexico is the Latin American paradigm of stability. The army stays in its barracks and supports the president who, every six years, goes from being the *tapado* ("concealed one") to the *nuevo ungido* ("newly anointed one") whom the president in power has designated as his successor with his *gran dedo* ("great finger"). The pact is broken in 1968 when the young people educated in the schools of the revolution and raised on the ideals of justice and liberty demand those very two things on the streets and meet with death, on the Night of Tlatelolco, October 2, 1968. That was the night the institutional revolution in Mexico ended, and something that had never died asserted every last bit of its strength: the social movement of workers, country peasants, students, the middle class. . . . But it took three more decades for the country to reach its definitive moment of transition, which occurred when the opposition finally triumphed in a presidential election. It happened on July 2, 2000, and there was no blood, no fighting, and no doubt that day. We all won, I wrote. The sitting president, Ernesto Zedillo, because he ensured nothing less than the strict fulfillment of the law. The elected president, Vicente Fox, because his determined, contentious gamble brought the opposition into power. And the entire Mexican populace, because the social struggle had finally joined forces with the political struggle, and the Mexican Revolution—betrayed, slandered, corrupted, constructive, liberating, contradictory as it was—achieved what other revolutions of the Third World could not. Revolution, sometimes, means remaining loyal to the impossible.

And it is not just victory over injustice but victory over the inevitable, which is sometimes a far more grueling battle. Under Stalin injustice and inevitability came together in a kind of perverse joke: for him, all Communists were traitors with one exception—oddly enough, the person who held the power, Joseph Stalin. We need not repeat the names of all those who carried out the same macabre political practice. We do, however, always need to reject and reverse any and all totalitarian pretensions, no matter how magnificent they may be, whether poetic or political (Rimbaud: we must change life; Marx: we must change the world). And we must replace them with the revolution that makes things relative, pluralizes the world, and renounces the illusion of totality, so similar to the word totalitarian. The revolution of the twenty-first century is about valuing differences: ethnic, political, religious, sexual, cultural. . . .

And so, the word *revolution* appears with the luminous meaning that Maria Zambrano gave it: revolution is annunciation.

S

Sex

And then there are the other ladies, I don't mean the ladies left over, the leftover ladies. The ladies of yesteryear whom François Villon evoked with a nostalgic beauty and precision that forever renounced the new encounter with the woman we love and who *was:* the ladies left behind, never the leftover ladies, who will forever remain, like restless ghosts, complicit in what once was and could have been. *"Dites moi où, n'en quel pays / est Flora la belle romaine. . . . ?"*

Eros first manifests itself in girls, in my case two classmates in Washington with whom I slowly came to discover who I was, in the marvelous penumbra they offered me: one of them had old-fashioned Mary Pickford ringlets while the other was a dauntless, freckled little thing, like Nancy or Mafalda in today's terms. In those dimly lit apartments free of parents, they were the first women to reveal themselves to me, and to themselves as well. We were but nine years old, and they did it with a kind of shameless innocence. Why, then, had they felt obliged to reveal our delicious secrets? Nobody had caught us unawares, ever. Yet they had had to confess it, expose it and make themselves vulnerable—it was almost as if they had wanted to be punished. And the punishment was that I would never be able to see them again. In Santiago de Chile, however, at twelve years of age, I had the misfortune of falling in love with a neighbor, a girl with a neat fringe, wild eyes, and a father who was a high official in the Chilean air force. When he discovered us together, he not only ended our puppy-love affair but drove my family to move to another house. And then, at age fifteen in Buenos Aires, after refusing to attend the fascist schools of the Minister of Education Hugo Wast, I discovered that at eleven in the morning, the only people in our apartment building on the corner of Callao and Quintana were me and my upstairs neighbor, a beautiful actress with a long mane of hair and silvery eyes. And so my very first sexual strategy consisted of going upstairs to her apartment with my copy of the radio magazine *Sintonía,* ringing the lovely lady's doorbell and asking, "Who will Eva Duarte be playing today in the series *Celebrated Women of History,* Joan of Arc or Madame Dubarry?" I still remember the half-open eyes of my illusory silver goddess when she answered, "Madame Dubarry. Less saintly but far more entertaining. Won't you come in?"

The Mexico of the 1940s was an adolescent's sexual wasteland. Saintly little girlfriends handed over their sweaty, cakelike palms in the movie theater, and little else. The Mexican brothels, on the other hand, were exciting, garish, melancholy, and quite varied in style. The majority of the madam's "pupils," so to speak, were poor girls who had either migrated to the capital or been recruited from the slums, though all were inevitably trained to tell you, "I come from Guadalajara," as if hailing from the capital of Jalisco gave the world's oldest profession some kind of cachet. They never allowed you to kiss them on the mouth and before sex would solemnly cover up the inevitable picture of the Virgin of Guadalupe lurking nearby. Very rarely would you ever encounter a belle de jour type, the thirty- or forty-year old woman incapable of hiding two things: her innate dignity and her insatiable sexual appetite. No, they were more maternal with us, taking it upon themselves to educate us. The cathedral of brothels was the Casa de la Bandida—that is, the House of the Bandit Lady—and was run by a lady composer of revolutionary *corrido* songs who was rumored to have been the lover of Pancho Villa. Insurgentes was a theatrical brothel that specialized in lesbian shows. Darwin was a refuge of decent women in search of love, while Centenario was a spot where exotic women would waft down marble staircases under the light of fin de siècle chandeliers. And Meave, with its open windows overlooking the fish market and its incongruous combination of aromas, its linoleum beds set inside office workstations without ceilings, and its temptation of latent crime. . . . such austere discipline the morning maids displayed as they cleaned those sheetless linoleum chaises.

Sexual graduation consisted of finding a married lover, a woman who presented problems no more complicated than those of discretion and stealth. Serious girlfriends, on the other hand, were increasingly more beautiful and independent. On occasion, religious hypocrisy would get the best of them and send them headlong into other, more conventional marriages. On other occasions, distance would slowly erode a love affair with some unforgettable woman who emerged from a tropical lagoon with a face shining like dawn and dusk. A woman like Venus, of course, the star of both moments of the day. These loves were followed by a lengthy list of women whom I hesitate to include in my catalogue of Don Juan exploits because they were women of whom I never took advantage; I accompanied them and I experimented with them always as a couple, with all the rights and obligations that go with being part of a couple, and we gave equal intensity to our relationship, certain that we were united in the search for lasting emotion even though we knew that our union might only be temporary. Looking back, one by one, I can recall cases of erotic passivity, occasionally even submission and servility on the part of one or the other, but I also remember complicity. I remember moments of sudden exasperation and other moments of lasting gratitude. Sometimes stimulation would lead to anguish and at other times, abundant plenitude. In the end, to know sex is to know the harbinger of the words of love, and to not know what follows because the harbinger is enough and interrupts the very thing it promises.

I was, many times, a passenger of sex, a privileged but fleeting actor among a circle of beautiful women, foreign actresses accustomed to taking on a palatable companion for the brief period of filming. They gave me so much more than I gave them. I remember them as life's great gifts, impassioned precisely because they were so transitory, goddesses for one season, occasionally cruel enchantresses, always magnificent and magnanimous, and at times vulnerable to the point of death. The dead lover. I remember one, particularly lovely, courted and adored to distraction but always dissatisfied, gripped by an aching void that nobody could fill, and which she herself was never quite able to describe. And then she committed suicide. I remember another, deceitful and delightful, for her cunning, duplicitous antics, which she left transparent and exposed as a testament of her independence. She knew how to exploit her sexual games: two balls in the air at all times but only one true arousal. To share and to arouse alike. The opposite of the marvelously tender, vulnerable woman who was not submissive but simply eager to give and receive pleasure, knowing that I would soon leave her, yet dignified by the manner in which she received the experience; a woman with whom I felt I received far more than I gave on those early mornings in Rome.

Then there are the sexual relationships that I remember with a smile. The feigned suicides. The ideological champions who confused the bed with the pulpit. The superficial ones for whom sex was a social game. But I also remember the intelligent ones, intellectuals who made demands on a man's brain as well as his sex. The deluders who would write false letters and show them to their friends. The ones who shared and nurtured, waiting and hoping to play the role of wife, mother, daughter, bride. . . . I looked for them as lovers. I remember them as ghosts.

But there were also those women who so vividly—perhaps inevitably, perhaps in spite of themselves—embodied a desire that transcended them as individuals, and coalesced in my search for one woman who could encompass them all, yet who was at the same time singularly her own woman. I found her and have lived with her for a quarter of a century. With the others, it always ended. Each was a constant reminder of all the things that could never be mine because they were women who engendered so many things that obeyed their own laws, far beyond the confines of the sexual relationship. That was always the moment to leave.

It was also the moment to transform sex into literature. A body of words crying out for the closeness of another body of words. Are these words real? Are they a lie? We all run the risk of falling in love with a woman or a man who, like Swann's Odette, is not "our type," who is not right for us, and who is really only a ghostly extension of our own libidos. . . . We must be grateful to them all. Each represents not only a moment but words, so many words. These, for example, by Lope de Vega: "*Mas si del tiempo que perdí me ofendo / tal prisa me daré, que una hora amando / venza los años que pasé fingiendo.*" (And if all the time I lost is my offence / I will move so swiftly that with one hour of love / I will conquer all those years so falsely spent.) One is always thankful for this hour of fleeting, fatal plenitude, no matter how brief it may be. And to invoke the poet-author of *La Dorotea* once again, we are thankful despite the protraction, the frustration, and the disillusion brought about by sexual relationships that drive us to vilify sex and fervently wish that the crows flying over "the beds of battle, tender ground" would scratch out the eyes of such ungrateful women when in reality the only eyes to scratch at are our own. *More bestiarum,* in the manner of animals, as St. Augustine described sex, which he enjoyed so much in his early days. Perhaps we would best change the subject, not only because of a man's need for discretion when it comes to sexual relationships but also, perhaps, because of the secret irony that the English have turned it all, practically, into a proverb: "Pleasure is momentary, the position ridiculous, and the expense damnable," they say. After all, who on earth would want to renounce, despite its brevity, cost, and position, that radiant center of the world that is the lovers' bed? And, as we silently arise from it, who wouldn't want to leave these words by Góngora behind on the pillow: *"Aun a pesar de las tinieblas, bella / Aun a pesar de las estrellas, clara"* (Even in the face of darkness, lovely / even in the face of stars, luminous)?

Shakespeare

"Adieu, adieu! remember me." This phrase, uttered by Hamlet's father as he alternately appears and disappears is the trigger of the tragedy. Hamlet doubts because he remembers. He acts because he remembers. Where others forget or wish to forget, Hamlet shoulders the burden of remembering and of reminding everyone of their obligation to be or not to be. His location is anomalous. Hamlet is a prince and lives in Elsinore, a palace filled with dynastic memories. A monarchy is sustained by tradition remembered; therein lies its legitimacy. Hamlet rebels, specifically, against the subversion of legitimacy committed by King Claudius, his father's brother and murderer. Memory, succession, and legitimacy are the true "bare bodkin" that Hamlet brandishes, though the price he pays will be the "hush" of death.

Don Quixote, in contrast, emerges from an obscure village in an obscure province of Spain. So obscure, in reality, that the even more obscure author cannot or will not remember the name of the place. Cannot or will not: the place grows dark, it hides, it fades to black. The place is *la mancha*—that is, "the stain." Right there, in the middle of Cervantes's blank memory, the modern novel begins, sketching a vast circle that culminates with the obsession of Proust's narrator, in search of lost time, or with the narrators of William Faulkner, who are there so that nobody will forget the burden of history, race, the Sartorises, the Snopes, the South. . . .

Hamlet promises his father's ghost that he will banish from "the table of my memory" all but that which was his father's legacy. We live in a "distracted globe," as the Prince of Denmark observes, but as long as memory has a place at his table, all "trivial fond records" will be "wiped away." The memory, after all, is the "warder of the brain" and Hamlet wishes to keep it that way, in living, breathing color. Macbeth, on the other hand, wishes to forget, to render memory nothing more than "fume." Hamlet wants to remember a crime: Macbeth wants to forget one; he wants to pluck from the memory a "rooted sorrow"; he needs to banish all the burdens etched upon his mind, to find the sweet antidote that will "cleanse the stuff'd bosom of that perilous stuff"—that is, memory, the heart's remorse. . . . What a contrast with Hamlet and his fervent desire to maintain his memory ever "green," like the everlasting plant of life.

Such tension between memory and oblivion, such a *mise en abîme* of memory, reveals the sonorous modernity of both Shakespeare and Cervantes. Hamlet, Macbeth, and Quixote are all protagonists of a difficult and selective memory. Hamlet wishes to remember a crime. Macbeth wishes to forget one. Quixote only wants to remember his books, in the plural, yet he ends up remembering his own book, in the singular. A dilemma that is completely anathema to the epic of antiquity. According to Eric Auerbach, the omni-inclusivity of the epic is precisely what makes it an epic. Everything fits, everything must fit into the epic. Homer and Virgil forget nothing. Balzac's Colonel Chabert, on the other hand, has been forgotten by his wife, his friends, his society. Everyone thinks that he has died on the fields of battle at Eylau. Penelope, however, weaves and unweaves, convinced that Odysseus has neither died nor will be forgotten. The characters of antiquity possess names and attributes that are unforgettable, immutable, eternal: Odysseus is the prudent one, Nestor is the subduer, while the light (and choleric) one is Achilles. But then, between two steps on the staircase, the housemaid forgets the name that Walter Shandy wishes to give his newborn son, Trismegistus, and thanks to the slipshod memory of a house servant, the "hero" of the novel finds himself forever saddled with a most undesirable name, Tristram.

Gogol adds a sublime twist to the relationship between memory and identity. His rogue Khlestakov is remembered by all, not as who he is but rather as something he is not: the feared Inspector General. With Kafka, we return to the tradition of Cervantes: nobody remembers the Land Surveyor K. And then Milan Kundera puts the final touch on this tradition in *The Book of Laughter and Forgetting,* in which those who remember forget. Kundera, writing this from within a repressed, disguised society, where nothing is what it claims or appears to be, tells us that forgetting is the only memory of those who cannot or will not identify themselves or others.

In his magnificent story "Instructions for John Howell" Julio Cortázar offers us yet another clue to the question of memory and forgetting. The eponymous character attends a play in a theater. A look of sheer terror comes across the face of the actress, who whispers to Howell, the spectator, "Save me. They are trying to kill me." What is happening? Has Howell entered the play, or has the heroine entered the daily life of Mr. Howell?

What Cortázar proposes here is a circularity of genres, a blasphemy for which the minds of the Enlightenment—most notably Voltaire—reproached Shakespeare, for offering what they considered to be a vulgar salad of tragedy and comedy, characters both noble and burlesque, who could both spout lyrics and belch grotesquely, all in the same work of literature. Cervantes also broke through genres, mixing the epic and the picaresque, the pastoral novel and the love novel, but most of all mixing novels within the novel. This is where Shakespeare and Cervantes converge: in this circulation of genres, in that "impurity" that so offended Voltaire: Quixote's Manchegan maculation and Macbeth's soiled hands.

In the end, Shakespeare and Cervantes come together in this circulation of genres, effectively baptizing the freedom of contemporary creative life. With these two authors, the circulation manifests itself in a clear and parallel manner: in Cervantes, the novel within the novel, which becomes the theater within the theater in the puppet stage of Master Pedro which, in turn, leads directly into Shakespeare's play within the play, the objective of which, in the case of Hamlet, is to "catch the conscience of the king." Harry Levin, analyzing these two plays within plays, suggests that *Hamlet*'s King Claudius interrupts the performance because the play has come too close to reality. In *Don Quixote,* however, the Knight of the Sorrowful Countenance abruptly interrupts a performance that has come too close to his imagination. Claudius would like his reality, the death of Hamlet's father, to remain hidden behind a lie. Don Quixote, however, would like his fantasy to become a reality: a princess imprisoned by the Moors, rescued by Don Quixote's impassioned valor.

Claudius must kill the theater so that he can kill reality. Quixote must kill the theater so that he can give life to his imagination. Quixote is the ambassador of reading. Hamlet is the ambassador of death. To make the world remember, Hamlet, the hero of the North, imposes death upon himself and others as the only acceptable solution to his historical energy. To make the world imagine, Quixote, the hero of the South, imposes art upon the world, an absolute art that takes the place of a dead history. Hamlet is the hero of doubt, and his mad skepticism discharges a torrent of mortal energy. In the end, Hamlet offers a sacrifice to reason, the triumphant daughter of his ills. Don Quixote is the hero of faith. Our gentleman believes in what he reads and his sacrifice is the recovery of reason. And so he must die. When Alonso Quijano comes to his senses, Don Quixote can no longer imagine.

Hamlet and Don Quixote have something else in common as well. Both are nascent figures, characters that were inconceivable before Shakespeare and Cervantes shaped them with the clay of their imagination and set them on their course of action. The heroes of antiquity are born armed, like Minerva from the head of Zeus. They are born in one piece, whole. Don Quixote and Hamlet are unimaginable before they are described; both start off as inconceivable figures and eventually become eternal archetypes thanks to the contaminating circulation of genres. Their impurity gives them form. Claudio Guillén describes *Don Quixote* as an intense dialogue of genres that confront each other, debate among themselves, make fun of each other, and desperately call out for something that is just beyond their reach. And doesn't *Hamlet,* in that Shakespearean freedom of genres, that magnificent stylistic jumble, that offers the sublime and the crass in the very same breath, as simultaneous as the rhetoric of Henry V and the belching of the cowardly Ancient Pistol, coincide exactly with the Cervantine stylistic confrontations?

Sancho Panza infuses this *démarche*—step, approach, demarcation—with its wildest meaning when he, the squire, the very representative of earthly realism, becomes the ersatz governor of the island of Barataria and, just like his master, Don Quixote, must act (though less happily) in another fiction within the fiction.

Shakespeare has his anti–Sancho Panza: the pompous Polonius who, in the most satisfying manner, declares his lack of respect for genre (which he obviously respects because genre is respectable and he is the guardian of courtly respectability) when he extols the virtues of the company of actors that has just arrived at Elsinore. "The best actors in the world, either for tragedy, comedy, history, pastoral, pastoral-comical, historical-pastoral, tragical-historical, tragical-comical-historical-pastoral, scene indivisible, or poem unlimited."

The limited and divisible worlds of Shakespeare and Cervantes reject the unity of the indivisible, the poetry of eternity. The man of La Mancha and the Bard of Avon are *here and now,* for they are men of the Renaissance. One is more sorrowful than the other because his Spanish history is flagging, exhausted by the imperial impulse to circumnavigate the globe and conquer a new world, and drained by persecution and intolerance toward its Arab and Jewish traditions. For this reason Cervantes adopts the mask of comedy. But then the other is even more sorrowful because he harbors no illusions about the actors that strut across the stage like peacocks for an hour or so, looking back fondly upon some glorious exploits in Rome or Egypt, England or Scotland. For that reason, at the height of the Elizabethan triumph, Shakespeare dons the mask of tragedy.

I don't think either of the two believes in God but then, neither of them can say so, and if the Englishman believes in the tragedy of will and the Spaniard believes in the comedy of the imagination, both certainly know how difficult it is willfully to hold on to one's imagination except through "words, words, words. . . ."

Quixote the good and Macbeth the bad wish to forget. Hamlet the undecided wishes to remember. But the Quixote character is of the novel; Hamlet and Macbeth, of theater. Quixote uses the mask of comedy; Hamlet and Macbeth, of tragedy. Quixote reads and is read. Hamlet and Macbeth act and are seen. Borges asks himself why we are so bothered by the notion that Don Quixote is a reader of *Don Quixote* and Hamlet a spectator of *Hamlet*. He ventures that these inversions suggest, in turn, that if the characters within a work of fiction may be readers or spectators, then we, as readers and spectators, may also be works of fiction. But Shakespeare is theater, spectacle, public space.

One day, when I was with the writer Terenci Moix in Barcelona, I remembered London's glorious old Gainsborough film studios, maker of movies featuring a Margaret Lockwood who could scarcely squeeze into her plunging necklines even though she hid her abundant bosom so that she might escape at night dressed as a man, to rob highways in the company of James

Mason, and, no doubt, to later reward her lover with that very bosom.

Today, those old studios have become condominiums. But in a kind of posthumous artistic tribute, one of Gainsborough's old soundstages was transformed into a theater for the duration of four months, to host a double bill of drama. On alternating nights, to packed houses, Ralph Fiennes performed two of Shakespeare's political tragedies, *Richard II* and *Coriolanus.* The dashing movie actor, well known for his roles in *The English Patient, Schindler's List,* and *The End of the Affair,* is, above all else, a creature of the stage. His Hamlet, performed on Broadway in 1995, won him a Tony Award. His Richard and his Coriolanus were the kind of award an actor bestows upon himself.

Both are among the most difficult roles of the Shakespearean canon because they are, to put it one way, naked works. In *Othello, Romeo and Juliet,* and *King Lear,* the protagonists do not know their fate but the audience does, so clearly that one almost wants to shout out to Romeo, "Don't kill yourself, Juliet's alive," or "Iago is deceiving you. Desdemona is faithful," to Othello. In *Richard II* and *Coriolanus,* the protagonists possess an absolutely perfect knowledge of who they are, and the audience is aware of this as well. In this sense, we have no surprises. What we do have—thanks to the decidedly public nature of both works—is the most intense dramatic reflection on the nature of politics and the exercise of power.

Richard II was written in 1595, between *Titus Andronicus,* the work of a beginner, and *Romeo and Juliet,* the playwright's first major triumph. *Richard II* is a work about how power is held and how it is lost. There are two Richards. The Richard of the first part feels he has been anointed by God. He embodies the divine right of kings and he exercises this right capriciously. The ceremony gives power an incarnation and Fiennes infuses his character with a ritualistic movement, almost that of a sacred dandy. He is a man with two bodies: one anointed, the other physical. The monarch's imagination closes in on itself in its attempt to reconcile man and king. Richard's obsession is that of being king in spite of being a man; in other words, he is obsessed with annihilating the man in order to be king.

Such an enterprise requires a tremendous exercise of imagination and Richard, as he imagines himself, loses his grip on himself and his power. For him, the crown is a decorative accessory. Power, for Richard, becomes an interior fact, the power of the imagination, a lyric metaphysic. Victim of the imagination of power, the king loses all notion of how to exercise that power. His frivolity leads him to behave arbitrarily. His arbitrary behavior sparks the enmity of those people hurt by his power. The mounting list of grievances explode in rebellion. Defeated, Richard learns that his crown is hollow and that the name of his court is Death.

Ralph Fiennes moves deftly from the first Richard, frivolous and autocratic, to the second, beaten and bruised. His pain does not remain inside him. He empties himself of it with a kind of guilty tenderness. His greatness is his defeat, his pain, his woe. History allows him nothing more than to "sit upon the ground and tell sad stories of the death of kings." In effect, he is telling the world, "You may crush my power and my glory but not my pain."

Fiennes gives a great performance of a rather unforgiving role in a theatrical work that has its fair share of formalistic flaws. It is absolutely appropriate to pair it with Shakespeare's most perfect political tragedy, *Coriolanus,* written in 1607, between *Macbeth* and *Antony and Cleopatra,* toward the end of the playwright's career.

If Ralph Fiennes doubles his breadth as an actor in *Richard II,* he quadruples it in his performance of *Coriolanus.* This is a character at war with Rome, his homeland, the enemies of Rome, his mother, and himself. Coriolanus, champion of the Roman patriciate and detested by the city plebes, returns home triumphant from the war with the tribes threatening his city. Elected consul, he manages to turn all the plebeians against him, exiles himself from Rome to join his old enemies, prepares to sack and set fire to the city, until his mother Volumnia is able to dissuade him. But his clemency will cost him his life. In plainer, uglier terms, Coriolanus somehow ends up getting on everyone's bad side. Except his mother's. But this is the felicity that will ultimately destroy him, because Coriolanus, in his mother's eyes, is not a creature made of flesh and bone. He is an icon of power, the product of maternal fantasy. She does not love her son, she loves the military and political conqueror. She does not allow him to be who he is. She wants to make him believe that "a man were author of himself, and knew no other kin."

What the mother—in a peerless performance by the extraordinary Barbara Jefford—does not know is that Coriolanus will never be a great politician because he does not understand the art of adaptation, the art of the chameleon. He is a man of principle, without vanity or airs of importance, vices that a patrician scorns because he has no need to appear a certain way or act in a certain manner other than his own. He *is*. But Coriolanus's integrity endangers the vanity and venality of those around him. He is doomed. He makes everyone uncomfortable. He will remain alone. And he knows this. He will be defeated if he acts, and he will be defeated if he doesn't.

The genius of Shakespeare—and of Fiennes as well—lies in his ability to give this fatal man (a man who is conscious of his own dismal fate) an extraordinary sliver of humanity. A surprising sliver for such a verbal, discursive, occasionally rhetorical author as Shakespeare. That sliver—or crevice, if you will—is silence. The character of the wife Virgilia calls Coriolanus to a love without words. During those quiet moments with his beloved, Coriolanus shows that he is also conscious of what he loses, and that is love, victim of the political web that transforms manna from heaven into bile.

A work of art with a commitment to the political act, with the themes of party and state, *Coriolanus* has given rise to all sorts of ideological confusion. The French Right, in 1933, applauded it and the Left prohibited it. The Nazis glorified it and the U.S. occupying army, in 1945, banned all performances of it in Germany for a period of eight years. Brecht turned it into a Communist epic about class struggle: the good plebeians versus the bad patricians.

Without these congested ideologies, *Coriolanus,* a superior work of the Shakespearean canon, is nothing more than the story of a man abandoned by everyone. Shakespeare lends a rather inconclusive air to the work, just as Beethoven, another genius, did with his own *Coriolanus,* by ending it in an indistinct musical penumbra.

There is, finally, another Shakespeare, and to see it one must turn to the film version of *Titus Andronicus,* brought to the screen by the famous set designer of *The Lion King,* Julie Taymor. Ms. Taymor does not beat around the bush; she gives Titus's daughter, whose tongue and virtue have both been mutilated, branches in place of hands. In this early work, Shakespeare decided to defeat Christopher Marlowe at his game of horrors that are more bearable when seen from the distance offered by the theater, as opposed to the close proximity the camera affords. Men buried up to their necks in sand, almost starving to death. Men who allow their hands to be chopped off in order to save their children's lives, only to see them in jars alongside the decapitated heads of young princes. Men strung up by their feet, their heads cut off so that the blood will spill out in thick torrents. The children of Tamora, the proto–Lady Macbeth (played by a raging Jessica Lange), served to their father as vengeful cakes cooked up by Titus Andronicus (the chameleonesque Anthony Hopkins).

The list is an endless one and it reminds us that there is truly nothing new under the sun. In the annals of horror, *Titus Andronicus* beats *American Psycho, Crash,* and Stephen King. This is what allowed Voltaire to write off the Bard of Avon as "the height of ferocity and horror. . . . a barbaric buffoon. . . . whose works deserve the audiences of county fairs of two hundred years ago."

Shakespeare's assault on "good taste" and "restraint" are truly admirable and remind us of the ferocity with which Octavio Paz responded to the description of Mexican literature as "refined and subtle." "Give it to them, let them bitch, the whores," he said.

Shakespeare grabbed words by the ass and made them shriek and bitch, showing us that the range of verbal expression cannot be constrained by the constipated or famished genres of literature. The savage, lyrical, and tragic abundance of William Shakespeare continues to be the greatest evidence to support the conviction that ironclad rules have no place in literature. As well as the fact that critics can often make the funniest, and occasionally most deplorable, mistakes.

Silvia

The first and the last, says the poet to Artemis in the marvelous poem by Gérard de Nerval. . . . *"Et c'est toujours la seule—ou c'est le seul moment"* . . . If all the women I have loved could be encapsulated in one, the only woman that I have loved forever encapsulates all the others. They are the stars. Silvia is the galaxy itself. She has everything. Beauty. Erotic pleasure as well as the simple pleasure of being together, eating together, sleeping and waking up, walking, traveling together, sharing friends, discussing doubts, making plans, understanding flaws, accepting mistakes, and loving each other even for the things that we find irritating or unpleasant in our respective personalities and behaviors. The joy of having children. The pain of losing them. The communion of memory. The respect that comes with the passage of time. Different tastes. Our complementary vocations, intellects, emotions: we are different and we each give the other what the other no longer even lacks because all that is mine flows into her just as all that is hers flows into me. The labyrinth of genealogies, friendships, favorite cities, the splendid detail lavished on food, restaurants, our common love of film, theater, opera. All that unites us and even those things that might separate us, become a meeting point, question mark and, in the end, alliance. We are very different physically. She is delicate, petite, blond, with sensual eyes that change from blue to green to gray as the hours go by. Her mien is European, but her skin is olive-colored, with a lovely oriental glow. Her penchant for clothes is extreme, to my delight. I love her because I am the most punctual man in the world and she always arrives, punctually, late. This is part of her charm. To be waited for. The Europeans of the seventeenth century hoped that death would arrive from Spain, so that it would arrive late. No, death arrived early for us when we lost our son Carlos. We were always united, and then death arrived to bring us together even closer than before. She knows how to keep Carlos present at every hour while I, either less sensitive or more cowardly, have learned to summon my son, with a force that surprises me, only at the moment when I begin to write. That is when he appears at my side, in some way fulfilling his truncated destiny through my daily effort to write. That is how everything is perpetuated and then comes back to live inside the union of the couple. Apollinaire once said that some people die so that they may be loved. In our case, my son is alive because the love that drew us (Silvia, Carlos, and me) together continues to live on in our lives. But it is she, the woman, who reveals the specificity and inclusivity of love. It is she, Silvia, who crowns my life's quest to pay attention— sexual, erotic, political, literary, fraternal. Pay attention, or you will not have the right to love me and be loved by me. When Tomás Eloy Martínez, our dear Argentinian friend, lost his beautiful wife, Susana Rotker, he wrote a vivid, searing requiem that ends by saying, "I would have given everything I am and everything I have to be in your place. I would have loved to watch her grow old. I would have wanted her to watch me die."

A couple can never know which person will outlive the other, or if they will die together. The one who survives will always be a delegate of death rather than simply grieving. The love that delegates itself through death is Eros. After all the nights, days, years of flesh united, its absence can only be filled through the erotic imagination. "Eroticism is the approval of life, even in death," Georges Bataille tells us, thinking of Emily Brontë's *Wuthering Heights.* Sexuality necessarily implies death because reproduction signifies eventual disappearance from earth. To understand this is to understand erotic life after the death of a lover. To understand this is to understand the sexual relationship in the present at its most intense degree and to surpass it, erotically speaking, each and every hour that the beloved does not return in the physical sense.

But then shouldn't there exist, even in the most complete love, an anticipation of loss that intensifies the sexual present? Sometimes, as I watch Silvia sleep, I wish I could steal her name, her appearance, her experience from her, so that I could be the absolute master of her existence, the jealous guardian of her secrets. Without her, I can only conceive of love standing before a mirror, trembling from the memory of her. And then, disturbed and hungry, I hastily return to her closeness. I treat her body as if it were mine. With Silvia I learn to feel both passion and respect for the female body united with mine. I only praise her in the name of the perfection that I ascribe to her, even if she does not possess it, the perfection that she offers up to me, even though she may not see it.

Every night I leave an invisible note on her pillow that says, "I like you."

Women are the fleeting voyagers of the dawn. Each one is the bearer of a different destiny. My destiny was to find Silvia and to make all that is mine hers.

T

Time

Quite some time ago, I was traveling through the Mexican state of Morelos with the New York playwright Jack Gelber and his wife. Having lost our way in the labyrinth of mountains, rice fields, and reedbeds, we stopped to ask an elderly local gentleman the name of the village we were in.

"It depends," the old man replied. "When there is peace, the village is called Santa María. And when there is war, Zapata."

That old country gentleman knew something that "modern times" seem to have forgotten: that there exists more than one time in the world. There exist other times, in the plural—alongside, above, or below the lineal times marked by our Western calendars.

An old man who could live depending either on Zapata time or on Santa María time was the living heir to a complex, multilayered culture. That man is indispensable to us and, perhaps more important, he is fraternal. He reminds us that he has a brother in India for whom the past is never the past but rather an eternal present, forever enriched by what the West considers to be the dead "past." I suspect he has a twin in China who con-

ceives of time as a purely dynastic proposition, and perhaps a
nephew somewhere in Morocco for whom time does not evolve
at all horizontally from past to present to future, but rather as the
vertical, parallel ascent of God and man.

I can even imagine that perhaps he has a young grandson living in Madagascar among the *imerima* who refuse to banish ancient times in order to make way for newer ones. Rather than
mutually reject one another, each of them comes together to
comprise a kind of continuous accumulation. Everything is alive,
and everything is present, now and always. The *imerima* perceive
all possible history as two declining realities: the legacy of the ears
and the memory of the lips. And as we enter the twenty-first
century, ears and lips tell us that we should broaden the channels
through which time flows, so that we can give both life and space
to the manifold cultures of a world that runs the risk of both
global uniformity and local dispersion. For this, we must examine the notion of time as we see it from inside our traditional
Western patterns, which means we must examine our concept of
future-oriented history, the notion of progress as an inevitable
linear ascent toward perfection and, finally, the question of international hegemony and servitude in the twenty-first century because the modern world also offers us the possibility of a time
without time, a time that might be the end of time if, as is eminently possible, we manage to murder nature and commit suicide
in the process.

The defense of time is, as such, the defense of culture and the
way we experience it throughout our history. That defense has a
dwelling place. It is called the present, the here and now. The past
occurs today, when we remember. And the future occurs today,
too, when we desire.

A living present cannot exist if the past is dead. We can throw
the past out the window, but it won't be long before it comes
right back at us through the front door, often in the strangest of
guises. Wars that fight memory are ultimately lost by those who
incite them. We must turn the past into the present if we want to

understand the reemerging cultures that are dissatisfied with the headlong race toward a headless future. We must do this so that we can understand the internal tension in those cultures, the tension that merges the technical, supra-national demands of the global village and the affirmation of local differences, regionalism, microcultures, and the rhythms of time that are their individual legacies.

All these tensions call upon us to reformulate our concept of temporality and the role of language and imagination in the interest of a redistribution of our shared civilizations so that we may coexist with deeper and less ephemeral traditions than our own. Mexico is a multicultural, Spanish-speaking country, but it also continues to be an indigenous country as well. A whole repertoire of possibilities that we have forgotten, postponed, or expelled from our own concept of progressive time quietly awaits us in the indigenous world, repository of all that we have forgotten and scorned: the intensity of ritual, atavistic wisdom, mythic imagination, the death relationship, the method of marking the passage of time—narration and sum—not only in the calendar of the sun but in the calendar of destiny, the *tonopuhali* of twenty-day cycles, each one with its own discrete, thirteen-day unit. We need to do this until we can assimilate a veritable *mandala* that reflects a more comprehensive, more expansive concept of time, oriented beyond our simple linear conceptions.

Time has always been a problem. Ever since the beginning of time. It is a redundant problem, for the problem of time is time itself. The root of the problem is that there are two ways to perceive it. From one point of view, reality is defined by constant change. The world is in flames. The law of opposites is bloody. Everything tends to become its opposite and this is what effects change. History is the history of violence. Time is struggle. Evolution and flow are the only temporal realities. If movement ceases, the universe collapses and time stops.

From the other point of view, only that which is permanent and lasting is real. Flow, movement, and change are merely cosmetic. Plato reconciled both sides but favors the second. If change is real, permanence is unreal. Plato's dualism tells us that there exists a world of forms, real and permanent, outside of time and free of change: an eternal world. But there also exists another world, one of sensory objects, predicated upon appearance and change, which reflects the world of forms in another world of changing times. In *Timaeus,* the Creator explains how He transformed original Chaos into Universal Order. The immensity of God does not rely on space. The eternity of God does not rely on time. But as time and space are occupied by things and events, those things and events coexist in space and occur in time.

Lessing divided the arts into forms that coexist in space (in painting and sculpture, arts of total and immediate impression), and forms that occur over time (music and literature). Hence, the great question posed by modern literature has been: why is writing beholden to succession instead of simultaneity? Because language is composed of successive, discrete units. To a large degree, the revolution of the modern novel resides in its rebellion against discrete, successive inevitability. But the same thing is true of music, physics, and poetry. The impossible dream of simultaneity rebels against succession, and transforms rather than destroys it: Picasso, Pound and Eliot, Apollinaire, Joyce, Faulkner, Virginia Woolf . . . their goal is its greatness, but their genius resides in their failure to reach the goal—that is, the measure of change achieved by their rebellion. Literature is time's great laboratory.

Plato states that it is impossible to declare the universe eternal. But the Creator "resolved to bequeath us an image of eternity in motion . . . and this is what we call time." Time is the image of eternity when it moves. Eternity in movement is time. I never cease to marvel at this idea, which is an image. But whether I am impressed, consoled, or inspired by it, I can never find release from the contentious relationship I have—and in the end, everyone has—with time, because as I continue to pursue time, I scratch at it but can never grasp it fully. Born, nurtured, loved and being loved, yearning, aging, and ultimately dying in time, I will never know what I was before I was—the past without me—nor will I ever know what I will be when I no longer am—the future without me.

No matter how much we rationalize time, its realm, original and mortal, is the realm of mystery. I ask myself about the wisdom of God and the Devil and I tell myself it is a relationship with time. The Kabbalah says that nothing disappears entirely; everything is transformed. What we believe to be dead has only moved on to another place. Places remain. We don't see them move on anywhere. And anyway, what is time if not our own measurement, invention, imagination? All that exists is thought. All that is thought, is. Times can move from place to place, they can join together or superimpose themselves upon each other and then they separate. We can travel from one time to another without moving from the space we inhabit. But if we travel from one time to another and don't return to the present on time, we lose our memory of the past (if that is where we went) or our memory of the future (if that was the starting point). It is captured in the present. Life is in the present. And all of us, without exception, return to the present sooner or later. Time does not stop to wait for us as we travel back to the past or forward into the future. And we always arrive late. A minute or a century, it makes no difference. By now we cannot remember if we are living before or after the present. Perhaps our pact with time is to live in the present without memory of the most distant past or future, for the past and future that are closest to us are precisely what enable us to return to the present. There are times when we exchange enigmatic glances, on the street, in an airport, on a boat, in a department store, on a staircase, in an elevator, in a church, in a theater, in a cemetery, and we are asked: Who were you? Where did you live before? Where did you die before? Do we know each other?

If I wanted to rid myself of an intolerably sad memory, my pact with God or the Devil would be this: take away my memory and I'll give you my soul. But not even God can reverse what has been done. The Devil, on the other hand, claims that he can reverse what was into what wasn't. That is how God challenges and tempts man, for by forgetting an abominable fact, don't we also risk forgetting the very best of our lives? Times that witnessed our parents' love for us, a woman's beauty, a man's passion, a child's pride, the joy of friendship, everything. That is the diabolical clause: forget everything or forget nothing.

I see a child and I tell myself that each person born might very well reincarnate another man who dies. If I want to know how some child's face will look after forty years, all I need to do is go to the place where he will be baptized, named. There I will find him. There I will see the future face of that child. There I will tell myself that nobody can end his own life. No one is ever able to live fully all his possible time.

Who, then, are the immortals? There are beings who do not speak to us, but who look at us. They do not see us, but they remember us. They do not remember us, but they imagine us. Who, then, are the immortals? Those who lived a long time, those who reappear time after time, those who had more life than death, but less time than life.

U

Urbanities

I believe in cities. Nature makes me too anxious. The terror she inspires in me strikes me as nearer rather than dearer. I am seduced by natural beauty. I can spend hours flying above the white thrones of the Andes or the Rocky Mountains, in a state of virtual ecstasy. How I would love to lose myself in the delicate, everlasting beauty of a Russian birch forest! The Irish coast, that turbulent ocean fortress that defends an entire continent, takes my breath away. And I could bury myself forever and ever in the lime-green clarity of the Caribbean, transparent tomb of all the silver and gold of the ghost cities of Indian America. And is there anything quite as serene, undulating, and blessed with eternity in movement as those wheat fields that are waves, the green followed by the gray-brown, followed by the tremulous blue of the Palouse, in Idaho?

And then I hear the sardonic voice of Schopenhauer: "For once, try to fully be nature," and then I emerge from my calendar dreams, my guilty rapture, my grudging separation from those people who so unconditionally revel in natural beauty. What is the intrinsic defect that prevents me from speaking with a true love of nature, desiring and desirable at the same time? For I admire nature, but I fear it as well. I envy it. All natural things and beings always seem to be in just the right place. We, as human beings, displace ourselves, we wish we could be something or somewhere else, we are always out of place, unlike the Colorado canyons or the waterfalls of the Zambezi River or the tigers of Bengal—that is, if there are any left in the world by now. Even migratory species fulfill cycles of eternal return that are comparable to the superlative beauty of the wild cherry tree as it comes into bloom time after time. Yes, we admire the order of natural beauty. But we know that behind its creation lies catastrophe. And we fear that the next catastrophe will not be the work of nature (with all the peril and convulsion she carries with her) but rather the hand of apocalypse, one that is worse than any earthquake or tidal wave: the final act of vengeance that human beings will perpetrate against nature. Today, for the first time, we possess the verifiable suspicion that we could die along with nature, at the very same moment. In times past, no matter what obstacle nature faced—stay here, abandon me—we always knew that nature would outlast us. The inevitable death of the human being has been accepted by a natural environment that, until now, has served as a consolation to us because it survives. Today, our own madness could orchestrate a simultaneous catastrophe. I die, and nature dies with me. *Après nous, le néant.* . . .

I have never believed that there exists an original bucolic Golden Age to which one day we shall return so that we may become as we were in those early times—that is to say, complete. The primeval Golden Age, Ovid's very explicit dream that is expressed, almost verbatim, by Don Quixote with his goatherds:

> Fortunate the age and fortunate the times called golden by the ancients, and not because gold, which in this our age of iron is so highly esteemed, could be found then with no effort, but because those who lived in that time did not know

the two words *thine* and *mine*. In that blessed age all things were owned in common. . . . In that time all was peace, friendship, and harmony. . . . there was no fraud, deceit, or malice. . . .

It is a regressive dream, one that brings us back to the illusion of that which never was. All the virtues we have lost but yearn to re-cover, we attribute to nature. It is a revolutionary dream: one in which we turn back to our starting point in order to discover the promise of the future. This, in the end, becomes utopia's desired incarnation, more than just a pretext reminiscent of origin. The return to nature is also the dream of the New World. America is invented (desired, discovered) by Europe so that in another part of the world, in an ideal *là-bas,* a perfect and natural society may be reborn—the very one that the Renaissance (More, Cam-panella, Bacon, Shakespeare, Cervantes) both dreamed of and de-nied. In Europe, it was denied by realpolitik, Machiavelli, the Borgias, and irresponsible power; the Fuggers and money with interest, Luther and the religious war with nationalism; Isabel, Ferdinand, and racial intolerance. The terrible Thirty Years' War and its Mothers Courage dragging their bundles of rags and eat-ing the scraps of their old illusions: with this image, Brecht ends the Renaissance.

America thus becomes the contradiction of Europe, its utopia. But *u-topos* is the place that does not exist. How can America—a place that indeed exists—be the place that exists only in the imagination? From Vespucci, Columbus, and the chroniclers of the Indies to Neruda, Carpentier, and García Márquez, we appear to be Europe's utopia, the felicitous return to the land of origins. Neruda most often sings to an idyllic, pre-Hispanic America, where the boorish conquistadors robbed the gold in the mines but left behind the gold of their language. Car-pentier goes back in time, traveling to the seed of all civilization at the source of the Orinoco. But it is García Márquez who closes the doors to regression with lock and key after discovering the re-claimed paradise. The communities that have experienced those symbolic "hundred years of solitude" will have no other oppor-tunity on this earth. The opportunity, García Márquez implies, of regressing to the *u-topos,* though yes, the opportunity of building a better city, a Latin American *civitas,* for the future. In this sense, utopia reassumes its true face. It is a project for the future.

The dream of a Golden Age, nevertheless, is a persistent one. At some time in the past, there must have existed an elemental age of natural joy and harmony. We may live in misfortune, but we must have been born into happiness. An abundantly loving mother, embracing all her children, making no distinctions among them, must have preceded the wretched patriarchy that imposes the survival of the fittest, appoints his firstborn heir, de-scendants, property, boundaries, and declares war to defend all those things. . . . Even if this theory were true, I can't help but think that, as with all human endeavors, nature is perfectly indif-ferent to the question of matriarchy and patriarchy. Perhaps we all suffer the offenses we have perpetrated against nature. For one thing, we can be certain that nature is utterly indifferent to our fragility, our vulnerability, our fatal disappearance from earth. . . . The setting sun does not know its own beauty. The canyons of Colorado do not know their own magnificence.

I am a creature of the pavements. I prefer cities because nei-ther they nor I are under any illusion about our respective perma-nence. A city is an accidental tribe, Dostoevsky said. But I am far better able to identify my mortal condition, my precarious des-tiny with that accidental tribe, precisely because of its accidental condition, its unpredictable and reckless movement, than with a natural environment idealized to the very apex of happiness and immortality, only to fall over and over again into the depths of the most destructive depravity. Nature's beauty is so deceitful. The metropolis is hostile but does not hide this fact. Natural beauty can be unfaithful: the lovely mask of an original or imminent chaos. For that reason I admire—though also fear—the city as a response to nature, so tumultuous and savage. Can't cities just as easily fall into the very same condition that makes us fear the harshness of the natural world: the *selva selvaggia*? The only difference is that the urban jungle is a jungle of our own making.

Cities risk danger, cities fall to their knees, they grow sick and they die. Our century, like no other, has shown itself capable of eliminating entire cities. Not even Scipio in his confrontation with Numantia or Carthage destroyed cities with the barbarity and technical skill of which we have been capable in our time, from Sarajevo to Sarajevo, with Verdun and Guernica in between, Chungking and Dresden, Hiroshima and Baghdad. . . . History is urbanicide. Some cities survive. Others disappear forever. Babylon no longer exists. The Cuzco of the Incan civilization is a ghost. The Tenochtitlán of the Aztecs is a petrified, tremulous underground above which we find the successive cities of Mexico— the indigenous, the Baroque, the neoclassical, the nineteenth-century, the modern. Rome continues to add almost geological layers to its age of antiquity. There are the partially subterranean cities. They invite us to penetrate their labyrinths. How easy it is to lose ourselves in them and never again see the light of day.

I adore the cities that instead of burying or hiding themselves away, stretch out, show themselves off, expose their spaces like jewels spread out on velvet. Paris is the perfect city in this sense. It changes, but it does not hide. It expands, but it does not disappear. Those of us who are inveterate lovers of this city can bemoan the disappearance, here and there, of a bookshop, a café, a market. . . . But in its essence, Paris does not change. The literary and musical references are always there. A novel by Balzac is a novel by Proust is a novel by Le Clézio. A poem by Villon is a poem by Apollinaire is a poem by Prévert. A song by Piaf, by Patachou, by Jean Sablon or Georges Brassens, or the marvelous Barbara, never grows old. The places cited are encircled forever by names like Pigalle, Montparnasse, the Rue LePic, the Pont Mirabeau, the Place Dauphine where dead leaves will fall forevermore.

What is this? Why is this? History, prestige, esprit, continuity, powerful evocations? No. It is light. To say "the city of light" is a platitude that some innocents believe to be a reference to the public lighting scheme. They don't realize that it refers to nothing less than a miracle: "Every afternoon, in Paris, one miraculous moment dispels the accidents of the day—rain or fog, sweltering heat or snow—to reveal, as in a Corot landscape, the luminous essence of the Île-de-France" (*Una familia lejana* [*Distant Relations*]).

Paul Morand, with whom I coincided on various occasions at the pool of the Automobile Club of France on the Place de la Concorde, told me that in his last will and testament he had included a provision stating that his skin should be used as a suitcase so that he might be able to travel for all eternity. Venice—or rather the Venices, in plural—was one of the favorite cities of that self-proclaimed "widower of Europe." For Morand, Venice was more than just a city; it was the confidante of his silent soul, the portrait of a man in a thousand different Venices. I, who spent six months living opposite the Chiesa de San Bastian, decorated by Veronese in that half of Venice that is the Dorsoduro, experience Venice as a city that requires absence in order to preserve its glory, which is the glory of wonder. As humans we possess the remarkably consistent capacity for turning the marvelous into the routine. When I realized that I was walking through San Marco looking at nothing more than the tips of my shoes, I finally broke free from my routine so that I might recover that feeling of wonderment, so that I might remember and write of Venice as the city where no footprints are left behind upon the stone or the water. In that place of mirages there is no space for any ghost other than that of time, and the marks it leaves behind are imperceptible. The lagoon would disappear without the stone it reflects, and the stone would disappear without the waters that reflect its image. What weak competition, I think to myself, are the transient bodies of men in the face of this enchantment. Whether we are solid or spectral is of little importance. It is all the same. All of Venice is a ghost. And it does not issue entrance visas to any other ghost. Here, nobody would recognize them as such. And so, they would cease to exist. No other ghost exposes itself to quite so much.

For me, the loveliest cities in Europe, in addition to Venice, are Prague and Cambridge. Prague, the dead lover of the Vltava. Prague, the city abandoned by its writers: Rilke, Werfel, Kundera, the exiles that left so that they could break "the curse of Prague." The city of ghettos, isolation, emotional walls, prohibited territories, the city of impersonal documents, where the true language is that of the passport, the identity card, the bureaucratic slip of paper that decides who is and who is not a person.

I speak of the city I visited in the winter of 1968. I had traveled there with Julio Cortázar and Gabriel García Márquez to support our friend Milan Kundera and the impossible battle for the Prague Spring. I don't know if there is any lovelier, sadder city in all of Europe. The most poignant spot is the Old Jewish Cemetery, a cramped, narrow plot of land encroached upon by old, soot-stained buildings. Instead of expanding horizontally, this cemetery rose upward: layer upon layer of tombs, earth upon earth. A geological ghost of the Jewish world of Bohemia. A tangle of dead leaves, black earth, and black tombs. The graves of Prague are like totems. One would have to burrow deep down, like a mole, to reach the very last man buried there. His name is Gregor Samsa. He doesn't move. He is suspended above the void that is both his tomb and urban precipice; there he clings with hands and feet above the void of Prague, the "little mother with claws," as Kafka called it.

Yet is there any other urban space that so majestically, with such admirable unity and purity of form, preserves its physiognomy, ever-changing and ever-singular, spanning the years from the High Middle Ages to the Baroque?

There is nothing more different from Prague than the beauty of Cambridge, whose "backs" are a necklace of precious stones, a successive parade of serene, immortal, architecture worthy of endless praise: from St. John's to Trinity to King's College to Queen's and Peterhouse; I cannot think of another university complex that marries such beauty with such great service, such tradition with such creation. This is the university of Erasmus and Samuel Pepys, of Wordsworth and Byron. There is the tree from which, gravely, the apple fell down upon Isaac Newton. But if there is one artist who comprises all the secret symmetries of Cambridge, it is Christopher Wren. I spent the most perfect year of my life reading and writing and gazing out, from my room at Trinity College, at the asymmetric quadrilateral of Wren's Neville's Court. This is an asymmetry that, breaking the apparent symmetry of Cambridge, opens the door to a mystery that can be called architecture as a prophecy of the past. . . . Cambridge assimilates the inhabitant, more than the visitor, to a life of work, discipline, and the pleasures shared by both solitude and companionship. I have never encountered a student body as informed or sharp-witted as that of Cambridge. And there is no uninterrupted succession of architecture more beautiful than those Cambridge backs. And accompanying the absolute serenity of immutable architecture is the fastest sky my eyes have ever seen. What pure delight it is to lie down on some green space in Cambridge, hands clasped behind the neck, to contemplate the passage of those "clouds of glory," as Wordsworth called them in the great poem of English Romanticism, *The Prelude,* comparing them with "God, who is our home," before the "shades of the prison-house begin to close" upon us. . . .

Granada, Ronda, Córdoba, Salamanca, Santiago de Compostela, Oviedo, Ávila, Cáceres. My rosary of Spanish cities goes beyond architectural beauty to embrace a human conviction. I imagine the ideal European city. Italian architecture. French cuisine. English theater. German music. And filled with Spaniards. One way to classify cities is by the number of friends we have in them. And outside of Latin America, I can't think of a single place where I have more friends than the cities of Spain. I am at home in Madrid, Barcelona, Mallorca, Sevilla. . . .

I always return to Paris—another city of friends—because it is where beauty and life coalesce so perfectly. There is no other European city where I have lived quite so intensely—politically, intellectually, romantically. My son was born there. I learned to love my wife there. There are cities I only visit—those in the north of Europe, the cities of the United States—and there are others in which I live. Mexico, as an act of amorous masochism, is my most well-lived city. It is my people, my history, my cross, my suffocation, my test, my challenge: remember me as beautiful, little mistress of New Spain, don't gaze down upon me as I fall to my knees, most accessible Virgin of Guadalupe, don't gaze up at me as I lie down, inaccessible whore of Orozco. . . .

I hear the echoes of kettledrums above the noise of engines and jukeboxes, amid the sediment of bejeweled reptiles. The serpents, animals with history, sleep heavy in your urns. Your eyes gleam with the voracious suns of the high tropics. In your body, a barbed-wire fence. Don't give up, brother! Summon all that you have in you, sharpen your knives, and refuse. Do not speak, do not pity, do not love. Let all your nostalgia and all your loose ends emigrate. Every day, start at birth. And recover the flame at the moment of that con-tained, imperceptible strumming, at the moment of the streetside barrel organ, when it seems as though all your memories have suddenly become clear, tight. Recover them on your own. Your heroes will not return to help you. You have come here, without knowing it, to find me at this plateau of funereal jewels. This is where we live, where our aromas blend together on the city streets, the smells of sweat and patchouli, new brick and subterranean gas, our idle and tense flesh, though never our gazes. We have never knelt together, you and I, to receive the same host; torn apart together, created together, only to die for ourselves, isolated. Here we fall. But what is to be done about it? Endure it, brother. And wait to see if one day my fingers touch yours. Come, let yourself fall into the lunar scar of our city, that city that is a panoply of sewers, glass of vapor, and mineral frost, the city that is the presence of all our forgotten memories, city of carnivorous precipices, of immobile pain, immense brevity, stagnant sun, long scorches, city of low flames, city up to its neck in water, city of picaresque lethargy, of black nerves, of three navels, of the contagious laugh, of warped stenches, rigid city between air and worms, old city in lights, old city in its cradle of birds of ill omen, new city living alongside sculpted dust, city living alongside the immense sky, city of dark varnish and stones, city beneath the resplendent mud, city of viscera and ropes, city of violated defeat (city that we could not suckle in the light of day, the secret defeat), city of humble outdoor markets, meat from clay pots, city that is the reflection of fury, city of desired failure, city in a tempest of domes, city that is the trough of the rigid jaws of the brother drenched in thirst and scabs, city woven in amnesia, resurrection of childhoods, incarnation of feather, city of bitches, city of starvelings, sumptuous villa, city of lepers and sunken pestilence, city. Incandescent prickly pear. Eagle without wings. Serpent of stars. This was what we were given. What can we do about it, in the most transparent region of the air.★

London is good to me, for it is where I write in peace because nobody calls me, nobody knows me. I look out the window. I

★Fuentes, Carlos, *La región mas transparente* (*Where the Air Is Clear*), 1958.

don't go out into the relentless rain. My voyage is my desk. My tropics are made of paper. I hear the incongruous telephone. The answering machine serves as testimony of my absence. I am here. I am not here. I write and I write. All I need to hear and understand, I hear from the mouths of my six or so English friends.

Nevertheless, I cannot abandon the cities that witnessed my growth, shaped me, and educated me. Panama, the city that calls itself the *corazón del mundo y puente del universo* (the heart of the world and the bridge of the universe), even though it is only a scar of the sea in the middle of the jungle. Montevideo, which I knew with no skyscrapers but full of old-world grace, the perfect capital city dreamed up for its writers, if not by its writers: Felisberto Hernández, Juan Carlos Onetti, and the ghost of Lautréamont. . . . And Quito, golden equatorial doubloon whose inhabitants only request, *"En la tierra, Quito, y en el cielo, un hoyito para ver a Quito"* (On earth, Quito, and in heaven, a crevice through which to gaze upon Quito). And then Rio de Janeiro, the *cidade maravilhosa* where, as I mention elsewhere in this volume, I learned about literature perched atop Alfonso Reyes's knees. Isn't literature, then, the lie that reveals the truth in a Janic city, that *"río de enero, río de enero, fuiste río y eres mar"* (river of January, river of January, once river, now sea) that Reyes himself sang? Santiago de Chile, where liberty and poetry were forever fused, Santiago of the Frente Popular, the beautiful women with eyes like grapes and schools of British discipline where the desire to write constituted a lack of discipline that was transformed into order and lessons in constancy in the face of the overwhelming obligation to prove, day in and day out, that the Battle of Waterloo had been won on the playing fields of Eton. . . . Buenos Aires, where I became a man and loved and walked about freely, and read Borges and refused to repeat the fascist mottoes of the regime, and understood why tango is a sad thought that one dances, and how a man could fall in love to the point of dishonor because of a woman like Mecha Ortiz or Tita Merello. Next to the lion-colored river, said Lugones, Buenos Aires is a city that was founded twice, the city where the Atlantic and the Pampa came together, equally vast and equally featureless, and gave Buenos Aires, a city privileged by distance and absence, the melancholy of being unique, of not being quite like anything else and bearing the cross of wanting to be like another city, Paris or Babel. There may be no other city as solid, as constructed, as "built" in Latin America, but there is also no other city quite so lost in the mist of its language, literature, music in motion, so wounded by its broken promises, inconceivable cruelties, its "disappeared," its tortured, its atrocities that cannot begin to equal the carnivalesque shock left behind by its dictators, its embalmed saints, its presidential ballerinas, its palace sorcerers. Buenos Aires endured all this and continues on, perhaps because the city exists thanks to a miracle, because the cannibals didn't eat it, and perhaps then that is why Buenos Aires eats meat. Founded twice, it could be refounded a hundred times over.

Washington was the city of my childhood, which was punctuated by summer vacations in Mexico under the charge of my splendid, valiant grandmothers. Washington remained with me as a long, burning, Faulknerian summer, with the smell of black men's sweat, of rotting parks, of slow, heavy rivers, of scratches the flavor of raspberries, of blazing movie theaters where Hollywood concealed the miseries of the Depression behind the erotic charm of Fred and Ginger dancing, the anarchistic, outrageous comedy of Laurel and Hardy, the marvelous reinvention of the comic Eve—as exemplified by Irene Dunne and Carole Lombard, accessible and ironic compared with the inaccessible sexual remove of Greta and Marlene, the divas of Europe. Why do I remember all of this as part of a summer I scarcely lived through, rather than the winters when I would ride my sled to school and was rewarded, each week, with two unforgettable trips to the movie theater, clutching my father's hand?

Today I detest Washington. Everything that loomed large in my childhood became dwarflike in my older age: the parks, the avenues, the houses, the politics, the politicians. . . . Comparable to a great cemetery of Greek mausoleums, Washington, like Buenos Aires, is an invented city, one without preexistence. But whereas Buenos Aires conjugates Pampa and ocean with the poetry of Cortázar, the music of Discépolo, and the voice of Goyeneche, Washington is nothing but a cemetery that stretches out toward the vast nothingness of Highway 1 that runs from the Atlantic to the Pacific, from the European entrance to the Asian exit, to a New York that has grown more and more repetitive, arrogant, vulgar, and, paradoxically, friendlier, more original and welcoming, but always Gotham, city of unbearable energy that imposes itself upon us, sucks our very existence from us, makes us believe that its vitality also belongs to us, passive and deceived by the whirlwind of the Big Apple and its nightmare of cocktail parties where nobody gives anyone else more than a fleeting glance and two seconds of conversation, but where the presentation of the film *Hamlet* can spark, at intermission time, some of the most animated and lucid debate ever heard among an audience of young people. . . .

My present distance from New York may very well be due to my former closeness. The New York where I lived during the 1960s was a tribal space of childhood recognition. We were a gang of friends, we shared women, reading, bars. The enthusiastic fervor of the age was what united us. The mutual discovery of the new Latin American literature by the North Americans, and the literature of North America by the Latin Americans united us as well. Manhattan stretched out to the farthest tip of Long Island and its tribe of young, dynamic playwrights, all the way up to Martha's Vineyard and then back down Second Avenue to end up inevitably in the fiefdom of Elaine's with all its habitués, and then the glorious young women showing off miniskirts, long manes of hair, and bodies that undulated to the rhythm of the Watusi amid the lights and shadows of the Peppermint Lounge, before waking up, melancholy, to the sound of the marvelous Cannonball Adderley and compensating for all that we lost out on in the nighttime with summer mornings in our penumbral bedchambers, barely allowing the July heat to filter through the brisk shadows of a youth we imagined would never end. . . . And as I have not rediscovered that thing that I can only evoke in my memory, I unfairly blame the city that I once felt was so very much mine and that now seems so foreign to me. Nowadays, who plays the African flute of the melancholy Brother Yusef Lateef in a city that has succumbed to celebrity, money, and Darwinian disdain? Oh, the paradox: the first and only world power, so full of itself, indulges in the luxury of scorning international information. With the exception of the two coasts—New York and Los Angeles—one looks in vain for international news on television or in the newspapers.

And one terrible day—September 11, 2001—horror would wake up New York, eradicating all its egotistical liturgy and resuscitating all its solidarity, all its heroism, all its human fraternity at this its most frightful hour. For how long? I don't know. I only know that nobody can destroy the energy of New York.

It takes longer to fly from New York to Los Angeles than to London or Paris. A Los Angeles increasingly lost in its labyrinth of freeways and its continental shock: how is it possible? This is where America ends, this is where everything crumbles into the sea, where there is no more frontier to conquer. California, the slide area. And then, right there in the middle of the continent, a great city, in love and beloved, the city that loves itself and makes its visitors fall in love with it: Chicago, *that toddlin' town,* the city of broad shoulders, where the men take their wives out to dance. . . .

The North American landscape invites all kinds of generalizations regarding uniformity, void, the immense and tedious plains, ignorance, lack of information, provincialism. . . . But those very stereotypes are what spur a person to prove it wrong, to celebrate the discovery of an unknown house by Frank Lloyd Wright in the Midwestern plains; Goya's marvelous portrait of

Pedro Romero, the founder of modern bullfighting, in Fort Worth, Texas; the largest, most complete bookstore in the world, tucked in between the lovely rivers of Portland, Oregon; Richard Ford on a quiet street in the hushed nostalgia and elegance of New Orleans; William Styron and his dog walking along the beaches of Martha's Vineyard; the Plaza hotel's perfect martini; Dorothea Straus conquering the streets of Manhattan every afternoon with the stride of an Amazon and an outfit straight out of the Belle Epoque; a bordello of Chinese gay men in San Francisco; the original manuscripts of the Spanish colony in the Ann Arbor Library; the melodious laughter and the warm breasts of the girls in Boulder, Colorado; the proud profile of the Chicano student in San Antonio, Texas; the heady aroma of ink, wood, and leather in Harvard's Widener Library; the ironic wisdom of the great Democrats, Arthur Schlesinger, John Kenneth Galbraith.

And so I reach a conclusion. Cities cannot bear to be compared. And "America" is a uniform illusion that is dreamed of in Hollywood like Gene Kelly and Cyd Charisse: "I dance, therefore I am." There is the "America" that endlessly bemoans the loss of its innocence in Boston or Long Island (Henry James, F. Scott Fitzgerald). There is the "America" that was never innocent in the first place (Richard Wright's Natchez, Mississippi, James Baldwin's Harlem), and the "America" that was always violent, corrupt, and supremely indifferent to the national idyll (Chandler's Los Angeles, Hammett's Poisonville).

There is one city to which I owe my passage from adolescence to adulthood, where I disciplined my life, focused my mind, and organized my work as a writer. That city, for me, is Geneva: my incomparable attic flat on the Place du Bourg-de-Four, the Forum Boarium founded by Julius Caesar; the Café de la Clémence right in front, for conversations with friends; the Café Canonica with the view of the lake for chatting up hookers with dyed-blond hair and lapdogs; the university for meeting and falling in love with women who bore the scent of youth and love-filled awe; the disciplined, *ancien régime* atmosphere of the Institut Universitaire de Hautes Etudes Internationales and its coterie of star internationalists such as Brierly, Bourquin, Ropke, Scelle, who graced me with their teachings; the bookshops of the Vieille Ville where I would buy old editions of the French classics and read them in the tranquillity of the Île Jean-Jacques Rousseau between the Rhône and the Léman. . . .

Cities of supreme peace and contemplation. The Sevilla of Muslim, Christian, and Jewish equilibrium. Jade-colored Oaxaca, the only city with a peacefully unified silhouette of the indigenous and the Spanish. A Berlin resurrected, amid the dreams rocked back and forth by the proximity of a hundred lakes. Cartagena de Indias, the perfect city of the colonial Caribbean, encircled by walls to fend off the English pirates of yesteryear and the drug-trafficking guerrillas of today: the miraculous oasis of a ghostly, blood-squeezed country. Savannah, Georgia, a city that Borges must have invented, plazas that branch off into streets, which lead to more plazas that branch off into more streets in an infinite, perfect geometric web, though in the end it is as desolate as a de Chirico painting.

There is no city without climate. Temperature is the vengeance of a nature that, when all is said and done, cannot be dominated by roof or street, by door, by the heat of a fireplace or the ice in a freezer. Nature all around us tells us, over and over again: choose. Nobody, nature says to us, can escape the dilemma between abandoning me to escape my suffocating embrace— even if the price is that of an errant orphanhood—and remaining forever in my savage and protective jungle, even if the price is that of abdicating the risks of freedom. . . .

Mexico: summer will arrive with the cry of dust defeated. London: spring will bloom in two youthful breasts behind a sheath of transparent organdy. New York: autumn will wear a crown of gold. Paris: winter will be a river of mist.

And outside the cities, the lakes and the fluvial waterways, forests and lands die at an unprecedented velocity. We are at risk of losing the equilibrium of the biosphere and condemning our descendants to live and die without nature. "The universe requires an eternity," wrote Jorge Luis Borges. "And in the heavens," he added, "the verbs *preserve* and *create* are synonyms." Preserve and create are our rival verbs at the dawn of this new century.

V

Velázquez

The artist asks questions. An image can be conceived of and executed in a thousand different ways. Which way would you prefer? The figure of the one who was, who is, or who will be? And where would you like to see it: in the place of the figure's origin, final destination, or present location? In which places and at which times?

In the iconic art of Byzantium, the extreme, culminating symbol of medieval painting, there is only one possible response to these eternal questions: the time within a painting is a singular time, and that time is eternity, the domain of a single figure: God, the *Pankreator*. The gaze of the Byzantine *Pankreator*, like Pascal's circumference, is everywhere and nowhere. It gazes at us and we gaze upon it, but there is a barrier separating us: divinity. We are here, now. He is here, everywhere. Tomorrow, we will no longer be here. He will continue to be here, for the centuries to come.

Fernando Botero is right when he says that it was Giotto who sparked the great modern revolution in art. Instead of the distant veneration of the Byzantine, Giotto infuses art with the urgent passion of the Italian and even perhaps the Franciscan world. St.

Francis's personal, passionate commitment is the very matter of religion and life, and is a mirror of the emotional engagement Giotto brings to the craft of painting. Piero della Francesca will strengthen the force of this revolution; the Arezzo and Sansepolcro frescos definitively yank painting out of its divine paralysis and its frontal gaze. Piero's figures sometimes even dream—or dare to dream, like the sleeping figures at Sansepolcro. But most of all they dare to look. In Arezzo, the figures look out beyond the painting, toward a horizon or a person that we do not see. Piero died in 1492, the very same year of the American Discovery, and perhaps he is looking as far away as the Mundus Novus baptized by another Italian, Amerigo Vespucci. It almost seems as if Piero is telling us, I am going to paint a piazza with a deep perspective, one that is as fluid as the time that witnesses birth, growth, and death, and as slippery as the boundless space in which the designs of God are fulfilled through human action. This is where we find real houses, doors, stones, trees, men—no longer space without relief, or time without the hours of the original God Creator, but rather space as place and time as scar of creation. After Giotto and Piero the painter can say, "Blind men, look, I paint to look, I look to paint, look at what I paint, and what I paint, by being painted, looks at me and, in the end, looks at all of you, who look at me looking at my painting." "Yes," says Julián, the painter in my novel *Terra Nostra,* "only what is circular is eternal and only the eternal is circular, but within that eternal circle, there is room for all the accidents and variants of the freedom that is not eternal but instantaneous and fleeting."

Paradoxically, Renaissance freedom is brought to its apogee by a Spanish court painter who produced commissioned works and used royal patronage to elevate the freedom of the artist to its very highest form and to revolutionize art itself. Just as Cervantes did in *Don Quixote,* Velázquez, in *Las Meninas* (*The Maids of Honor*), uses the restrictions of time and space not only to mock them (that would be easy) but to create an alternate reality alongside the orthodox "truth," and this reality is based on the freedom of the imagination. An infinitely more daunting task. While the Counter-Reformation orthodoxy accepts one single point of view, Cervantes in literature and Velázquez in painting offer multiple verbal and visual points of view. When they discover that their adventures have been made public—that is, published—Don Quixote and Sancho Panza realize that they have been read and seen by others. The others surround us. We read. We are read. We see. We are seen.

In *Las Meninas,* we surprise Velázquez while he is painting. He is doing what he wants to do, what he is able to do: paint. But this is not a self-portrait of the painter painting. It is a portrait of the painter who not only paints but is looking at what he is painting and who, moreover, knows that the people he is painting are looking at him as are the spectators who look at him from outside the painting, painting. Us. This is the necessary if uncomfortable or imperfect distance that Velázquez wants to eliminate, by introducing the viewer into the painting and projecting the painting beyond its frame and into the immediate, present space of the viewer.

But firstly: who is Velázquez painting? The princess, her maids, the midget girl, the sleepy dog? Or the gentleman dressed in black who appears at the entrance to the studio—the painting—upon an illuminated threshold? Or is Velázquez painting the two figures reflected, rather opaquely, in a cloudy mirror lost in the darkest corners of the atelier: the father and mother of the little princess, the king and queen of Spain—granting us, according to Michel Foucault's celebrated interpretation, the "place of the king"?

In any event, we can also believe that Velázquez is there, brush in one hand, palette in the other, painting the painting that we are looking at, *Las Meninas.* We can believe that this is the case—but only until we realize that the majority of the figures in the scene, with the exception of the sleepy dog, are looking directly at us. At you and me. Is it possible that we are, in fact, the true protagonists of *Las Meninas,* the painting that Velázquez, at this very moment, is painting? Well now, if Velázquez and the entire court are inviting us to enter the painting, then the painting, at the very same moment, is most certainly taking a step forward to become united with us. This is the true dynamic of this masterpiece. We are free to look at the painting—and by extension, the entire world—in various different perspectives, not just one that is dogmatic and orthodox. And we are aware that both painting and painter are gazing out at us. Just like the luncheon companions in Manet's *Déjeuner sur l'herbe,* which is scandalous because we find two clothed men and one naked woman *gazing at us.* Would there be any scandal at all in this painting if they weren't looking at us—if they were looking out toward the forest, for example, or the background, or the edges of their little picnic site? The circle is completed. The icon, at one time, gazed out toward eternity, frontally. Piero della Francesca looks toward both sides, beyond the formal limits of the painting. And Manet looks straight back at us, not from the eternal but rather the present moment. Braque and Picasso, finally, would multiply the gaze simultaneously in all directions—both the gaze of the painting's subject as well as our own gaze, directed toward a subject that we see simultaneously, in all its various perspectives.

For this reason, Velázquez is at both the center and the pinnacle, the base and the horizon, of modern painting. We must not forget that the canvas Velázquez paints—the painting within the painting—does not face us and is not yet finished, even though we are gazing at something we believe to be finished. Between these two central facts, however, two broad and shocking spaces open up. The first belongs to the painting's original scene. Velázquez paints, the princess and her maids are caught by surprise as they look out, the gentleman enters through an illuminated vestibule, the king and queen are reflected in the mirror. Did this scene actually take place? Was it posed? Or did Velázquez simply imagine some or all of its elements? The second space is occupied by another question: did the painter finish the painting? Not only the painting that he is executing, one we do not see, but the very painting that we are looking at. Is it finished? Ortega y Gasset reminds us that Velázquez, in his own day, was not a popular painter. He was often accused of delivering unfinished works. Quevedo even accused him of painting "distant stains." Today we can appreciate, from close up, that Velázquez's "realism" springs to life through a profusion of abstract brushstrokes. Observed at close range, his paintings dissolve into a splendid pictorial abstraction—meticulous, free, and, I would say, self-sufficient. I don't mean to suggest we dissect a Velázquez painting, but I do suggest that we approach him with a more inquisitive, intimate, microscopic gaze. That is how we may recognize the precision, the freedom, and the discipline of this "painter of painting," as Ortega called him, recalling as well that Velázquez is more than a realist—he is a de-realist whose modes of derealization are innumerable and even opposed to one another. But in every case, there is a representation that is a visitation in the Henry James sense of the word: power exercised by an intangible presence. Ortega, who was the precursor to Foucault's celebrated theories (the viewer occupies the king's position), reminds us that before Velázquez, painting created a false world on canvas, a world alien and immune to time, "the fauna of eternity." Although I believe that Ortega is wrong in this case, because that "fauna of eternity" pertains to pre-Renaissance art, I agree that Velázquez "does indeed paint time itself at the very moment that constitutes 'being,' just as it is condemned to stop being, to evolve, to become corrupted."

In *Las Meninas,* Velázquez establishes a principle for modern art. The reproaches he endured in his lifetime for painting "unfinished works," is, in today's world, the very emblem of his modernity and, I would add, his freedom. Velázquez deposits his work in the gaze of the viewer. As such, the viewer's responsibility is not to finish the painting but to continue it. . . . "A poem neither begins nor ends, ever," wrote Mallarmé. "It only pretends." This manner in which the work is a pose, or a fiction, that is open to all that preceded it and all that will succeed it, through the gaze of the present moment, is the great and eternal lesson of this greatest and most eternal of painters.

Velázquez does not finish his paintings. He opens them up to our reality. But he also tells us, with incomparable visual force, that in our world everything is unfinished, nothing is ever fully concluded. Why? Because we ourselves, men and women, have not finished, we have not closed the chapter on our own story, no matter how intently the borders of finality and certainty may close in around us. Unfinished, even in death, because whether we are remembered or forgotten, we still contribute to a past that our descendants must keep alive if they want to have a future.

The eternal aperture and innovation of Velázquez offer a response to the contemporary concern regarding the death of the artistic avant-gardes. These movements perished because they came to believe that art was something that progressed, something that was part of the modern world's general movement toward political freedom, economic satisfaction, and social well-being. But in the twentieth century, when progress stopped progressing, murdered either by political horror or physical violence, the avant-gardes ceased to exist. The singularity and the coexistence of artistic works, however, prevailed.

A simplistic Marxism, contrary to the complexity of Marx himself in terms of aesthetics, disseminated the notion that art progressed. To begin with, Marx underscored "the imbalance between the development of material production and the development of artistic production." Art provides people with a kind of pleasure that transcends the forms of social development that may prevail at the moment of the artwork's creation. "Why does a work of art continue to provide aesthetic pleasure when it is the mere reflection of a social form that has long since been replaced and that should only be of interest to the historian?" asks Marx in his *Grundrisse* (*Foundations of the Critique of Political Economy*). In the same work, he reminds us that Greek art is intimately connected to certain kinds of social development. But it continues to provide us with aesthetic pleasure and to represent, in some way, "an unattainable norm and model." Marx goes on to add, with an irony that escapes many stricter, square Marxists, that the discovery of gunpowder does not make Achilles obsolete, nor does the invention of the printing press condemn the *Iliad* to death. Industrial progress does not silence the song of the epic muse, Marx concludes.

Karel Kosik, the preeminent Marxist critic in Czechoslovakia, sheds even more light on the issue. Every work of art has a double nature within its indivisible unity. It is the expression of reality. But at the same time, it shapes the reality that exists, not before and not alongside the work, but more precisely within the work itself and only in the work. Kosik reconsiders Marx's question: how can a work of art provide aesthetic pleasure if the social conditions that existed at the time of its creation no longer exist? Dante is more than just a poet who participated in the struggles between Guelphs and Ghibellines in the Florence of the thirteenth century. Kafka is more than just a Czechoslovakian Jew who was terrorized by his father. Basic Marxism and psychologism believe that one's social or psychic foundations, which are determined by familial and economic foundations, will determine the work of art. Kosik solves the dilemma: how and why does a work of art outlast the conditions under which it was created? Because a work of art exists as a work of art because it demands interpretation, and interpretation produces, in turn, multiple meanings.

Velázquez shows us, like no other artist, how a work of art moves from fact (he painted *Las Meninas* in 1656, during the reign of Philip IV, in an absolutist, decadent Spain) to event (that is, the continuity that allows us to appreciate the painting today as something contemporary for us—just as contemporary as it will be to the viewer who observes it a century from now).

Kosik the Marxist, incidentally, was persecuted and imprisoned by the Soviet tyranny that seized his homeland in 1968. His papers were confiscated. The philosopher had to rewrite them from memory.

Yves Bertherat tells us that if society, economy, and politics exhaust the meaning of a particular work of art, the work of art will become illegible (invisible) by "everyone but those erudite souls of the past" when this community or society perishes. This is true because the other side of the coin is to believe that art "progresses" and the avant-gardes are the driving force behind such progress. The avant-gardes are dead, as is the notion that progress is the inevitable condition of the human quest for perfectibility (Condorcet: "progress. . . . will never be reversed as long as the earth occupies its present place in the system of the universe"). And so our awareness of limitations—the limitations of progress in a general sense and of the avant-gardes in particular—bring us back to our question. Can any kind of new movement come about at a time in which everything seems to indicate that newness is no longer possible because progress has ceased to progress—not in the fields of technology and science, but rather as a guarantee of happiness?

The catastrophes of the twentieth century have driven many of us to think of nature as a safe, idealized refuge. The great artists are not exactly nostalgic for nature despite the mastery with which some of them may render it in their works. Painting is a kind of paradoxical cloister. Like the light in Vermeer's windows, it comes from the exterior world but illuminates the interior. Géricault takes this double dispossession to its extreme in *The Raft of the Medusa*. The raft of the shipwreck victims is menaced and battered by the relentless forces of nature, a sea whose waves are briny ogres eager to devour the horrific confinement of a small group of shipwreck victims whose shelter from the merciless storm is the fragile raft that keeps them afloat; they are trapped in one of nature's vast prisons. It makes perfect sense that this work by Géricault was the inspiration for one of Luis Buñuel's greatest films, that incubus of confinement that is *The Exterminating Angel*. We live on the razor's edge of a natural world and a culture that are contiguous but separated, and that constantly invite us to partake in the brutal exposure of one or the protection of the other.

Schopenhauer does not beat around the bush: "Try, just once," he dares us, "to truly be nature." The horror that the philosopher feels for nature stems from the fact that nature has never really gazed upon us. Nature is a place of convulsion, tumult, jungle. But as another German philosopher, Schelling, reminds us, it is also "the incomprehensible basis of reality."

One of these realities is art and the example that is perhaps the most distant from nature—voluntarily so—is the painting of Velázquez, the extreme artifice that dares speak its name.

> Let my figures gaze beyond the painting that temporarily places them there. Let them gaze beyond the walls of this palace, beyond the plains of Castile. . . . beyond the exhausted continent we have defiled with crimes, invasions, greed, and lust beyond measure, and saved, perhaps, with a few beautiful buildings and elusive words. Let them gaze beyond Europe toward the world we do not know and that does not know us, though it is no less real. . . . And when you, my figures, also grow weary of gazing, cede your place to new figures that will, in turn, violate the rule that you will ultimately consecrate. Disappear, then, from my canvas and let other figures take your place.

These words, which I ascribe to the monk artist of the royal court in *Terra Nostra,* could be those of Velázquez in his eternal dialogue with the past and the future of painting. Like nobody else, he understood that we will always be blind without knowing it, we will always be bereft of vision. For that reason nature comforts us even as it threatens us. It is there, we see it. For this reason art provokes and disturbs us, because it is not there. As it is not there, we must imagine it. To understand this is to understand why Diego de Silva y Velázquez occupies, at least to my way of seeing things, a central place in the realm of art.

W

Wittgenstein

I believe in Wittgenstein because he endangers all our fixed ideas, all the truths we have acquired. He forces us to rethink everything, even the things we would rather not reconsider precisely because they constitute such a solid pillar of our mental architecture and moral armor. Whether we like it or not, he is the philosopher of the twentieth century. He goes directly to the heart of language and, consequently, the heart of literature because he is able to admit the unsayable.

The philosopher, traditionally speaking, has tended to emphasize thought and the perception of the senses, transposed onto the throne of reason. Wittgenstein transposes it onto language and within language; he distinguishes two approaches: language as the representation of facts and the measurement of propositions. Or language as the conductor of emotions. Let us distinguish, asks Wittgenstein, the austere, monkish Jew from Vienna, the impoverished millionaire living in a humble shack, without a penny to his name. Let us distinguish, he asks of us from his offensive poverty, his disturbing remoteness, his arrogant humility. Let us avoid confusion. The realm of value and meaning does not depend on the facts and propositions that comprise rational discourse. Value is the domain of paradox and poetry. Let us separate rational discourse from the worlds of ethics and aesthetics so that we may obtain a clear distinction, given that by doing so we will restore the objective rationality of science, so that it may be untrammeled by humanistic illusions or metaphysical disquisitions, and we will understand the subjectivity of ethics/aesthetics, which can only be expressed in an indirect manner, through poetry, fable, myth. From there we may say that only the unsayable has value, understanding the word *unsayable* to signify all that rational-philosophical can never say. In the world of positivist thought, so paradoxically dominant in a continent of myth and fable like the so-called New World, silence is inconceivable. All that exists is what can and cannot be said. (Or, in a more political sense, what should and should not be said.) But this effectively banishes everything that truly matters—that is, all those things that we cannot express rationally. The silence of reason does not create monsters. It only suggests that what is unsayable in philosophical terms is, in fact, eminently *sayable* in aesthetic terms.

The writer knows that Wittgenstein is right. The historian, the economist, the jurist, and the man of science are all beholden to a single definition of things. Napoleon invaded Russia in 1812. Bad money expels good money. The case has been judged. Two plus two equals four. For the writer, Napoleon invades Russia every time a reader opens the cover of *War and Peace.* Gold, in Shakespeare's *Timon of Athens,* is a "yellow slave" that "will knit and break religions; bless the accurs'd; / make the hoar leprosy ador'd; place thieves, / and give them title, knee, and approbation." Justice, warns Francis Bacon, can sometimes be nothing more than cruel vengeance. And for Lewis Carroll, two plus two *never* equals four. In literature, everything is plurivocal. The multiplicity of signs is what sustains poetry. A rose is a rose is a rose, said Gertrude Stein, poker-faced. But when Carlos Pellicer says, *"Aquí no suceden cosas / de mayor importancia que las rosas"* (In this place roses are the event / of greatest consequence), the flower becomes transfigured like the one Coleridge dreams of and wakes to find in his hand.

My appreciation of Wittgenstein, rather than precluding my appreciation of other philosophers, transforms it. Nietzsche's particular style, so famously aphoristic, is a kind of refusal to create a philosophical "system" that, in order to present itself properly to the world, must present unquestionable premises for the thinker's consideration. For Nietzsche, "systems" of thought are "delectable, though erroneous." Great systematic constructions do not have the capacity to criticize their own assumptions, and as such their buildings will collapse. Nietzsche sets out to write aphorisms, each of which encompasses everything—or at the very least, illuminates it. The very brevity of the aphorism helps us to see things in a new way and also to break loose from the multiple prisons that philosophical systems create to confine thought. In *Die fröhliche Wissenschaft* (*The Gay Science*), he tells us that it is "despicable" not to question things. In a world of exhausted virtues, we have no choice but to take the scalpel to all those things that, in our time, pass themselves off as virtuous. There are more idols than realities in this world of ours, and convictions have a tendency to be prisons. It is almost as if the entire universe was one of Piranesi's splendid, spacious yet cavernous gray jails. To break out of prison: perhaps this is the action that Nietzsche suggests we take against received truths, against complacency, against the notion of existence as mere accident or carelessness.

Yet the Nietzschean proposal is as difficult as the question he asks, once again, in *The Gay Science:* "What does your conscience say? You shall become the man you are." *The man you are,* revealed or stripped naked in one step, through the movement from negation to difference, from reaction to action, from resentment to sentiment. To be the man you are requires gift, sacrifice, education, values. Of course this is true. But for Nietzsche, skepticism and disenchantment are also required. "There is no preestablished harmony between the development of truth and the good of humanity." When a person believes that everything has a purpose, in the end nothing has any purpose. There is no causal relationship between happiness and history. Objective history, in fact, tends to become "furious subjectivity" because while the hero may exhibit his greatness to his fellow man, his fellow man is unable to endure it, and the hero himself will be unable to maintain it. From here emerges the historical violence of the hero who feels he has been misunderstood by the citizens who do not understand him. The hero tyrannizes his fellow man because his fellow man neither comprehends nor appreciates the hero.

With Nietzsche, the Hegelian-Marxist dialectic cannot be optimistic until history can prove it. Few other thinkers—perhaps no other—have been so frequently accused of saying things that they never said, and so frequently dispossessed of the things they did say. Nietzsche racist? "The place where the different races come together is the source of the greatest cultures." Nietzsche chauvinist? "Greece is original because it did not close itself off from the Orient." Nietzsche a Germanophile? "The military victories of the Reich do not imply German superiority in any sense. On the contrary, the deification of the German triumph may signify the death of the German spirit." Nietzsche anti-Semitic? "For me it is a question of honor that it remain absolutely, unequivocally clear that I am opposed to anti-Semitism" (Letter 479 to Franz Overbeck). And while Wagner unabashedly wrote that racial mixing was "ignoble," that Germany could only achieve purity by "liberating [itself] from the Jews," and that "the Jewish race is the natural enemy of a pure and noble humanity," Nietzsche breaks with Wagner, among other things, because the composer "was condescending to the Germans and became a German imperialist."

I could continue with more of the distortions imposed upon Nietzsche's thought, most specifically by his sister Elizabeth; Nietzsche would have been thrilled for her to have gotten lost in Paraguay forever but she returned to censure, ban, deform, and invent whatever her prejudices and phobias called for, taking full advantage of the reclusive nature and subsequent death of her brother. "I may be a bad German," Nietzsche wrote to Over-beck, "but in any event I am a good European."

There is no way that such a radical thinker, sometimes so contradictory and intolerant, could not incite scandal, opposition, and manipulation. In him I see not only the skeptic that rejects the facile temptations of history but also the living being who celebrates "the joy of affirmation" and who, in an oblique foreshadowing of Wittgenstein, tells us that when logic exhausts hope, a new form of knowledge emerges, one that calls for "the preventive virtue of art."

According to the classification of Nicolai Hartmann, Nietzsche belongs more to the realm of the philosopher of problems than the philosopher of systems. In this he shares a bond with Plato, another philosopher that Wittgenstein clarified for me. And the problem that Plato elucidates for me is the literary problem of nomination (just like the problem of poetic language as the seashell where one can hear what logic does not utter in Wittgenstein, just like the understanding of art that one acquires when logic is exhausted in Nietzsche). *Cratylus* is perhaps the first work of literary criticism, and its central concern is a discussion about the meaning of names. Cratylus tells us that all things have their proper name, granted them by nature—that is to say, something inherent to the thing and independent of convention and nothing else. Hermogenes, on the other hand, asserts that names can only be the product of convention: the name that is given to a certain thing is the correct name; if that name is exchanged for a new one, then the new one will be correct. And that is not all: the same thing can be given one name by one person and another name by another person. Nothing is intrinsic to the name. Everything rests on convention.

Socrates supposes that there exists a legislator of names who grants names and distributes them according to the nature of things. But this law allows too many exceptions. The qualities of a human being, for example, may contradict the meaning of his or her name. And if the gods are the ones who give us our names, well, it turns out that we don't know what the gods are called, or what they call one another. All we know is how we have chosen to name them: Zeus, Cronos, Hera. But all too frequently a name is a mask, most especially when the person who has it is the bearer of a secret. Hermes carries a message, he bears the power of language, he makes language circular, but that language may be true or false: the important thing is that language flows and moves, and that wisdom (*sofía*) is wise because it touches all that moves, swiftly baptizing all things. The purpose of the name is to indicate the nature of the designated thing in question. But the name belongs, in a broader sense, to the process of language itself—the formation of letters, syllables, nouns, verbs, and sentences. Can it escape nomination by bringing the flow of things into the flow of language? Can we be certain that a given thing has been given the correct name, one that denotes its true nature? Socrates warns that "it is possible to assign names incorrectly" and if this logic is taken a step further, it is also possible to create false sentences, false languages, verbs that disguise.

In the event that this is true, Socrates searches for another, more solid principle by which to name things, and this principle ultimately consists neither of knowing the natural or intrinsic name of a world in flux, nor of surrendering to the whim of nominal convention. Instead, his principle—lucid, human—truly consists of naming things according to the relationship that is established between them. While Socrates may reject Heraclitus's "runny nose," immersed in the interminable flow of all things, he also rejects pure nominal convention that is derived from an essence we do not know. It is with great liberty, great veracity, and great reality that Socrates proposes that when we name things, we observe the relationship between them, the manner in which things recognize and act among themselves. This is, in reality, the true name of things: their relationship.

The greatest living Spanish philosopher, Emilio Lledó, very astutely observes how the Platonic dialogues are a continual critique of language. In an earlier section I have alluded to the paradox of language as the expression of silence broken by animal sound—the *moo* or moan of the cattle whose etymology, as Erich Kahler tells us, is the very same as that of the word *myth:* moo, mutter, murmur, and mutism. The Greek verb *muein* comes from the same root, to close, to close the eyes, the same place where mystery and mystique come from. And that is how the process of language takes us from *mu* to *mythos,* according to Kahler's linguistic process, which consists of giving a word its opposite meaning. The Latin *mutus* (mute) becomes the French *mot* (which means word), and the onomatopoeic *moo,* the unarticulated sound, becomes *mythos*—that is, word. In his *New Science* of 1725, Giambattista Vico, the philosopher of Neapolitan Spain asserts that we only know what we create, and the first thing we create is language, the basis of all human knowledge. The linguistic dynamic is a process of course and recourse (*corsi e ricorsi*) that allows us to understand the progression of history, descending from the darkness of its own origins and then, later on, ascending to the light of its own idea, which is its own necessity.

In the same vein, Lledó also sees language as the active, creative link of society, and he bases this notion on four levels of evolution. The first is that of necessity: hunting, fishing, the need for communication as sustenance. Necessity creates language. Language creates images, and images can be reactivated by "all kinds of external and internal stimuli," as he says in *Lenguaje e historia (Language and History)*. At the second level, the city is the creator of symbols, and language becomes committed to *paideia,* the formative ideal of the human being, both personal and collective history. At the third level, language not only identifies, it connects, debates, revises. . . . And finally, in our own time, the homogenization of language returns to the identification between individual and social collective, and the price we pay is that of generating a forest of useless symbols.

From here, once again, we find ourselves before Wittgenstein's "preventive virtue," his arduous task of verbal cleansing, of linguistic hygiene. Wittgenstein is eternally aware of the "risk" that living and, therefore, thinking, implies. Most especially in matters of religion, he notes, "the honest thinker. . . . is like a tightrope walker. He seems to be walking on air. His support is the most fragile imaginable. And yet it is possible to walk upon it."

This sentence echoes something Pascal once said: despite their best efforts, human beings are like tightrope walkers, forced to assume risk. People can choose to go to sea or stay at home, but nobody escapes risk. Like Wittgenstein and Nietzsche, Pascal is the philosopher of fragments and aphorisms. Like Wittgenstein and Plato, he questions the nature of language. Like Kafka, he condemns part of his work to silence, but unlike Kafka, he wagers that it will be found in a simple inventory of his meager possessions. Pascal's *Pensées* were, in fact, found sewn inside an old shirt.

Pascal's thousand fragments may be, in their aphoristic brevity, an ironic response to his criticism of the philosophical tradition. Montaigne once noted that the one issue that has troubled philosophers more than any other is the question of what constitutes sovereign good for man. Pascal, who constantly reelaborates and sequesters Montaigne's writing, answers that there are "280 kinds of sovereign good in Montaigne." Pascalian pessimism with respect to philosophical systems extends, prima facie, to human beings themselves. Man is a sorrowful enigma. The justice he imparts is wrongful. The more wealthy his life is, the more empty it becomes. Vanity—"gaming, hunting, visits, theater, false perpetuity of one's name"—is the object of the most intense Pascalian disdain. "What a chimera then is man! What a novelty, what monsters! Chaotic, contradictory, prodigious, judging everything, mindless worm of the earth. Storehouse of truth, cesspool of uncertainty and error; glory and reject of the universe!"*

Blaise Pascal was, as we know, a practical man. His early renown grew thanks to his scientific ingenuity and his pragma-

---

*Translated by Honor Levi.

tism. He devised the first public transportation system in France. He invented the adding machine, the *pascaline*. And he discovered the laws of hydrostatic equilibrium. In addition, however, he may also be the person who turned a corporeal, physical organ—the heart—into the seat of knowledge and emotion. Symbol for love, name for central location, "the heart has its reasons, of which reason does not know," as Pascal tells us. Skeptical of human reason and human institutions in general, Pascal turns to the heart in the hope of finding a dimension of the human being that reason cannot completely encompass or grasp. Pascal makes reason complete with three reasons that could well be—when seen from a certain perspective—those of Wittgenstein. The heart says those things that cannot be said rationally. That other knowledge tormented Pascal because the young French philosopher believed that there was a void there, an abyss that encroaches upon us in two ways. As the discoverer of hydrostatic equilibrium, Pascal the physicist is aware of the void's existence. "The eternal silence of these infinite spaces frightens me," he said.

But then Pascal turns the physical void into a void of the soul, and asks himself, "What can fill it, what can balance it?" Pascal is the philosopher who inches precariously—once again, the tightrope walker—between void and plenitude. His thought emerges from the void and inserts itself into society, religion, and history. His perspective could not possibly be more pessimistic. God is hiding from us. Nature is corrupt. "Larceny, incest, infanticide, parricide, have all been accounted virtuous deeds. . . . Justice, like finery, is dictated by fashion. . . . Thus opinion is the queen of the world, but might is its tyrant." And then, in the final analysis, he observes that "might is the sovereign of the world, and not opinion." And even when opinion prevails over might, opinion itself will become the enforcer of might. At his most pessimistic, he states that this world "is not the land of truth. It wanders unknown among men."

Pascal does, however, warn us that the political order is supported by physical, not spiritual, realities. And that is a virtue, insofar as corporeal realities are identifiable and can justify obedience. There is an implicit deceit in political life. The majority of people obey because they believe that the legal order of things is just, and would rebel against it if they perceived it to be arbitrary. For that reason, governments prefer to maintain the illusion and, occasionally, even fantasies—the opiate of the people, to make a pre-Marxist allusion. As an observer of politics, Pascal fears "the art of opposition and of revolution" and rejects the idea, pre-Rousseauian as well, that it is possible to return to "the natural and fundamental laws of the State, which an unjust custom has abolished." The people rise up. Power uses its advantage to further destroy the people. Sometimes it is "necessary to deceive men for their own good."

It may seem as though I am criticizing the politically reactionary and realistic Pascal—Machiavelli after the fact. I am. But I also feel that I am making an inventory of sorts of the Pascalian skepticisms, which are those that emerge from the void, permeating society and history. Once there, having said all the negative things that can be said of the multitudes, government, power, revolution, and even a hidden God—*le Dieu caché*—and a corrupt nature, Pascal deposits his thoughts in the human race and conceives of them as a lifelong journey of gains and losses. The quality of this journey will depend upon the quality of the conscience of the person who learns—or does not learn—that "nothing is simple which is presented to the soul" (world, subject, society, politics, history) but that at the same time "the soul never presents itself simply to any object."

God hidden. Nature corrupt. God forsakes us to blindness—until, that is, the arrival of Christ. All of Pascal's thought, all his skepticism, all his irony, all his denial, are clearly directed toward an affirmation of Christ. The double path of man, his double passion—path and suffering—on Earth is what, in Pascal's eyes, brings us all closer to the path of Christ himself on Earth, and through the Passion. I cannot help but feel certain that all the apparatus Pascal puts in place for our role as tightrope walkers is like a bridge that stretches out from the *Dieu caché* that forsakes not only Jesus but also all of humanity, and from Jesus himself. . . .

"Thou wouldst not seek me if thou hadst not found me," says Christ in the disjointed Pascalian packages I continue to cite so copiously. That is to say: Pascal cannot and will not elude the question of faith, the question of the human being who believes. Not because of his allegiance to one or another religion, but because he searches for the most precious thing of all, the thing that he already carries inside him (the heart that knows the reasons that reason does not) and he searches for it, conscious that it begins at one demarcation point (birth) only to end at another (death). What determines the value of life for Pascal is not his probable religious affiliation but rather his faith in its most ample meaning: the conviction that we can be bearers of values that we wish to anchor in the world precisely because we ask ourselves the question "What else is there beyond this?"

Received ideas and the inertia of practice are what Pascal rejects, and for this reason—and many others—he exalts the figure of Christ as active, contentious, demanding with his time, the model that we have already found without knowing it, but that we must pursue so that we may always be conscious of what each of us can be, can exhaust, or can renounce.

"I believe because it is absurd," was Tertullian's most sublime reflection on faith, which can be explained not by reason, but by that "heart" which has reasons that reason does not know. Wittgenstein, a Jew who found himself irresistibly drawn to Catholicism, admits that the religious thinker is a "tightrope walker." And so is he. On the one hand, he tells us that faith is absurd, that Christianity is characterized not by faith but by practice—that is, by living as Jesus did. Yet on the other, he declares that faith is faith in terms of what the heart and soul need, not what "my speculative intelligence" requires. As such, "my soul with its passions. . . . is what needs saving, not my abstract thought." From this point the faith-practice contradiction in Wittgenstein's thought becomes less clear, less apparent, whenever his "soul" and his "passions" subject faith to the practical challenge to live as Jesus did. "Only Christian practice, a life like the life that died on the cross, is Christian. . . . and even today it is possible." And then he adds that "for certain men, it is even necessary: genuine, primitive Christianity is possible at every moment." Christianity appears to Wittgenstein, in the end, as faith that is action—not just "belief" but action. Christianity cannot reduce itself to simply sustaining that one or another thing is true. Christianity is practice, not dogma.

The vast intelligence of Ludwig Wittgenstein leads him to believe that there is no reason why religious faith cannot be part of the cultural heritage "that allows me to distinguish between true and false." Only a man of this kind of philosophical and moral integrity could say, as he lay dying, "God said to me, I judge you for what has come from your mouth. Your own actions have made you tremble with disgust when you have seen others repeat them." Because "my soul and its passions, not my abstract intelligence, are what need saving."

I don't know if there is any philosophical assertion more valiant or more definitive than this.

Women

I believe in women. With sex. With names. With biographies. With experience. With destiny. The German Jewish philosopher Edith Stein (1891–1942), a disciple of Edmund Husserl, entered the Carmelite order in 1933 to become Sister Benedicta of the Cross, yet she never renounced her Jewish roots. She declared that anti-Semitism was tantamount to "Christicide" and in 1933, when Pope Pius XI declared that "the Church prays for the Jewish people, bearers of the Revelation until the arrival of Christ," she felt emboldened to ask his successor, Pius XII (Eugenio Pacelli), for an encyclical to protect the Jews. "Spiritually, we are all Jews," the Jewish nun said to the pro-German pontifice. She received no response. Pius XII would not protect the Jews, and Edith Stein would be wrested from the Church and the protection it offered. Despite the fact that she was a nun, she was deported to the first concentration camp, Dachau. Who can ignore these facts when speaking of the destiny of women in history, our history? Edith Stein died in Auschwitz in 1942. Some time before, in her book *Science of the Cross,* she had said: "Reason divides us. Faith unites us." I had heard of Edith Stein and began to read her work at a very young age, at nineteen, thanks to the ill-fated Mexican philosopher Jorge Portilla, a devotee of this woman, thinker, and martyr. The word *martyr,* etymologically speaking, means *witness.*

Anna Akhmatova (1889–1966) was, with the possible exception of Osip Mandelstam, the greatest Russian poet of the twentieth century. Men loved her, but they did not understand her. They all admitted it, too: Anna was prouder and smarter than they were. Beneath her fragile appearance lay an iron will. Fragility and will gave wings to her marvelous poetry, which can perhaps be epitomized by a poem that fuses, in one earthly and eternal moment of recognition, writer and reader: "Our time on earth is fleeting, / The appointed round constricting, / But he— the poet's unknown friend— / Is devoted and everlasting." This tremendous faith in poetry is Anna Akhmatova's glory as well as her prison. Determined to forge her own path, free from the restrictions of Zhdanov and "socialist realism," she was vilified and hounded by Stalin. The artful dictator saw in Akhmatova a double force, a dangerous and intolerable one. She was both a woman and a poet, one who might dispute a small parcel of his power. "I take from the left and from the right. . . . And everything—from the silence of the night," she writes, warning the tyrant lest he misunderstand that the chorus of poetry is always "on the other shore of hell." In 1935 her poetry was banned by the regime, and she was labeled a "whore" and a "counterrevolutionary." Her poems remain in the memories only of those people who read her in time. But war has a way of restoring honor and renown: her voice resonates with the deepest echoes of the Russian literary tradition and the resistance of her people. She has been deified. Too deified. The poems and speeches she wrote in defense of her city, Leningrad, under siege, have brought her renown, ovations, awards. And still, she knows that "like a vampire, an executioner will always find a victim, otherwise he cannot survive." The executioner waits in the shadows. When the war ended, Stalin wondered if this brilliant, independent woman did not deserve—as soon as possible—to be robbed of the hope that she had won her freedom through her contributions to the victory. He ordered her glory and her freedom to be seized. She lost her apartment and her income as a writer. She lived in squalor, cold and hungry. She scraped by thanks to the charity of her friends. And to remove any lingering doubts as to whether creative freedom does not come at the highest of prices, her son was sent to a concentration camp. Liberated in 1956, son and mother no longer recognized each other. They had nothing to say to each other. The son transferred on to his mother all the rage of his own suffering. "Ask my contemporaries," says Akhmatova in the great "Poem Without a Hero," "And we will tell you / How we lived in unconscious fear, / How we raised children for the executioner, / For prison and for the torture chamber. . . ." With good reason she says, "I don't often visit memory / and it always surprises me." It is far wiser for her to listen closely to the growth of the ivy and convince herself that "someone small has decided to live." When Akhmatova died, the line of mourners outside the Writers' House in Moscow stretched several blocks long. This is her testament: "I am sure that even now we do not entirely know the magic chorus of poets that we possess, that the Russian language is young and flexible, that we only just recently began writing verse: that we love it and believe in it. . . ." They say she always walked with a firm, serene stride. They say that she never let herself be defeated by the attempts to humiliate her.

The German-Jewish philosopher Simone Weil (1909–1943) was a disciple of Alain and his mandate to rethink everything based on the reading, each year, of one philosopher and one poet, such as Plato and Homer. Alain claimed to be neither Communist nor socialist. "I belong to the eternal Left, the Left that never exercises power, which by nature tends toward abuse."

Not only did Simone Weil rethink everything, she decided to turn her thoughts into action, put them to the test on the street, at the factory, on the battlefield. As a student, she was known as the "Red Virgin" and she manifested her leftist tendencies by going to work in a factory, fighting fascism in Spain, and, later on, rejecting the "patriotism of the Church" and the French Catholic voices that claimed: "Better Hitler than the Popular Front." But Simone Weil also rejected Soviet Communism once she learned of the Stalinist purges. And she made her convictions known: "Very soon, the true revolutionaries will come to be recognized because they will be the only people who will not speak of revolution. Nothing, in this age, deserves such a name." And the more firmly she planted herself in the fields of labor and politics, the more attracted she felt to God, in terms of both gravity and grace. Nevertheless, she will always be a Christian outside the Church, which she believes to be a dogmatic, bureaucratic structure. She wants to be with God, to act freely. And she will be with God because she is convinced that "God did not create anything but love itself, and the means to love." God is real, Simone Weil tells us, because my love is not imaginary. And for this reason she feels she is the master of her own free will. Her acceptance or rejection of God depends on her freedom. On April 15, 1943, Simone Weil died of starvation in an English hospital. She was prohibited from joining the French resistance, and so she refused to consume more than the daily ration of a prisoner in a concentration camp, despite the fact that tuberculosis was eating her alive. All my life I have believed in Simone Weil, ever since I read her marvelous essay "The *Iliad,* Poem of Might," and memorized the lessons that she draws from Homer: "the fact that nothing is sheltered from fate. . . . never admire might, or hate the enemy or despise sufferers."

X

Xenophobia

We are all subject to the test of the Other. We see but we are also seen. Over and over again, we find ourselves facing the things that we are not—in other words, things that are different. We learn that the only identities that do not change are dead identities. All of us are in the process of being. Nothing can make us understand—or reject—this reality better than the movement that has increasingly come to define life in the twenty-first century: the massive migrations from South to North and East to West. Nothing tests our prejudices, our generosity, and our capacity to give and receive in quite the way this phenomenon does.

We witness the reemergence of fascism, exclusion, and pogroms, anti-Semitism, anti-Islamism, anti–Latin Americanism—all of them violent forms of xenophobia or hostility not only toward foreigners but, in a larger sense, toward all that is different. Homophobia, misogyny, racism. In the name of what? The supposed purity of a superior race, an untouchable national identity, a parthenogenic culture that conceives of itself as free of external contamination. National purity? In a France that is Gallic, Latin,

Germanic? A France that is as Jewish as Chagall, as Spanish as Picasso, as Italian as Modigliani, as Czech as Kundera, as Arab as Ben-Jeleum, as Romanian as Ionesco, as Argentinian as Cortázar, as German as Max Ernst, as Russian as Diaghilev? National purity in a Celto-Iberian, Phoenician, Greek, Roman, Muslim, Jewish, Christian, and Gothic Spain? Exclusionary purity in an indigenous, European, African, multiracial, mulatto Latin America?

An isolated culture will perish rapidly. It may become folklore, madness, or experimental theater. Incompetence and lack of comparative elements can weaken us irreparably and, most of all, degrade us when we carry the denial of foreign identities to the most extreme levels of horror, to the realm of the concentration camp and the Holocaust.

Nothing, however, brings together the dangers of xenophobia quite like the opportunities presented by migrant labor.

We celebrate the so-called globalization process because it facilitates the movement of goods, services, and securities around the world in a truly extraordinary manner. Things are free to circulate. But workers, human beings, are not.

John Kenneth Galbraith, professor emeritus at Harvard University, reminds us that migration is a phenomenon that benefits both the country that receives the migrants as well as the country that sees them off.

Between 1846 and 1906, 52 million émigrés left the European continent. Sweden, one of Europe's poorest nations in the nineteenth century, became one of its most prosperous after massive numbers of its neediest citizens emigrated to North America.

Irish immigration, in the wake of the potato famine that caused half the Irish population to die of starvation in 1845, benefited both the United States and Ireland, which is now a prosperous republic that made the leap from an agrarian to a technology and service economy. Today Ireland has had to attract foreign workers to help maintain this growth pattern.

In today's world, migration is almost uniformly a movement from South to North. But the reasons behind migration remain the same as ever: the need to escape local poverty and break the cycle of hopelessness.

In today's world, just as before, the migrant obeys what is known as the "pull factor": the First World economy's demand for workers who can fill jobs that can no longer be filled by those in the domestic labor force—because they have grown old, because they refuse to perform certain kinds of tasks, or because they have achieved a more comfortable, technically advanced professional status.

Another reason is the compelling illusion of prosperity that is promoted on the television screens, magazines, advertisements, and movies of the societies of the Northern Hemisphere. Some ten years ago, when Albanian émigrés, traveling by boat, reached the Italian coast, the first thing they asked of the authorities there was: "Show us the way to Dallas."

But the migrant laborer never makes it to Dallas. Nor to Disneyland. More and more they are becoming victims of racial violence. The Turkish worker in Germany, the Algerian worker in France, the Mexican worker in Arizona, the black worker in Italy, the North African worker in Spain. No ethical development policy or properly managed globalization program can neglect to include in its considerations the protection due to the migrant worker—for that is exactly what he or she is: a worker, not a criminal.

For five hundred years, the West traveled South and East, imposing its economic and political will upon peripheral cultures, never asking anyone's permission.

Now, those exploited cultures are returning to the West, effectively testing the values that the West itself championed as universal: freedom of movement, freedom of markets based on supply and demand of both workers and goods, and respect for the human rights of each and every migrant worker.

I repeat, instantaneous global interaction and communication are not possible without simultaneous, instantaneous global migration.

One of the great novels of the Spanish language in the twentieth century anticipated this trend and elevated it to dizzying dramatic heights. I am referring to *Paisajes después de la batalla* (*Landscapes After the Battle*), Juan Goytisolo's remarkable book published in 1982. In this work, Goytisolo translates one of the greatest and oldest novelistic traditions—the theme of displacement—to the modern city, its unwanted immigrants and its challenge to any and all notions of purity, be it linguistic, sexual, culinary, or ethereal. Goytisolo is able to imagine the physical space of this new mixed-race city: both Western and Eastern, Southern and Northern. And he gives a voice to each and every one of its inhabitants.

Whether we like it or not, the polycultural city is already here; it is among us. The energy of the Hispanic cities of the United States—Los Angeles, Miami, Chicago—is inextricable from their heterogeneity. Los Angeles, which is not only a Hispanic but a Korean, Vietnamese, Japanese, and Chinese city, will be the Byzantium of the twenty-first century, beckoning from its border with Mexico (which is also its border with all of Latin America) to the great community of the Pacific, toward Vladivostok, Tokyo, Shanghai, Hanoi. . . .

I believe in the questions posed by a fraternal act surrounded by abyss. Perhaps there is another voice out there, and perhaps it is also mine. Perhaps there is some other historical moment that I can affect and that I can be affected by. Are there not other faiths, other stories, other dreams that may be the same as my own?

We exist in the world, we live with others, we live in history and we will have to defend our memory, our desires, and our presence on this earth for the sake of the continuity of life. Xenophobia obstructs and assassinates life.

Cultures influence one another. Cultures perish when they exist in isolation, and they prosper in communication. As citizens, as men and as women from both worlds—the global and the local—it is incumbent upon us to challenge prejudices, to broaden our own limits, to increase our capacity for giving and receiving, and to open our minds to all that we perceive as foreign. If the locality is weak, the globality won't work. For this concept to come to life we must embrace the cultures of the Other so that the Other may embrace our own. Let us remember, at this dawn of a new century, that history is not over. We live in a continually incomplete history. The lesson of our unfinished humanity is that when we exclude we are made poorer, and when we include we are made richer. Will we have time to discover, touch, count the number of our brothers and sisters that we can say we have embraced and counted among us? Because none of us will ever be able to find the humanity within us unless we are able to find it first in others.

Y

You and I

"The 'I' is detestable." Arthur Rimbaud, who knew how to inspire both love and hate in equal degrees, also loved and hated himself, possibly to an even greater degree. The proclamation of his detestable ego is diametrically opposed to the love that we all feel for ourselves as we caress, admire, dress up, and deck ourselves out in that interior mirror that nearly all of us would wish to externalize, as the Italians do so magnificently in their cult of *la bella figura* and their steadfast belief in it. Many, many people cannot, will not, or do not dare emerge from that vanity of vanities, and this occurs because in this world there is both ugliness and imperfection, and the two know each other. There is also humility and even humiliation, and the two love each other as well.

The typical "I"—the ego, that little Argentinian we all carry inside us, as the old and rather unjust Latin American joke goes— can often manifest itself, beautiful and admiring, like a serious moral defect. It can be a psychic state that becomes an end in and of itself, excluding not only others but, in the end, the "I" itself— that is, personal virtue. Wrapped up in its own vanity, the "I" is the pygmy of existence. And it can very easily come to represent that part of ourselves in which we unwittingly deposit the things we most despise in other people. How easily the "I" turns against itself! The egotistical dwarf becomes gigantic, eventually turning into the vengeful monster of our own detestable selves.

The "I" can lose itself thinking that it exists in perfect, egotistical isolation. This means that the "I" tricks itself into thinking that it can exist without any need of what it already is. The Socratic "know thyself" is, in part, a commandment directed to our interior being, a challenge to the intelligence of that part of our interior selves that we sometimes lose amid egotism, complacency, and the mirror of vanity. But the Socratic invitation, in a broader sense, is a challenge that criticizes the "I" that does not have the courage to admit its defects, and exhorts the "I" to cultivate those defects that can only truly flourish within the framework of the "I." Because even though the Earth existed before we did and will continue to exist long after we are gone, all that exists outside of us passes through us. The "I" filters, assimilates, reflects upon, and adds something to the world, but only because—detestable as it may be—it exists. It is there.

The "I" is the framework, if not of all reality, at least of one crucial aspect of reality without which it would have no stage upon which to act. Perhaps "I" is not the most honorable pronoun. But there is no "you" that does not come from or direct itself toward the "I," nor is there a "you" and "I" that can be extricable from the "we." Yet at the same time, can there be a "we" that expels the "I" and the "you" from its dangerous community without also becoming a perilous political abstraction?

The Stoics and Rousseau proposed a notion of the "I" as the citadel of the soul. "Do not let yourself be vanquished by anything but your soul," said Seneca, native of Latin Córdoba. And the citizen of Geneva exclaimed: "Oh, virtue! To learn your laws is it not enough to retreat to our 'I'?" Taken to its extreme, the protection of the "I"'s intrinsic value abandons us in Pascal's chair; Pascal, the man for whom "all the unhappiness of men arises from one single fact, that they cannot stay quietly in their own chamber." But perhaps the "I" can exhibit many of its merits from the Stoic citadel and from the Pascalian chair. For example, it can cherish all that remains of childhood. It can also nourish the imagination and exercise itself creatively.

Writing, painting, composing, thinking. These are all solitary occupations of the "I." Only an oppressive dictatorship can look upon the solitude needed to write a poem and regard it as egotism and betrayal of solidarity, of which Stalin accused Anna Akhmatova. In the "I," desires make themselves manifest, virtues are cultivated, and errors are redressed. At least part of the life force finds its roots in the "I," which uses it for self-preservation. This is the indispensable side of egotism. To renounce self-preservation is to renounce the "I" in favor of another value that may be homeland, political conviction, love, justice. Our hope is that the sacrifice strengthens rather than annihilates our "I." And moreover, when the "I" is strengthened, doesn't it then ascend to a higher level, a place where it is free from the vices of egotism? Isn't that the moment when the "I" becomes a *person?*

I already know that *person,* etymologically speaking, means mask. The mask of classical drama, nevertheless, was not invented to hide but rather "to sound," *per sonare.* That is, to be heard. The "I" that is a person is conscious of himself because he is conscious of the world. The narcissistic "I" drowns itself in its mirror. The person rescues the "I" from agony, protecting and exhibiting the reservations that the egotistical "I" may not be aware of. Know thyself. The solitary "I" then becomes a person who can describe the evolution of his heart and his mind, how they nurture his imagination and passions. In this sense, the solitude of the creative individual is an illusion. What the individual writes, paints, composes, creates, imagines, possesses, is already the personal "I," the "I" with attributes. The *I am* becomes inextricable from the *why am I?* and *for what am I?*

Knowing oneself, then, does not imply loving oneself.

As a stage of creation, the personal "I" can be heroic in its capacity to unleash the most powerful imagination. But it is also rattled by the equally powerful traditions of Romantic disorder (Byron) or post-Romantic disorder (Burroughs) as a condition of creation: the derangement of all the senses, to recall Rimbaud once again. Few and far between are the examples of this illusion of combustible creation, fueled by alcohol, sex, drugs, excess, that actually render lasting and fruitful results. Just as Pascal commanded, Flaubert eventually no longer left his house, Velázquez no longer moved from his court, Beethoven remained in his village, Kant changed neither the schedule nor the route of his daily walk. Balzac's spirit for living needed no other vice than gluttony, women, and the 50,000 cups of coffee that killed him in the end. Cervantes, the model of restrained irony, spent time in jails and under bureaucracies that were in no way noble, and de Sade, the epitome of extreme disorder, also found himself obliged, in jails and madhouses, to imagine more than he could actually do in the real world. Shakespeare was too busy acting and managing theaters to be able to give his "I" more life than what he put into his writing, and for Dante not even the turbulent political scene in Florence could tear him away from a *Commedia* that takes place neither in Heaven nor Hell but rather at the midway point in the journey of life, in the dark jungle of one's own "I." . . . And so there are no strict rules governing the creative "I." Wordsworth is normality personified. His friend Coleridge, disorder. Baudelaire brings discipline and disorder together. Hugo eventually writes about how to be a good grandfather. Dickens, to his own chagrin, is a domestic animal, whereas Wilde transgresses domesticity, perhaps even to his own chagrin. The list of contrasts goes on and on, but the rule of creativity is still a strict one. It is called discipline. It is called knowing how to be alone. It is called framing the "I" in a projection that transcends the person.

The creative personality tells us that the worst sin known to the "I" is that of dispersing ourselves in banal occupations. And to go a bit further, that of working in a field that we dislike. The truly unfortunate "I" is he who fritters away his days in an occupation he detests and that, to make matters worse, he cannot abandon and unconsciously transforms into habit and eventually, inevitability. This category goes from the young restaurant waiter who takes no pains to hide the dissatisfaction he feels with his occupation, to the veteran waiter, who has resigned himself to the notion that serving customers is his destiny. In the middle of this category we find the happy waiter, proud of the service he provides, capable of attaching value and meaning to the fortune—not the misfortune—of contributing to the well-being of the world. The curmudgeon and the defeated soul generally find themselves in the Anglo-Saxon world, a world of bitter displacements and visible dissatisfaction. The individual who is proud of his work because he knows that all work is a worthy and creative pursuit is generally found in the Latin American and Mediterranean world. But the social location is the least important element in all this. The aristocrat who is venomous if poor, *fainéant* if rich, and disdainful in both cases has been displaced and replaced (and this is true almost anywhere in the world) by the businessman who can be generous, artless, and full of energy, or else sophisticated, miserable, and also, always, full of energy.

I speak from our own Faustian tradition; I do not concern myself with the Eastern spirituality that many of my friends understand and practice, mainly because I am unfamiliar with it. Perhaps, however, we do share the conviction that knowing oneself does not imply adoring oneself or possessing absolute truth, but rather implies the ability to live in accordance with a series of very basic guidelines regarding discipline, professional projects, and an understanding of how to operate in the world, whether alone or through the appreciation of friendship and love. Everything else is gone with the wind. Romantic heroes grow old. The most beautiful women develop wrinkles. Heroines die premature deaths from heroin. And the "I" can lose sight of itself thinking that the "I" simply *is,* without having to think about what the "I" *should be.*

The "I" establishes one set of hierarchies and the world another. The challenge, then, consists of understanding the point to
which the order external to the "I" is acceptable and justifiable,
and then, the point to which the "I" is able to accept, change, re-
order the world. The mystic can do this, anew, from Pascal's
chair. As for the rest of humanity, forced to go out into the world,
we also find ourselves obliged to reflect upon our relationship
with all that *is* outside of ourselves. I think I know myself because
I live inside my own skin ("full of myself, laid siege by my own
epidermis"—Gorostiza), but when I emerge from myself, I feel
that I do not know, or perhaps I un-know myself because I experience the feeling that the world does not know me. How can I
come to know the world without losing my knowledge of myself? How can I enrich the world and still enrich myself at the
same time? To emerge from the self is to transform the self; it
means discovering some "other" that has always lived within us.
Love, friendship, experience. Naturally, the categories contained
in this volume, in effect, explain how one travels from the "I" to
the real person, and from the real person to the world, to others,
to society.

The road is not an easy one. Without falling into egomania,
we sometimes find we experience moments in which we are
struck by the strong feeling that the more alone and isolated we
are, the closer we feel to those things that belong to everyone but
which we feel are exclusively ours. The word, the dream, the rec-
ollection, the desire, the sun, the beach we ran across bare-
foot. . . . do these things belong only to us? Or is it that by
belonging so profoundly to us, they actually belong to everyone?
The primary "I" can feel that it reigns over a world invisible to
everyone but itself.

The "I" can also experience a kind of satisfaction that consists of knowing oneself to be different from everyone else and
even alien to a given moment. But that same quality of the "I"
only exists because it is visited by something outside of the "I."
We can celebrate our original plasticity, the illusion of a solitude

that identifies itself with the very first creation. The world does not enslave us. We are different from the truths that are received and the virtues that are consecrated. The young soul does not shrink before his singularity, which is his freedom. The "I" perceives this to be his most stellar moment. But the "I" that remains too long in this glorious instant of youth runs the risk of beginning with self-definition only to end up in self-defense, of denying the enrichment of the "I" by allowing the undesirable and unpredictable to invade it and youthful courage to turn into immature fear, of finding itself, in the end, old and destroyed by those things that we all loved when we were young. . . .

Sooner rather than later, the "I" must learn that it can be its own worst enemy. That our personal mirror can be our most vexing ghost. And that, in the end, as Mexican novelist Salvador Elizondo warns us, a person can be his own worst disguise. Youth can be a terrible pleonasm when a person lacks the valor to be himself, expose himself to failure, not knowing if the door opens to a free fall. Nevertheless, even those of us, like myself, who have already reached the age of wills and testaments, treasure those moments of youth that continue to sustain our "I" throughout the years. We would do well to stop for a moment and ask ourselves, what is it that sustains my "I?" What is it that always remains with me? Paradoxically, the answer is almost always found in things that we received from outside ourselves, those sacred moments of love, friendship, and creativity that we shared with others.

The "I" believes in pleasure, laughter, good food, sex. The "I" believes in itself, sometimes feeling proud of itself and sometimes ashamed. After all, who doesn't bear the blemish of shame, the faux pas, the lost opportunity, the mere memory of which can cure us of that dangerous hubris which leads us to think of ourselves, in Mexican terms, as the *mero mero*, the cat's meow, the king of the forest, the bee's knees?

Kierkegaard said that he was never able to forget himself, not even while sleeping. "I can abstract myself from everything but myself." Defect? Virtue? Or, based on its philosophical manifestation, is this an invitation to transcend the "I," to empower it, to cultivate it so that it may grow and be valued in contact with others? And the "others" are not to be taken lightly. The "I" can only achieve plenitude when it leaves itself and creates its own life while still inhabiting it. The "I" that lives in the world is somewhat like people who live in a house that is still under construction. And the work never ends. With luck, we manage to give it a shared value. My subjectivity, my "I," only gains meaning if it is linked to the objectivity of the world outside of my "I" and to which I connect through a collective subjectivity that we call civilization, society, culture, work.

But once there, in the center of that star that grants us such feelings of plenitude—me, the world and my subjectivity enriched by the society and the culture that my work enriches—we all gaze, once again, into the mirror of the "I," we gaze upon our wounded vanity, the detestable egotism, the things we most hate in others that we see reflected back in our own image, and we feel guilty if we close our eyes. Wouldn't we love to replace the Socratic mandate with an adamant "ignore oneself," and then we open our eyes once again and look at ourselves in the mirror, naked, and in the end we recognize the things that most desperately identify us, each one in solitude and each one in communion with our brothers.

It is a bitter host. It has no answer. We don't know what the body is. We don't know what the soul is. And nothing identifies us more than the fact that we don't know what we are. As St. Augustine said, "Man cannot understand the manner in which the body and the soul are united and yet, that is precisely what man is."

Z

Zebra

Somewhere (I cite from memory) Ortega y Gasset says that for Aristotle, the centaur is a possibility. This is not true for us, because biology forbids this.

The zebra, despite its visible presence among us, always produces bewilderment. His black and white stripes give him away. Without this stamp, he would be a horse. Thanks, however, to his singular design, he has bestowed a name upon both a butterfly (the *papilio marcellus*) and a plant (the *zebrina,* commonly found in Mexico and Guatemala). The fact that its name is reflected in things as dissimilar as a butterfly that reproduces several times a year, and a plant that creeps like a serpent and whose generic name in Spanish is *araña,* or spider, makes a person think that one day the zebra, like Ortega's centaur, will be rendered inadmissible by logic but admissible by fantasy. Once upon a time, the zoologists tell us, there were zebras that only had stripes on their head, neck, and breast. One day there will be zebras that exist only in the imagination and that will be worthy representatives, as in this book (instead of Zanzibar, Zeus, Zacatecas, Zapata, *zagal, zafarrancho, zapato, zanahoria, zorro, zumo,* or zoology), of the most difficult letter in my personal A to Z.

Fantastic zoology. The novelty of the American continent is no stranger to the imagination of that continent. The chronicles of the Indies are replete with fantastic sightings of fauna that had never before been seen, adding indispensable detail to illustrate the very notion of "discovery."

If the fantastic is, as Roger Caillois has defined it, a duel with fear, then imagination is the first exorcist of the fear of the un-known. The European fantasy of America evolved through the fabulous *bestiarios,* or beastly inventories, compiled in the Indies, where the Caribbean Sea and the Gulf of Mexico are described as the habitats of mermaids that Columbus himself spotted on January 9, 1493. Apparently the mermaids "left at very high tide," although the admiral also admits that "they were not as lovely as they were reputed to be, and in some way their faces in fact bore the contours of men."

And then there was Gil González, explorer of the Panaman-ian isthmus, who traveled across a wide swath of dark sea to en-counter "fishes that sang in harmony, as they say the mermaids do, and who sleep in the very same manner." And Diego de Rosales tells of "a beast that rose up from the water and exhibited its frontal side, with the head, face, and breasts of a woman, well-formed, with cascading blonde tresses and manes, and a small child in its arms. As it dove back under, they noted it had a tail and the back of a fish. . . ."

It may be that the feverish imagination of the sailors who ex-plored the Caribbean and the Gulf of Mexico did not, in fact, see mermaids but whales, given that the latter were described as hav-ing "two breasts on the torso" (thank goodness) "so as to give birth and suckle their young," as Fernández de Oviedo wrote.

More problematic, however, is the configuration of the so-called fish-sharks of these waters, also described by Fernández de Oviedo, with even greater anatomical precision this time. "Many of these sharks I have seen," he writes in his *Sumario de la Natural*

Historia de las Indias (*Compendium of the Natural History of the Indies*), "have their virile or generative member doubled. What I mean to say," Oviedo adds, "is that each shark has two penises. . . . each one is as long as the distance between the elbow and the most extreme fingertip of a very tall man."

"I cannot say," the chronicler discreetly admits, "whether in practice he uses both of them together. . . . or each one separately, or at different times. . . ."

As far as I am concerned, I can't decide whether I ought to envy or pity those sharks in the Gulf of Mexico and the Caribbean, but I do recall, thanks to the chronicles of Pedro Gutiérrez de Santa Clara, that luckily these beasts only give birth once in their lives, something that seems to contradict the very existence of such an organ and its functions—one, abundant, and the other, barren. . . .

The letters of Pedro Mártir de Anglería, recounting the astonishing bestiaries of the American seas, were the object of scorn in papal Rome—that is, until a man named (also astonishingly) Juan Rulfo, who was both the archbishop of Consenza and the pope's legate in Spain, confirmed the tales that Pedro Mártir had told and further broadened the realm of all that was "marvelous yet real" to include things like the guitar-fish that was capable of sinking an entire ship with its mighty horn; or the *cocuyo,* a glowworm whose light allowed the natives to "thread, weave, sew, paint, dance, and do other things in the nighttime. . . . they are the lanterns of the coasts."

The pelicans that cloak the air in search of sardines. The vultures or buzzards that Columbus spied on the coast of Veragua, "repugnant, abominable birds" that would swoop down upon the dead soldiers and who were "an intolerable scourge to those of the land." This is the night of the iguana, and Cieza de León does not know "if it is meat or fish," but he does know that when young it glides across the waters, just grazing the surface, and when old it lumbers slowly across the floor of the lagoons.

The list of enchantments continues. The turtles with shells large enough to cover a house. Fertile tortoises that lay broods of a thousand eggs upon the sands of our seas. Beaches of pearls "some as black as jet, others tawny-colored, and others as yellow and resplendent as gold," writes Fernández de Oviedo. And the mythical salamander that burned in its own skin but at the same time was so cold, as Sebastián de Covarrubias recorded in his *Tesoro de la Lengua Castellana* (*Treasure of the Castilian Language*), that "as it walks over coals it extinguishes them as if it were made of pure ice."

The marvels of the seas and shores of the Discovery soon took their place among the great wonders of civilization, magnificently described by Bernal Díaz del Castillo as he and Hernán Cortés's troops entered the Aztec capital, México-Tenochtitlán.

Bernal's vision almost seems to take us into another branch of fantasy, that of science fiction. The most brilliant writer of this genre, Ursula K. Le Guin, notes that science fiction is almost always the history of the future, even though everything seems to occur outside of time in the fantastic psychomyths of fantasy literature—in the living region of the mind, as Le Guin conceives of it, where there is no temptation of immortality at all, where spatial and temporal limits no longer seem to exist. This, in turn, allows what H. P. Lovecraft, American master of the macabre, proposed to such resounding success: the invention of worlds that are not outside time and space, but that in fact possess time and space that are probable and perhaps even memorable. This is what the Polish writer Stanislaw Lem achieves in his marvelous story "One Human Minute": he takes an inventory of each and every person inhabiting the earth, in one single minute.

Given that the "modern" list of these timeless writers extends from Voltaire (*Candide*) and Beckford (*Vathek*) in the eighteenth century through to Ray Bradbury, Arthur Clarke, and Isaac Asimov in the twentieth, and given that their themes run from the evocation of the most remote past (Frazer and Frobenius) to the creation of a future that is quite close at hand (Verne and Wells), my own selection leads me from the fantastic imagination of the American explorers and their bestiaries of the Indies to the most repulsive form of replicating nature: the artificial creation of the human being in the scientific laboratory, the progress of mechanics, and the substitution of the divine: Mary Shelley and *Frankenstein*.

Mary Shelley envisioned the horror of an anti–birth: the conception of a creature created with the leftovers of death. Victor Frankenstein is the name of the father that wishes he were a mother and gives birth to the anonymous monstrosity that grows more and more like its creator—reclusive, cruel, born without a past, but different from the God who might also possess these characteristics because God is not curious, God is not the mother Eve who eats the apple from the Tree of Knowledge; God is not Pandora who spills the secrets of a box filled with calamities; God does not covet an identity, a name or a perception: God is, knows all; *to name him is to diminish him.*

Frankenstein's monster is doubly monstrous: it is not a man, as its creator wishes it could be; nor is it a God, as its creator wishes *he* could be. Mary Shelley's modern Prometheus does not steal God's fire: he goes out looking for it. But that flame is an illusion, it is the false fire of polar light, it is the funeral pyre that awaits creator and creature alike: the icy bonfire of science when it is not man who creates science but rather science that either creates or destroys man. Mary Shelley's modern Prometheus does not create a human being, she creates an *anonymous* one. Perhaps this is why the widow of the poet Shelley chose not to sign her book with her own name. Where could one find the name of such a monster, a monster that is the fruit of the union between an inquisitive man and a wordless death?

One stormy night during the summer of 1816, a group of people gathered at a rented villa on the shores of Lake Geneva. It included Lord Byron, who had rented the house, his friends Percy Shelley and his wife, Mary, the insufferable Doctor Polidori, and an assortment of women representing Byron's various paternal, incestual, and amorous relations. Together they decided to tell horror stories to pass the time during the thunderstorm. Byron invented the vampire; Mary Shelley, the monster. Dracula and Frankenstein were born here. The Villa Diodati, as it is called, can still be visited today. The vistas have scarcely changed, though now there are jukeboxes, television sets, and Ping-Pong tables in the house. I prefer the vision offered by James Whale's film *Bride of Frankenstein,* in which the actress Elsa Lanchester plays Mary Shelley in 1816, recounting a tale that occurs in 1935, and in which Lanchester also appears, this time playing the role of the monstrous woman that Dr. Frankenstein creates so that his first monster, played by the actor Boris Karloff, might have a mate. The time-game is fascinating, and is made even more compelling by the fact that these monsters, which literature either could not or would not properly name (how very brilliant and wise of Mary Shelley!) now bear the names lent them by their photographic images.

The monster has a name thanks to photography. And that name is the name of its creator. The audience names the monster after its creator, Frankenstein. This is like giving the name "God" to each and every one of his creatures. But, as Borges observed, isn't the genre of fantasy the trunk of the tree, and theology one of its branches?

In the realm of fantasy literature, God has no greater enemy than Dracula, the man-vampire that conquers all laws divine and human. He fornicates without love, he drinks because he must, desires no one and nothing other than his own immortality, and conquers death. His image is reflected in no earthly mirror. He sleeps by day. He kills by night. And he travels to flee his own legend and to replenish his source of both life and pleasure: blood.

Roland Barthes has noted that in de Sade's universe, travel has just one purpose: to shut oneself away. To isolate and protect lust. But also to experience confinement as a quality of existence, a voluptuosity of being. Does Dracula do anything other than this when he leaves his Transylvanian cloister and gets himself onto a death ship, hidden inside a box filled with newly dug earth, bound for the heart of the imperial, bourgeois metropolis, London? All characters of extreme identities, from the Gothic novel to the Surrealist film, embark on that journey, from one prison to another: they exhaust their place of origin and so they travel to a corruptible future.

Dracula seeks the blood that nourishes him. But this metaphor of horror conceals a love story. Dracula seeks recognition, even if he must turn the life that he needs and loves into death. And his victims, all those women so captivated by him, who always forget to close their windows at night, to sleep beneath crucifixes, or to hang necklaces of garlic around their throats—aren't they invoking the presence of that "other" who, by identifying himself with them, allows them to identify themselves with him? Do Dracula's ladyfriends seek the peculiar desire that can only be satisfied by the monster who desires nothing other than immortality itself, on the borderline between dream and nightmare?

Dracula and Frankenstein are literary zebras whose habitats preceded them: castles in ruins, Transylvania and the Alps, laboratories that work thanks to a kind of faith in progress, villages that are sanctuaries of millenarian tradition. . . . From its popular legends to the legacy of lineage, Europe possesses the landscape for fantastic literature. America does not. I mean English America, Protestant and Puritan North America.

Nathaniel Hawthorne complains of the lack of mystery in a country with nothing more than a rather common, ordinary prosperity, a country that has no shadows and no real age. How very imaginative a writer must be in order to discover mystery in that humdrum, prosperous world! Old maids that live in perpetual darkness, houses painted in blood, walls that murmur, and Hawthorne's own mother, a widow locked away, her food growing cold at her bedroom door, a ghostly sister who only allows herself to be seen as night falls. . . .

The person who truly reveals the terror of the North American fantastic, however, is Edgar Allan Poe, whose great discovery is that fantasy occurs not in castles on the Rhine or in Roman dungeons but in the heads and hearts of human beings. "The Tell-Tale Heart" could be the title for everything he ever wrote, for he is an author who rejects the North American enterprise of happiness and progress ("I have no faith in human perfectibility," he once said) and instead reveals the very opposite of North American optimism. His narratives do not take place in the solar meridian of the United States but rather in the murky daybreak of the Earth. It is at that hour of dawn, still not fully wrested from the night, that the most intranquil beings emerge. The dead listen. The tombs open. The ghosts rap their knuckles at the entrances to graves. With good reason it has been said that Poe was born and raised inside a coffin. Henry James takes this brand of imaginary terror to its highest degree: the duel with the world that occurs only inside the minds of his characters. There is no exterior setting as there is in Frankenstein or Dracula. London, Boston, English weekends, aristocratic society life, well-appointed country homes. No: his terror is inside the imagination, in the turn of the screw. . . .

Poe, who was Stalin's preferred writer (a case of power fascinated by torture and terror), could also be, somewhat paradoxically, the favorite author of the most logical Cartesian of them all. The deductive logic of "The Gold Bug" and "The Purloined Letter" elevate reason to the level of mystery in a foreshadowing of that great Latin American fabulist, Jorge Luis Borges, the perverse neo-Platonist who first suggests a totality, only to immediately prove its impossibility. Borges opens many of his stories with the ironic premise of a hermetic totality. He evokes the age-old nostalgia of original unity. But then he immediately betrays all yearnings for the idyllic (which echo the founding utopia of the New World) with the comic incident and the peculiar accident. Funes the Memorious remembers everything (fantastic premise). But if he wants to live he must reduce, select, limit himself to a manageable number of memories (comical conclusion).

In the universe of Tlon, time is denied. The present is infinite. The future has no more reality than current hope. The past has no more reality than the present memory. And there is no dearth of people in Tlon who declare that all of time has already occurred and that our lives are nothing more than the falsified, mutilated, crepuscular memory of an irrevocable process. At the foot of the page, Borges makes note of Bertrand Russell's theory: that the universe was created only a few minutes ago and was instantly provided with a human race capable of remembering a past that never occurred.

The literature of fantasy proposes that reality is found on the other face of things, just beyond the senses, in a place that is invisible only because we didn't know enough, because we didn't extend our hand in time to touch its elusive presence. This, then, is what was behind Julio Cortázar's sweeping vision. He looked out at the parallel reality, just around the corner, a vast and latent universe filled with its patient treasures, the contiguity of beings, the imminence of the forms that wait to be summoned by a word, a brushstroke, a gesture of the hand, a melody hummed, a dream. . . .

Imagination: mediation between sensation and reason, but with the ulterior motive of dispelling any logical relationship between cause and effect. This forces us to re-create everything, once we are freed from the pressure of convention, from that quotidian normality that so bothered Hawthorne.

Gregor Samsa wakes up to find he is an insect. And Odradek, the most mysterious of all of Kafka's messengers, rambles through the tombs of Prague in a work filled with invalid Hermes. Odradek is a flat, star-shaped spool made of various multicolored threads. Odradek is treated like a child; his immediate appearance is absurd, but he is a totality, a complete specimen of his genre. Odradek might seem like the kind of person who was once, but is no longer, useful—though this, Kafka warns us, would be a grave mistake. Odradek, who hides on the stairs, in the corridors, in the halls: in communication. Odradek, who disappears for months at a time and then returns, invisibly but faithfully. Odradek, the guardian spirit, the ghost of the House of Kafka. Odradek is a myth, half-living and half-dead, half-object and half-living being, forgotten but present, without origin; without future and without goal.

Is the literature of the fantastic the ghost that restores all that is forgotten among the living?

Zurich

In early 1950, just after my twenty-first birthday, I traveled to Switzerland to continue my studies at the University of Geneva and the Institut Universitaire de Hautes Etudes Internationales. Employed by the Mexican mission to the International Labor Organization (ILO), I served as secretary to Roberto Córdova, the Mexican member of the International Law Commission of the United Nations. All of this lent a terribly formal air to my arrival in Switzerland. Geneva, as always, was a very international city. I made friends with international students, diplomats, journalists. I met a beautiful Swiss student and fell in love with her, though our clandestine encounters were thwarted by two circumstances.

First, I was expelled from the strict pension where I was living on the Rue Emile Jung, for the clandestine reasons mentioned above. And second, my girlfriend's parents ordered her to stop running around with a young man who came from such a dark, uncivilized country whose inhabitants, as the rumor went, ate human flesh.

The day my girlfriend broke it off with me, I consoled myself by going to a cinema on Rue Mollard to see Carol Reed's celebrated movie *The Third Man,* which at the time was the greatest cinematic spectacle in the world. Its heroine was Alida Valli, one of the most beautiful women ever to grace the silver screen, and who years later would be my neighbor at the San Angel Inn neighborhood in Mexico City. In *The Third Man,* Valli was a perfect mask of frozen sensuality with clear, flashing, vengeful, resigned eyes.

Most important, however, the movie featured Orson Welles. I had first seen *Citizen Kane* as a child in New York, and from that day onward, I have always regarded it as the greatest talkie ever made in Hollywood. Its formal beauty, its bold lighting, its camera angles, and its great attention to detail were values that converged to tell the Great American Story: Money: how to make it and how to spend it. Happiness: how to search for it and never find it. Power: how to attain it and how to lose it. Kane was at once both the American Dream and its antithesis, the American Nightmare.

Now, at the Cinema Mollard, Welles emerged from the shadows of the Vienna sewers as Harry Lime, the cynical black marketeer who justifies his illegal activities with a phrase that became famous around the world and that affected Switzerland quite directly.

"In Italy under the Borgias," said Orson Welles as Harry Lime, "they had warfare, terror, murder, and bloodshed, but they produced Michelangelo, Leonardo, and the Renaissance. In Switzerland, they had brotherly love, they had five hundred years of democracy and peace, and what did they produce? The cuckoo clock."

I don't recall how this observation was received by the audience in Geneva. I do know, however, that I had moved from that puritanical pension to a bohemian attic flat on the Place du Bourg-de-Four and from there, in the company of a Dutch cohort, I began to explore the dark side of cuckoo-land, the night life of Geneva. We discovered seamy cabarets teeming with third-rate Harry Limes, prostitutes with bleached blond hair eternally seated with their poodles at the Café Canonica, and a pair of beautiful dancers whom the Dutchman and I quickly befriended. My gleeful ardor, however, was somewhat dampened when I asked the ballerina out for a Saturday date, only to be responded to with a "Oh, no. Saturday is my husband's day."

Ah, the ghost of Calvin. Even the cabaret dancers were no more than animated cuckoo clocks, it seemed. After all was said and done, was Harry Lime right?

Before going to Geneva I had read Joseph Conrad's novel *Under Western Eyes,* which had filled my mind with visions of a city of political intrigue, teeming with Russian exiles and fearsome anarchists. But even in the tragic hothouse atmosphere Conrad described, there was nevertheless something that resembled cuckoo-land: the protagonist Sofia Antonovna says to the traitor Razumov, "Remember, Razumov, that women, children, and revolutionists hate irony."

He might very well have added, "And the Swiss, too?" As a Mexican, I have never appreciated generalizations regarding my country or any other for that matter (with the one exception of the United States: I am, after all, Mexican). Reading Conrad in Geneva, I could only echo his thoughts that "there are phantoms of the living as well as of the dead."

And so, in the summer of 1950, I was invited by some very old and dear German Mexican friends, the Wagenechts, to visit them in Zurich. I had never been to Zurich before and harbored the preconceived notion that it was the very crown of the Swiss prosperity that stood out in such stark contrast with the rest of Europe, still convalescing from the war—London, where they were still rationing the most basic of items; Vienna, occupied by the four victorious powers; bombed-out Cologne; Italy, with no heating, its third-class trains packed tight with men in ratty pants carrying suitcases held together with twine; children collecting cigarette butts on the streets of Genoa, Naples, Milan. . . .

It was a beautiful city, Zurich. The balmy days of June exhaled the last deadening breaths of May and heralded the imminent arrival of the July heat. It was difficult to separate the lake from the sky—it was as if the waters had become pure air and the firmament, the very mirror of the lake. The feeling of tranquility, dignity, and reserve was irresistible and only heightened the physical beauty of the surroundings. Where are all the gnomes? I would ask myself. Where is all that gold hidden away? In this city where the Nibelungen ostensibly made themselves visible, dressed in frock coats and top hats as in George Grosz's caricatures?

I must admit that all my potential for irony, well established on the shores of Lake Leman, fell to pieces the night my friends invited me to dinner at the Baur au Lac, a hotel by the lake. In reality the restaurant was a barge, a terrace that floated on the lake. Reached only by a narrow gangplank, it was lit by Chinese lanterns and flickering candles. As I unfolded my stiff white napkin amid the tinkling sounds of silver and glass, I looked up and my eyes came to settle on the group at the table next to us.

Three ladies were dining with an older gentleman in his seventies; he was as stiff and elegant as the starched napkins, dressed in a white double-breasted dinner jacket and an immaculate shirt and tie. With his long, delicate fingers he sliced a cold pheasant with the utmost refinement. Even as he ate, he seemed as erect as a candle, and his bearing was one of military severity. His face betrayed "a growing fatigue," but his lips and jaw were set in a semblance of pride that sought desperately to hide his exhaustion. His eyes shone with "fiery and playful caprice."

On that summer night in Zurich, as the carnival lights twinkled against those of the restaurant upon the features that I finally recognized, the face of Thomas Mann was a theater of hushed, implicit emotions. He ate, letting the ladies do the talking; he was, to my very captivated attentions, the creator of times and spaces in which solitude is the mother of a "beauty unfamiliar and dangerous" but also the soul of the perverse and the illicit.

There was no way I could prove the accuracy of my intuition that evening of my youthful, if distant, encounter with an author who had literally shaped the writers of my generation. From *Buddenbrooks* to the great novellas to *The Magic Mountain,* Thomas Mann had been the securest link in our Latin American literary connection to Europe. Because if Joyce was Ireland and the English language, and Proust was France and the French language— well, Mann was even more than Germany and the German language. As young readers of Broch, Musil, Schnitzler, Joseph Roth, Kafka, and Lernet-Holenia, we knew that the German language was more than just Germany. It was the language of Vienna and Prague and Zurich, sometimes also that of Trieste and Venice. But it was Mann who pulled all of them together into a European language based on the European imagination—a whole that was far greater than its various parts. To our young Latin American minds, Mann was already what Jacques Derrida would later call "the Europe which is what has been promised in the name of Europe." Watching Mann eat his dinner that evening in Zurich, the two spaces of that spirit, Europe and Zurich, became united together in my mind and would remain as such forevermore. Thanks to that meeting without a meeting, I crowned Zurich as the true capital of Europe that night.

It was odd. It was impertinent. Did I dare approach Thomas Mann—me, a twenty-one-year-old Mexican student with many nights of reading under my belt but with little of the intellectual sophistication that was still so far beyond my grasp? In a memorable essay, Susan Sontag recalls how she, at an even younger age, penetrated the inner sanctum of Thomas Mann's home in Los Angeles in the 1940s, and discovered that though she had precious little to say, she had plenty to observe. I had nothing to say but, like Sontag, much to observe as well.

And there he was again the next day, at the Hotel Dolder, where he was staying. Dressed all in white, dignified but one degree short of the stiffness of the previous night, his eyes were somehow more alert, more horizontal. Out on the courts, a group of young men played a game of tennis but he had eyes for only one of them—who seemed to be the Chosen One, Apollo in tennis whites. To be sure, he was a very beautiful young man, no more than twenty, twenty-one years old. My age. Mann could not take his eyes off him and I couldn't take my eyes off Mann. I was witnessing a scene from *Death in Venice,* only thirty-eight years later, when Mann was no longer thirty-seven (his age when he wrote the sublime novella of sexual desire) but seventy-five, older even than the feeble Aschenbach, yearning for young Tadzio from afar on the Lido—where, twenty years after seeing Mann in Zurich, I saw Luchino Visconti in the company of Carlos Monsiváis, filming *Death in Venice* with Silvana Mangano, a woman who encompassed all forms of beauty and desire, even those of androgyny.

That morning in Zurich, the situation was replayed—astoundingly, famously, painfully the same. Mann—dignified man of letters, Nobel Prize winner, septuagenarian—could not hide, from me or anyone else, his passionate ache for a twenty-year-old boy playing tennis on a court at the Hotel Dolder one radiant morning in Zurich in June of 1950. That was when a young woman found her father, seemed to chide him affectionately, and forced him to abandon his passionate post and return with her to everyday life—not only that of the hotel but that of this tremendously disciplined author whose Dionysian impulses were forever being controlled by the Apollonian dictate to enjoy life only if you are able to give it form.

I saw it that morning. For Mann, the artistic form preceded the forbidden flesh. Beauty was to be found in art, not in the formless, fleeting, and ultimately rotten carcass of our desires. It was a dramatic and unforgettable moment for me: a true commentary on the life and work of Thomas Mann—the arrival of his daughter Erika, visibly admonishing her father for his weaknesses, gently pushing him to return, if not to the order of cuckoo-land, to the order of the spirit, literature, and the artistic form, where Thomas Mann could have his cake and eat it too, be the master and not the plaything of his emotional life.

I sat down to eat lunch with my German Mexican friends in the dining room at the Dolder. The young man who waited on us was the one whom Mann had been admiring that morning. He hadn't had time to bathe and smelled lightly of healthy, athletic perspiration. The headwaiter imperiously turned to him—"Franz"—and he went scurrying off to another table.

And so there was something of mystery in Zurich, something more than cuckoo clocks. There was irony. And rebellion. There was the Café Voltaire and the birth of Dada, in the middle of the bloodiest war ever waged on European soil. There was Tristan Tzara giving rationalism the finger: "Thought is made in the mouth." And there was Francis Picabia creating art out of nuts and bolts. There was Zurich, telling a decaying, bloodstained, hypocritical world that sanctioned death in the trenches in the name of some kind of superior rationalism, "All that we see is false." From this simple premise, uttered by the impertinent, monocled Tzara from his spot at the Café Voltaire, sprang a revolution of sight and sound and humor and dream and skepticism that in the end buried the complacency of nineteenth-century Europe, though it could not prevent the barbaric events still to come. Was Europe still not quite "what had been promised in the name of Europe"? Could it ever be? Would Europe be reduced to the night and shadows of Treblinka and Dachau? Yes, if we accepted the notion that everything that came out of Zurich—Duchamp and the Surrealists, Hans Richter and Luis Buñuel, Picasso and Max Ernst, Arp, Magritte, Man Ray—was not "what had been promised in the name of Europe." But it was. The thing that had always been promised in the name of Europe was the criticism of Europe—Europe's own warning to herself against her own arrogance, smugness, and surprised confusion when the first blows of adversity finally began to fall. It was the same warning that the artists of Zurich had issued in 1916. And it should be issued once again, now that the ghosts of racism, xenophobia, anti-Semitism, and anti-Islamism are rearing their heads again, reminding us once more of Joseph Conrad's words in *Under Western Eyes,* that "there are phantoms of the living as well as of the dead."

Who had seen these phantoms, painted them, given them corporeal horror? Another citizen of Zurich, Füssli, the greatest of the pre-Romantic painters. Füssli, who from the eighteenth century had embodied all the themes of the dark night of the romantic soul just as Mario Praz described them in his celebrated book *Flesh, Death, and the Devil in Romantic Literature.* Füssli and the Belle Dame Sans Merci, Füssli and the beauty of the Medusa, Füssli and the Metamorphoses of Satan, Füssli and André Gide's warning that not believing in the Devil means giving him all the advantages of surprising us. The baptismal waters of Romanticism—the beauty of the horrible—spring from Füssli, citizen of Zurich. Darkness shattered by unattainable light. The joy in crime that the anti-cuckoo Harry Lime embodied so well. The Fatal Man and Fatal Woman who have bewitched our impossible imaginations, from Lord Byron to Sean Connery and from Salomé to Greta Garbo. . . .

Zurich, as repository of the archetypes of the modern world? Why not, if we take a broad view of things? James Joyce sang lusty songs in the Café Terrasse, playing with the words in joyous anticipation of *Ulysses,* his work in progress. Lenin was a habitué of the Café Odeon before he left for Russia in a famously sealed railway car. Did the two ever meet for real, as Beckett recalled, or did they only encounter each other in Tom Stoppard's play? Didn't all these ghosts walk upon the waters of the lake in Zurich?

And yet, for me, dazzling as a Füssli painting and shocking as all the Dada pranks may be, tensely opposite as the Zurich life and work of Joyce and Lenin may be, it is always Mann, Thomas Mann, the good European, the contradictory European, the critical European, who comes back to my heart and mind as the figure I most closely identify with the city of Zurich.

How many times was he there? Can we really separate Mann from Zurich? What a long life he lived there, with all the comings and goings between his villa at Kusnacht and his homes at Erlenbach and Kilchberg; places of rest, spaces for work. But then there is also the Zurich to be remembered as the setting of certain high points in Mann's life. The 1921 visit, when he dared to raise his speech fee to 1,000 marks. The day in 1926 when he read "Disorder and Early Sorrow" to students. The joyous 1936 celebration of his sixtieth birthday; he had chosen Zurich not as a foreign place but as "a homeland for a German of my ilk." Zurich as "an ancient seat of Germanic culture, where the Germanic fuses into the European." The disturbing visit in 1937, on the precipice of the Nazi night and fog, preparing *Lotte in Weimar* as a desperate attempt at a new *Aufklärung,* a new Enlightenment, ignoring Gerhart Hauptmann's refusal to shake hands with the philosophical desire for "other times," perhaps better ones. And then his struggles to keep his son Klaus off drugs—a world, wrote Mann, "where moral effort. . . . earns no gratitude of any kind."

And then there is the Thomas Mann who returns to Zurich after the war, to embark upon a period of ceaseless activity, as if age and exhaustion held no sway. The room at the Hotel Baur au Lac, endlessly invaded by mail deliveries, requests for interviews, tiny scraps of glory in the writer's boots, more and more until they became an insufferable nuisance. And then retreating to the beauty of a young man he yearned for, waiting for "a single word from the boy" and knowing that nothing, nothing in the world can empower an old man to love again.

And then, on August 15, 1955, "the throne became vacant." And I turned around and looked back on that serendipitous encounter in Zurich in the spring of 1950, and wrote, "Thomas Mann, out of his solitude, had finally found the affinity he sought between the personal fate of the author and that of his contemporaries." Through Mann, I had imagined that the products of his loneliness and this affinity were called art (created by one) and civilization (created by all). He had spoken with such assurance in *Death in Venice* about the duties imposed upon him by his own ego and the European soul, that I, paralyzed by my admiration of him, saw him that night in Zurich as something so distant that I was unable to imagine anything at all comparable in our own Latin American culture, where the extreme demands of a ravaged and often silenced continent very often annihilate the voices of men and turn the voice of society into a hollow political monster, sometimes even killing it or turning it into a kind of sentimental, pathetic dwarf.

Yet as I looked back on my impassioned reading of all that Thomas Mann wrote, from "The Blood of the Walsungs" to *Doktor Faustus,* I could not help but feel that despite the vast differences separating his culture and my own, both (that is, Europe, Latin America, Zurich, Mexico City) were cultures where literature, in the end, asserted itself through a relationship between the visible and invisible worlds of narrative, between nation and narration. A novel, said Mann, should weave together the threads of many human destinies in the task of crafting a single idea. The "I," the "you," and the "we" were dried and separated out by our own lack of imagination. I understood what Mann was saying and I was able to put those three "people" together many years later, when I wrote my novel *La muerte de Artemio Cruz* (*The Death of Artemio Cruz*).

But then the 1950s meandered into the 1960s and we turned our attentions to another citizen of Zurich: Max Frisch and *I'm Not Stiller.* We got wind of Friedrich Dürrenmatt and "The Visit." We even realized that Jean-Luc Godard was, in fact, Swiss and that the proverbial cuckoo was as dead as the equally proverbial duck, as dead as the equally proverbial doornail. Harry Lime emerged from the sewers, only to become fat and smug, doing television spots about drinking "no wine before its time." Welles himself suffered the same fate as Kane, indulgent and tragic, and perhaps he left behind scraps of his tremendous talent in the hands of hard, tragic, implacable Swiss writers like Frisch and Dürrenmatt, those whom Harry Lime saw as nothing more and nothing less than cuckoo clocks.

I have two endings for my tale of Zurich; one is much closer to my age and my culture. It is the image of the Spanish writer Jorge Semprún, a Spanish Republican and Communist who was sent to the Nazi concentration camp of Buchenwald at age fifteen and who, when he was liberated by the Allied troops in 1945, could not recognize his own face, that of an emaciated young man who had been rescued from death, who would never speak of his wrenching experience until his face said to him, "You can speak again."

In his extraordinary book, *La escritura o la vida* (*Writing or Life*), Semprún waits patiently until he is fully restored to life, even if it takes him decades (and it does) to speak about the horror of the camps. And so, one day, in Zurich, he dares to enter a bookshop for the very first time since his liberation so many years earlier, and he surprises himself by staring at his reflection in the shop window. Zurich has given him back his face. He does not need to rediscover the horror. Recovering his face is enough to tell us the whole story. The life of Zurich surrounds him.

The second ending is closer to my own memories. It happened that night in 1950 when, without him knowing it, I left Thomas Mann sipping his demitasse as midnight was approaching and the floating restaurant of the Baur au Lac gently swayed and the Chinese lanterns slowly flickered and went out.

I will always be grateful to that night in Zurich for silently teaching me that in literature, you know only what you can imagine.

ABOUT THE AUTHOR

CARLOS FUENTES, Mexico's leading novelist, was born in 1928. He has been his country's ambassador to France and is the author of more than twenty books, including *The Death of Artemio Cruz, Terra Nostra, The Old Gringo, The Years with Laura Díaz, Diana: The Goddess Who Hunts Alone,* and, most recently, *Inez.* Fuentes has received many awards for his accomplishments, among them the Mexican National Award for Literature in 1984, the Cervantes Prize in 1987, and the *Légion d'Honneur* in 1992.

ABOUT THE TYPE

This book was set in Bembo, a typeface based on an old-style Roman face that was used for Cardinal Bembo's tract *De Aetna* in 1495. Bembo was cut by Francisco Griffo in the early sixteenth century. The Lanston Monotype Company of Philadelphia brought the well-proportioned letterforms of Bembo to the United States in the 1930s.